classic WINES of new zealand

classic WINES of new zealand

MICHAEL COOPER

Hodder Moa Beckett

ISBN 1–86958–759–6

© 1999 – Original text Michael Cooper
The moral rights of the author have been asserted

© 1999 – Design and format Hodder Moa Beckett Publishers Ltd

Published in 1999 by Hodder Moa Beckett Publishers Limited
[a member of the Hodder Headline Group]
4 Whetu Place, Mairangi Bay, Auckland, New Zealand

Designed and produced by Hodder Moa Beckett Publishers Limited

Printed by Chong Moh Offset, Singapore
Film: Microdot, Auckland

Contents

🍇 Introduction

Which are New Zealand's greatest wines? What do they taste like and how well do they mature? What are the secrets of their success?

This book is a celebration of classic wines – those which achieve outstanding quality from one year to the next. The goal of *Classic Wines of New Zealand* is to cut through the bewildering array of New Zealand wines on the market – between 1500 and 2000 – to focus on those with a track record of consistent excellence.

What is a New Zealand wine classic? As defined in my annual *Buyer's Guide To New Zealand Wines*, it is "a wine that in quality terms consistently ranks in the very forefront of its class (which rules out highly important but not top–flight wines, such as Montana Marlborough Sauvignon Blanc). To qualify for selection, each label must have achieved an outstanding level of quality for at least three vintages; there are no flashes in the pan here."

A small, elite group of Super Classics recognises wines which have achieved brilliance in at least five vintages (compared to three for Classic status). The Super Classics are all highly prestigious wines of the calibre of Cloudy Bay Sauvignon Blanc, Kumeu River Chardonnay and Ata Rangi Pinot Noir.

As a guide to brilliant emerging wines, there is a third category – Potential Classics. The pool from which future Classics will emerge, Potential Classics are wines of outstanding quality which look likely, if their current standards are maintained or improved, to qualify after another vintage or two for elevation to Classic status.

The selection of classic wines is based on my thousands of tastings each year for *Winestate* and *Wine Star* magazines, plus a multitude of other tastings at wineries, competitions, media presentations and at home. Many of the wines are tasted "blind" (with labels hidden), but not all. Other wine lovers (not least the winemakers themselves) will inevitably disagree with the inclusion of certain wines or the omission of others. Both in terms of the wines featured and the specific tasting notes, it must be emphasised that this book is a collection of one person's opinions.

The goal of this book is to give you a clearer picture of the country's top wines than you'll find anywhere else. For each wine, key aspects of its production are outlined and major reasons for its quality are highlighted. My notes from a "vertical" tasting of past vintages, in some cases stretching back 15 years, give insight into the style of the wine and its cellaring ability.

This book aims to fill a major gap in New Zealand wine writing. Specialist wine and food magazines typically focus on reviews of infant wines – one-year-old Chardonnays and 18-month-old reds. Such a relentless focus on young wines reflects the media's reliance on advertising – in this case the purchase of "bottle shots" to highlight favourable reviews. Because wine companies are normally only interested to advertise vintages they still have for sale, the magazines have little incentive to arrange tastings of older wines. Once a particular vintage of a top wine is sold out, although it is still resting in cellars around the country, it is rarely written about again.

Before paying $25 to $40 for a premium young Chardonnay or Pinot Noir, you need to know you can mature it for a few years and that when it comes out of the cellar it will be drinking better than when it went in. That confidence comes from "vertical" tastings, which by examining the past enable you to predict the future with a fair degree of accuracy.

In a vertical tasting, several – perhaps all – vintages of a wine are tasted side-by-side. A vertical tasting lets you assess several things: the overall quality of a wine, the evolution of its style (reflecting changing viticultural and winemaking techniques), the impact of vintage variation, and its maturation potential.

For a winemaker, looking at his or her life's work strung out along the table, exposed to critical dissection, a vertical tasting can be a nerve-wracking experience. However, for the wine lover, a vertical tasting offers an unparalleled opportunity to get to grips with a wine – its quality, style and longevity.

In the final analysis, the tasting notes in this book can apply only to the individual bottles I tasted. As they mature, wines often display marked bottle variation. Recent research has shown that 20 per cent of corks are gradually infiltrated by air, causing precocious development and early oxidation of the wine.

Cellar conditions also vary, with a significant effect on the way wines mature. The ideal conditions that produce the best results are more likely to be found at wineries than in domestic cellars. As André Simon observed: "There are no great wines; only great bottles."

The book is organised by grape variety and, within each section, the wines are treated in alphabetical order. The wines are also classified as Super Classic, Classic and Potential Classic.

quality ratings

The quality ratings are the same as for my annual Buyer's Guide:

☆☆☆☆☆	Outstanding quality (gold medal standard)
☆☆☆☆⚡	Excellent quality, verging on outstanding
☆☆☆☆	Excellent quality (silver medal standard)
☆☆☆⚡	Very good quality
☆☆☆	Good quality (bronze medal standard)
☆☆⚡	Average
☆☆	Plain
☆	Poor
No star	To be avoided

The Classics

Classic Wines of New Zealand

Sauvignon Blanc
Grove Mill Marlborough
Jackson Estate
Kumeu River
Matua Valley Reserve
Nautilus Marlborough
Nga Waka
Palliser Estate
Te Mata Cape Crest
Vavasour Single Vineyard
Villa Maria Reserve Wairau Valley
Wairau River Marlborough
Wither Hills Marlborough

Sweet Whites
Corbans Cottage Block Noble Riesling
Giesen Botrytised Riesling
Glazebrook Noble Harvest Riesling
Rongopai Winemaker's Selection
    Botrytised Riesling

Bottle-fermented Sparklings
Amadeus Classic Reserve
Daniel Le Brun Vintage Brut
Deutz Marlborough Cuvée
Domaine Chandon Marlborough Brut
Pelorus

Branded Reds
Esk Valley The Terraces

Cabernet Sauvignon – predominant Reds
Brookfields Cabernet/Merlot
Church Road Reserve
    Cabernet Sauvignon/Merlot
Te Mata Awatea Cabernet/Merlot
Vidal Reserve Cabernet Sauvignon and
    Reserve Cabernet Sauvignon/Merlot
Villa Maria Reserve Cabernet
    Sauvignon/Merlot

Merlot
Esk Valley Reserve Merlot-predominant Red

Pinot Noir
Dry River

Syrah
Stonecroft

POTENTIAL CLASSIC

Chardonnay
Babich The Patriarch
Montana Ormond Estate

Gewürztraminer
Montana Patutahi Estate

Riesling
Pegasus Bay

Sauvignon Blanc
Goldwater Dog Point Marlborough
Kim Crawford Marlborough
Villa Maria Reserve Clifford Bay

Bottle-fermented Sparklings
Hunter's Brut
Mills Reef Traditional Method

Branded Reds
Cross Roads The Talisman
Te Awa Farm Boundary

Cabernet Sauvignon – predominant Reds
Babich The Patriarch
Fenton Cabernet Sauvignon/Merlot/Franc

Merlot
Clearview Reserve

Pinot Noir
Gibbston Valley Reserve
Martinborough Vineyard Reserve
Palliser Estate

With 31 classic wines featured out of a total of 97, Chardonnay plays a pivotal role in this book. The country's most popular grape variety, it accounts for over 30 per cent of all vine plantings, and there are well over 300 different labels on the shelves.

What are the key technical ingredients shared by the country's premier Chardonnays?

New clones (especially clone 15) are becoming important, but the classic Chardonnays rely heavily on the widely planted Mendoza clone, favoured by quality-orientated winemakers because its smaller berries give a higher skin to juice ratio and richer flavour. For the classic wines, grape yields are normally restricted to no more than 3-3.5 tonnes per acre.

Mechanical harvesting is common, but hand-picking of the best fruit is increasingly recognised as a key factor in the wine's ability to mature well. So is whole-bunch pressing, whereby bunches of hand-harvested grapes go straight into the press, bypassing the crusher. This gentler technique involves much less skin contact, and so yields juices with less colour, solids and phenols, (flavour compounds), but greater delicacy.

In New Zealand the classic Chardonnays are all partly or wholly barrel-fermented. At least part of the final blend is also usually barrel-matured on its yeast lees – with regular stirring of the lees (*bâtonnage*) another option – for six months to a year. Barrel fermentation, lees-aging and lees-stirring contribute a yeast-related flavour complexity to the wines, promote a more harmonious integration of the wood and wine characters and add a soft, creamy texture. Most of the classic New Zealand Chardonnays also undergo, at least in part, a secondary, softening malolactic fermentation. The search here is for a softer-acid style with heightened complexity.

Most classic Chardonnays are at their peak (or on their high plateau) at between three and five years old.

chardonnay

Ata Rangi Craighall Chardonnay

The word "seamless" often crops up in Oliver Masters' conversation. A brother-in-law of Ata Rangi founder, Clive Paton, Masters has been a partner in the company since 1995, with special responsibility for producing one of Martinborough's – and New Zealand's – most distinguished Chardonnays: Ata Rangi Craighall. What does he mean by "seamless"?

"The great white Burgundies of France don't have fruit, oak or 'malo' characters sticking out," says Masters. "They're integrated wines, with complexity and persistence." In my own tasting notes over the years for Craighall Chardonnay, that same word features again and again: "seamless". Powerful, mouthfilling and lush, it's a beautifully balanced and harmonious wine with an outstanding concentration of peachy, nutty, mealy, biscuity flavour and a smooth, ultra-rich finish. This is one of New Zealand's most opulent Chardonnays.

Masters sees the Martinborough district as ideal for growing Chardonnay. "You need a balance between too hot and too cold. That balance is especially important with Pinot Noir, but it's also vital with Chardonnay. Marlborough produces a tight, more limey style of Chardonnay with high acidity. In Hawke's Bay and Gisborne, you can get extremely ripe tropical fruit flavours, but the wines can be less focused. In Martinborough, we get rich stonefruit/peach flavours – sometimes, almost into figs – with real concentration and weight, and the wines still have a focus."

Stony and sheltered, the Craighall vineyard lies straight across Puruatanga Road from the winery.

Ata Rangi has sourced fruit from Craighall for a decade, but not until 1997 did it acquire a financial stake. Now the front block is jointly owned by Ata Rangi and Dry River, and the back block jointly leased with Dry River.

Craighall's Chardonnay vines are all of the low-cropping Mendoza clone. In free-draining soils of moderate fertility, the vines' canopies are not dense and yields are low. "We put in a lot of work in the vineyard to get concentrated fruit, and if you get that, you really can't go wrong," says Masters. The age of the vines is also giving fruit weight, which "sucks up the oak", contributing to the wines' seamless quality.

The grapes are hand-picked. Because there is no need to schedule the harvest date around the availability of a mechanical harvester, Ata Rangi's owners are more inclined to take the risk of hanging the grapes out late, in search of extra ripeness. "At the end of the ripening period, Chardonnay gets very fragile," notes Masters. "Persistent rain makes Chardonnay fall to pieces quickly, so Martinborough's typically dry autumn weather is ideal for achieving that extra ripeness."

Once at the winery, the grapes are all whole-bunch pressed, rather than crushed. Some of the juice is run straight from the press to barrels for a high-solids ferment; the rest is clear-settled. The wine is all fermented in French oak barriques (20 to 25 per cent new). Handling is semi-oxidative, with little use of sulphur dioxide. The young wine is matured on its gross lees, and about 30 per cent undergoes a softening malolactic fermentation. The amount of lees-stirring is gradually increasing, as Masters and Phyll Pattie – Paton's wife, who originally controlled the Chardonnay production – gain greater confidence in the ability of the fruit to absorb such handling.

(Left to right) Alison Paton, Oliver Masters, Clive Paton and Phyll Pattie.

Although the Ata Rangi partners look to classic white Burgundy for inspiration, they are not trying to emulate its style. "Our wine will always have greater fruit character," says Masters. "But many New Zealand Chardonnays have obvious oak influence, or obvious 'malo'. We're aiming for that seamless character, the integration that fine Burgundy shows – that's the mentality that runs right through our approach."

Craighall Chardonnay (retail around $32) is a rare wine. Only about 400 cases are made in a good year, dropping to 250 cases in a light year. Although the wine is rarely exhibited in competitions, the 1996 vintage won a gold medal at the Air New Zealand Wine Awards, and was runner-up for the Chardonnay trophy.

Craighall Chardonnay has only recently begun to emerge from the shadow of its illustrious stablemate, Ata Rangi Pinot Noir. Yet the vertical tasting (below) demonstrated that the wine is improving almost on a vintage-by-vintage basis, and is clearly one of New Zealand's lushest, most powerful, most concentrated and downright delicious Chardonnays.

tasting notes

These notes are from a vertical tasting of the 1991 to 1998 vintages, held at the winery in November 1998.

1998 NR Light yellow. Big, fresh, rich wine with very ripe, citrusy, mealy flavours and a touch of butterscotch. Creamy texture. Beautiful fruit shining through. Full of promise, with commanding mouthfeel. (Not rated, because tasted as a representative barrel sample, prior to bottling.)

1997 ☆☆☆☆☆ Light-medium yellow. Strikingly fragrant. Lush, harmonious, beautifully rich wine with concentrated, ripe citrus fruit flavours, a touch of butteriness and unobtrusive acidity. Plump, mealy, complex wine with a long, spreading finish. The best of the bunch – a gorgeous wine with enormous depth. **Drink 2000-02.**

1996 ☆☆☆☆☆ Light-medium-yellow. Soft, succulent, seamless wine with superbly rich citrusy fruit and hints of fig. Great weight, with biscuity, mealy complexities and sweet-fruit delights. Looking back, the breakthrough wine for the label. Ready now onwards. **Drink 1999-2001.**

1995 ☆☆☆☆✦ Medium yellow. More refined than the 1994, but slightly less majestic than the 1996 and 97 – a bit less fragrant and ripe-tasting. Impressively rich citrusy fruit characters, showing higher acidity than usual. **Drink 1999-2000.**

1994 ☆☆☆☆ Medium-full yellow. Rich, toasty, mature bouquet. Big, very toasty wine, slightly less complex than the later vintages, with rich, citrusy, limey fruit flavours and a creamy texture. Ready. **Drink 1999.**

1993 Not made (Martinborough and Hawke's Bay blend).

1992 Not made (Hawke's Bay).

1991 ☆☆☆☆ (Grown in the Craighall vineyard, but labelled simply as Ata Rangi Chardonnay.) Full yellow. Toasty/peachy bouquet. A big wine, still very alive, with firm acid spine and rich, slightly buttery, citrus fruit and peach flavours. Just past its peak, but holding well for a 1991. **Drink ASAP.**

Babich Irongate Chardonnay

CLASSIC

When Joe Babich made the first Irongate Chardonnay in 1985, he told no-one – not even his brother and partner, Peter. "I was making it in a French style, and kept it a secret in case it was a failure," recalls Joe. "I used to furtively stir the barrels after work, when nobody was around."

Steely, intensely flavoured, lean, Irongate is one of New Zealand's most subtle, classically proportioned and long-lived Chardonnays. Although far from a blockbuster style, show success was swift. The 1985 won a gold medal and the Vintners Trophy for the best current vintage dry white at the 1985 National Wine Competition – a feat repeated in 1987. Until the arrival of The Patriarch Chardonnay in 1995, Irongate was Babich's white-wine flagship, and it remains a classy, distinctive wine that often performs outstandingly in the cellar.

In its youth, Irongate is typically fine and elegant, tight and restrained, only hinting at the power and richness it later unfolds. "I've never been a fan of blowsy, excessively woody Chardonnay that tastes good for 18 months and then falls away," says Joe Babich. "My goal with Irongate Chardonnay has been to create a wine that in style fits somewhere between the flintiness of Chablis and the opulence of Montrachet."

Irongate is in essence a single-vineyard wine – although the name Irongate recently leapt a fence. The 1985 to 1996 vintages were sourced exclusively from the Irongate vineyard (now renamed Hastings vineyard) in Gimblett Road, Hawke's Bay, then owned by David Irving and

Gavin Yortt. Today, the name Irongate is applied to the property right next door. Owned by Fernhill Holdings (in which Babich is the major shareholder), this new Irongate was previously known as Mara Estate Gimblett Road vineyard. The 1997 to 1999 vintages of Irongate Chardonnay contain a decreasing proportion of the original vineyard's fruit, but from 2000 onwards the grapes will be sourced entirely from the new block.

Named after the Irongate aquifer, which flows deep beneath the surface, the vineyard once formed part of the bed of the Ngaruroro River. In shingly, arid, extremely free-draining soils, the irrigated vines develop small, open canopies of foliage, maximising the grapes' exposure to the sun. The typical smallness of the berries – giving a high skin to juice ratio in the "must" – is a key factor behind the flavour concentration in the wine.

Key aspects of the wine's handling include hand-picking (rather than machine harvesting) of the fruit since 1998; full barrel fermentation since 1988 (previously partial); maturation in 225-litre French oak barriques since 1989 (previously in larger puncheons); one-third new oak; no malolactic fermentation (except in 1988 and 1993); and six to eight months' maturation of the wine on its yeast lees, with regular stirring "to fine the harsh extractives".

Why does Irongate Chardonnay have the ability to flourish for over a decade, when many New Zealand Chardonnays decline after three or four years? "We handle the wine very, very carefully," says Babich. "It's Old World handling to the end of the lees-aging stage. For example, at the beginning we don't take precautions against oxidation of the juice, because it doesn't hurt the finished wine. Some oxidation of the juice means the wine will be less prone to oxidation afterwards, and you get better, paler colour. However, once the wine's out of the barrel, it's New World, anaerobic handling, and the wine's bottled under nitrogen."

Between the 1985 and 1998 vintages, production of Irongate Chardonnay has risen from 250 to 2000 cases. The early gold medals and trophies got the label off to a great start, but for Joe Babich, the greatest satisfaction lies elsewhere. "The ultimate reception is the marketplace – and people keep buying it." The normal retail price is $25.

Finesse and delicacy are the hallmarks of Irongate Chardonnay, rather than brute power. Because it is not opulent and fast-maturing, the wine requires understanding in its youth. However, after at least four years, when it's in full stride, Irongate unfurls into one of New Zealand's finest Chardonnays, intense, finely structured and graceful.

tasting notes

These notes are from a vertical tasting of the 1985 to 1998 vintages, held at the winery in November 1998.

1998 (NR) Tasted just after final blending, about three weeks before bottling. A high alcohol style, giving an impression of real scale and power. Intense citrus fruit flavours intermeshed with mealy, biscuity complexities. Looks outstanding.

1997 ☆☆☆☆☆ Highly fragrant – unusually so for a young Irongate. Richer on the palate than most past vintages (apparently reflecting the riper fruit achieved in the company's own vineyard). Powerful wine with deep grapefruit-like characters, quality oak and a crisp, mealy, beautifully modulated finish. **Open 2001-10.**

1996 ☆☆☆☆ ⚹ Light lemon/green. Classic Irongate style – youthful, tight, lemony, appley, mealy, still unevolved. Long, nutty finish with fresh acidity. Needs time: **Drink 2000-08.**

1995 ☆☆☆☆☆ Youthful yellow/green. Wonderfully fragrant nose, very complex and inviting. Robust, immaculate wine with concentrated, ripe fruit flavours (harvested before the wet end of the season). Lemony, mealy, perfectly poised palate. Taut, terrific – the best-ever Irongate? A great drink now or cellaring proposition. **Open 1999-2007.**

1994 ☆☆☆☆ Medium yellow. Lemony, biscuity fragrance. Elegant wine with good depth. Complex wine with citrusy, mealy, slightly earthy flavours and good acid spine. Maturing well but less intense than the 1995. **Drink 1999-2005.**

1993 ☆☆☆ Golden. Honied, slightly dull nose. Still some pleasure here, but not a top vintage. Full bodied and citrusy, with firm acid, *Botrytis*-derived honey characters and a toasty, crisp finish. Starting to fade; drink up. **Open 1999.**

1992 ☆☆☆☆☆ Light gold. Notably lush fruit flavours, but also firmly structured – long and tight. Bigger than the 1991. Full bodied wine with loads of grapefruit-like, mealy, toasty,

appetisingly crisp flavour. Powerful, persistent wine, maturing well. **Open 1999-2003.**

1991 ☆☆☆☆☆ Light gold. Classic Irongate, exemplifying the refinement typical of the label. Attractive, nutty fragrance. Lovely, slightly lean palate with fresh, citrusy, incisive flavours and a tight, long finish. Beautifully modulated wine that should be very long-lived. **Open 1999-2003.**

1990 ☆☆ Gold/amber. Dull, honied nose. Strong *Botrytis* influence on palate. Mouthfilling, crisp wine, now past its best. **Drink ASAP.**

1989 ☆☆☆☆☆ Deep yellow/light gold. Still very lively on the nose – rich and toasty. Mouthfilling and crisp, with intense citrus/lime flavours. Slightly toasty. Long, lemony finish, full of vigour. Firm acid style. Very typical of label. **Drink 1999-2000.**

1988 ☆☆ ⚹ Deep gold/brown-tinged. Clearly reflects cyclone Bola with its *Botrytis*-derived honey characters. Drying out, losing its fruit. Toasty bottle-aged characters and a firm, crisp finish. Always a lesser wine. **Drink ASAP.**

1987 ☆☆ Deep gold. Well past its best. Orangey, oxidised flavours. Still drinkable but very tired.

1986 ☆☆☆☆☆ ⚹ Deep yellow/light gold. Toasty, slightly honied fragrance. Strong, citrusy flavours braced by good acid. Complex, mealy, nutty characters add complexity. Currently slightly less pleasureable than the 1985, but has lasted well. **Open 1999-2000.**

1985 ☆☆☆☆☆ Deep yellow, greenish tinge. Toasty, developed bouquet, nutty, buttery and rich. Soft, full palate, rich and concentrated, slightly earthy and mealy. Complex, extraordinarily long-lived wine, starting to dry out on the finish but still remarkably enjoyable. **Drink 1999-2001.**

Babich The Patriarch Chardonnay

POTENTIAL CLASSIC

O nly three vintages of The Patriarch Chardonnay have been released, but they are all such distinguished, multi-faceted wines that this is clearly a classic in the making – provided that Babich stick with Chardonnay as the varietal foundation of their white-wine flagship. Which is not guaranteed.

Named in honour of Josip Babich, who founded Babich Wines in 1916, The Patriarch range features one white and one red wine, selected by the company's winemakers as the most outstanding wines of the vintage, regardless of variety. So far the white wines have all been Chardonnays from the company's vineyard in Gimblett Road, Hawke's Bay, but future releases may be based on other grapes – Sauvignon Blanc, Sémillon, Chenin Blanc, Gewürztraminer, Riesling or Pinot Gris. The Patriarch label is not permanently attached to any particular vineyard, region or variety. Quality is the sole selection criterion.

An arresting wine with great power, complexity and harmony, The Patriarch Chardonnay is the fruit of Babich's determination to investigate the boundaries of winemaking. "We want to explore things," says Joe Babich, "to push the boundaries out all the time. It doesn't come from textbooks; we're working things out for ourselves."

For its much longer established Irongate Chardonnay, the winery has a very clear idea of the style it wants. "With The Patriarch, we haven't yet," says Babich, "except we do have an overall goal – complexity and finesse." Winemaker Neill Culley adds: "We do want a Chardonnay that's more

interesting at the end than the beginning ... most New Zealand Chardonnays are the opposite."

The grapes are hand-picked in the company's Gimblett Road vineyard. In 1998, the vines were crop-thinned to 2.5 tonnes/acre (compared to 3.5 tonnes/acre for the Irongate Chardonnay), which had "a profound effect" on the grapes' flavour concentration, according to Joe Babich. For the journey from Hawke's Bay to the Henderson winery, the fruit is packed in 20 kg bins, stacked in a refrigerated 20-foot container.

In Auckland, the grapes are whole-bunch pressed and fermented with a high proportion of indigenous yeasts (100 per cent in 1996; 50 per cent in 1998). All of the wine goes through a secondary, softening malolactic fermentation – partly to differentiate it from Irongate Chardonnay, and partly because winemaker Neill Culley believes that most top Chardonnays are characterised by a low malic acid content in the juice, and also go through malolactic fermentation.

Like Irongate Chardonnay, The Patriarch Chardonnay is fully barrel-fermented. However, The Patriarch spends longer in oak casks (11 months, compared to six to eight months for Irongate), and the new oak influence is stronger (50 per cent for The

Patriarch; one-third for Irongate).

Retailing at $30, The Patriarch Chardonnay is only made in small volumes – around 350 cases per year. The first 1995 vintage performed brilliantly in shows, scooping three gold medals. The 1996 won no golds, but Joe Babich emphasises The Patriarch "is not made specifically to win gold medals".

How will it mature? Babich wines typically perform strongly in the cellar; Irongate Chardonnay has a proven ability to age gracefully for a decade or longer. Markedly lusher and softer than Irongate, The Patriarch is a more seductive wine in its youth, drinking well from the beginning. The debut 1995 vintage is developing well, but its peak drinking period is still unknown.

A powerful, high alcohol style, The Patriarch Chardonnay possesses great weight, impressive fruit concentration and deliciously deep, figgy, biscuity flavour. Rich and harmonious, it also has an extra dimension – a rare degree of complexity that makes it truly absorbing drinking. 🌿

Joe (left) and Peter Babich – sons of The Patriarch.

tasting notes

These notes are from a vertical tasting of the 1995 to 1998 vintages, held at the winery in November 1998, supplemented by a further tasting of the 1998 vintage in March 1999.

1998 ☆☆☆☆☆ Weighty, bone-dry wine with impressive power. Deep citrus and fig flavours, with mealy, nutty, butterscotch-like complexities and finely balanced acidity. A big, multi-faceted wine, still a baby. Very powerful, yet beautifully delicate and harmonious. The presence in the mouth is quite commanding; everything is there for a great future. **Open 2000+.** (This tasting note is from a blind tasting of various 1998 Chardonnays held in March 1999.)

1997 Not made.

1996 ☆☆☆☆☆ Pale straw hue. Complex, nutty, mealy, slightly oxidative bouquet. Very big and rounded, powerful style with deep citrus, fig and oak flavours. Great texture – weighty and soft. Very long finish. **Drink 1999-2005.**

1995 ☆☆☆☆☆ Light yellow. A hedonist's delight – big, soft, lush wine with rich, ripe tropical and citrus fruit flavours, very delicate and deep. An opulent wine with nutty, mealy complexities in a very concentrated style with mouth-encircling flavours. Sheer pleasure. **Drink 1999-2005.**

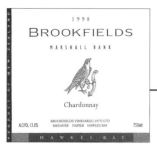

Brookfields Marshall Bank Chardonnay

(formerly Brookfields Reserve Chardonnay)

CLASSIC

Don't expect to find this wine in the medal lists of major competitions. Hawke's Bay winemaker, Peter Robertson, avoids the show circuit. "I stopped entering the Chardonnay when the 1986, a real beauty, was thrown out. We sell out at the price I want [$34], so why bother entering it in competitions?"

Robust and flavour-packed, Marshall Bank Chardonnay was labelled Brookfields Reserve Chardonnay up to and including the 1997 vintage, but was recently renamed Marshall Bank Chardonnay, after Robertson's grandfather's property in Otago. It is typically a rich, concentrated wine with a lovely depth of peachy, toasty, buttery flavour. Lush and complex, it drinks well in its youth, but top vintages (such as the 1992) also mature gracefully long term.

Initially grown at Fernhill, since the 1997 vintage the wine has been entirely estate-grown at Meeanee. Based on hand-picked, Mendoza clone grapes, cropped lightly (at an average yield of three tonnes per acre), it is fully barrel-fermented in all-new French oak barriques. Although it typically spends eight months in wood, the wine is only lees-aged for three to four months: "I don't want bready flavours," says Robertson. The degree of malolactic fermentation varies with the season – none in 1998; 50 per cent in 1997; 66 per cent in 1996.

If you ask Peter Robertson about key factors contributing to the standard and style of the most recent vintages of his top Chardonnay, he highlights three points. "We're now taking grapes off mature vines [10 years old]; since 1994 we've moved away from Nevers to Alliers oak; and since the mid 1990s we've moved to quite a lot of malolactic fermentation." Older vines, he believes, give greater flavour intensity; Alliers oak gives a more restrained wood influence than Nevers oak, boosting the wine's harmony; and the increasing degree of malolactic fermentation has broadened the palate and added another flavour component. Robertson's goal is "to make a Chardonnay that when young is somewhat restrained, but from a year onwards offers integrated flavours."

When to drink it? "I often think winemakers enjoy their wines when they're still a bit too young; younger than the punters do," says Robertson, who recommends drinking his top Chardonnay at three to four years old.

Brookfields Marshall Bank Chardonnay is a small volume wine – only 400 to 500 cases are made each year. Most is sold in New Zealand, but the wine also trickles out to Australia and Asian markets. Sturdy and overflowing with ripe grapefruit and stone-fruit flavours, Marshall Bank is a classic example of the Hawke's Bay regional style, with notable richness and strength. 🍷

Peter Robertson makes substantial, flavour-crammed Hawke's Bay Chardonnays and Cabernet-based reds.

tasting notes

These notes are principally from a vertical tasting of the 1991 to 1997 vintages, held at the winery in December 1998. The 1998 was tasted separately, in March 1999.

1998 ☆☆☆☆☆ Pale lemon hue. Fat and rich, with a surge of very ripe and sweet fruit flavours, figgy and peachy. Very lush yet delicate wine, deliciously approachable in its youth, with oak and lees-aging complexities in a mealy and creamy style with mouthfilling body. Clearly capable of unfolding well. **Drink 2000+.**

1997 ☆☆☆☆☆ Medium yellow. Oaky/peachy bouquet. Powerful wine with rich citrus fruit and peach flavours and a firm, slightly buttery finish. A complex, slightly oxidative style with crisp acidity, still developing. **Drink 2000+.**

1996 ☆☆☆☆☆ Full, bright yellow. A more "malo"-influenced style than the 1997 (two-thirds of the 1996 went through malolactic fermentation.) Strapping, soft, rich, citrusy wine, powerful and very harmonious. Intense, ripe fruit fleshed out with balanced oak and malolactic fermentation characters. Lovely now. **Drink 1999-02.**

1995 ☆☆☆☆☆ Full, bright yellow. Similar to the 1996, but tighter, with rich grapefruit flavours and mealy, biscuity oak and lees-aging complexities. Good acid spine. Taut wine, still developing, and likely to be long-lived. **Drink 1999-02.**

1994 ☆☆☆☆☆ Light gold. Big, characterful wine, with some parallels to the 1997. Taut, slightly cheesy (100 per cent malolactic fermentation), buttery and honied. Complex and very robust. **Drink 1999-01.**

1993 ☆☆☆ Medium gold. Strong, *Botrytis*-derived honey characters on nose. Strong citrusy fruit, distinctly honied, with firm acid. A lesser vintage, lacking its customary power and richness. **Drink ASAP.**

1992 ☆☆☆☆☆ Light-medium gold. Beautifully structured, very rich wine with intense flavours of citrus fruits, honey and nuts, braced by firm acidity. Impressively concentrated, tight and focused. A real standout. Lovely now. **Drink 1999-2000.**

1991 ☆☆☆☆ Medium gold. Less power and concentration than the 1992. Mellow, but still alive and holding well, with rich citrusy fruit, firm acid backbone and considerable complexity. **Drink 1999-2000.** (This was the winery's last bottle.)

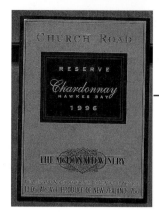

Church Road Reserve Chardonnay

If you taste your way through every vintage of Montana's top Hawke's Bay Chardonnay, one thing is blindingly obvious – the winemakers at the country's largest wine company are learning as they go. The 1994 and later vintages of Church Road Reserve Chardonnay are markedly finer and more delicate, and likely to be much longer-lived, than those from the early 1990s.

Church Road Reserve Chardonnay is a bold, punchy style built on Hawke's Bay's rich fruit flavours, strongly seasoned with wood. Compared to its stablemate, the standard Church Road Chardonnay, the reserve wine is more powerful and concentrated. "It's a full-on Chardonnay, in terms of fruit and oak," says Peter Hurlstone, winemaker at The McDonald Winery, home of the Church Road range. "It's a blockbuster with a generous amount of oak, lengthy lees-aging and lots of *bâtonnage* [lees-stirring], but we're also building in more and more elegance and complexity."

Much of the fruit is grown in Montana's warm, sheltered Korokipo vineyard on State Highway 50, between Fernhill and Taradale. The heavy soils with a high clay content develop "really ripe, pineappley characters" in the grapes, says Hurlstone. Another important source of fruit is Montana's Phoenix vineyard, closer to the coast near Clive, where in the slightly lighter and siltier soils, the grapes develop "stone-fruit and melon characters". Only the low-yielding Mendoza clone of Chardonnay is used for the Church Road Reserve label, with the vines' yields restricted to an average of three tonnes per acre.

About 80 per cent of the grapes are mechanically harvested, giving a degree of skin contact that strengthens the wine's flavour and develops "a broader, richer palate," says Hurlstone. However, about 20 per cent of the fruit is hand-picked and whole-bunch pressed, in the search for greater finesse and elegance. The total amount of skin contact is gradually decreasing, in order to achieve a slightly more delicate wine that will mature better over the long haul.

The wine is fully fermented in French oak barriques, typically two-thirds new, with the rest one year-old. Montana avoids the "louder, sweet vanillan characters" of American oak, preferring the "lifted spice and toast characters" (in Hurlstone's words) of medium-toast French oak (with a small proportion of heavy toast). The wine remains on its full yeast lees for the total time in barrel (up to 10 months), with fortnightly lees-stirring to enhance the yeast characters and add suppleness to the palate. On average, about 40 per cent of the wine goes through malolactic fermentation, to provide additional complexity and soften the acidity.

After some of the earlier non-reserve Church

Road Chardonnays faded early, Montana's winemakers learned the importance of preventing post-ferment oxidation. "We're not worried about oxidation of the unfermented juice," says Hurlstone. "But once the ferment has finished, we've learned to maintain a reasonably high sulphur regime and use gas blanketing, in order to keep the wine's freshness."

Of all New Zealand's top Chardonnays, Church Road Reserve (which retails at around $30) is one of the easiest to find. Production has soared from 1000 cases in 1991 to 5000 cases in an average year and 8000 cases in a favourable vintage like 1998.

When is the best time to drink it? Unlike the winery's rarer Cuvée Series Chardonnay, a fully whole-bunch pressed, delicate, slow-maturing Burgundian style, Church Road Reserve Chardonnay is made for fairly early drinking. Although the latest vintages are aging more gracefully than their predecessors, the wine is in full stride at three to five years old.

Montana rarely enters New Zealand wine competitions, so its top Hawke's Bay white wine does not have an impressive haul of medals. Given its upfront appeal, if it were entered in shows, it should do well. Church Road Reserve Chardonnay is very much a "style" wine – powerful, smooth and packed with ripe citrus and tropical fruit flavours, fleshed out with strong toasty oak.

Montana's Korokipo vineyard, the source of its finest Hawke's Bay Chardonnay.

tasting notes

These notes are from a vertical tasting of the 1991 to 1996 vintages, held at The McDonald Winery in December 1998.

1997 Not made.

1996 ☆☆☆☆☆ Light yellow. Powerful wine, more upfront than the 1995. Broad, rich and soft, with deep peach and grapefruit flavours, toasty oak and a buttery, rounded finish. Very typical of the label. **Drink 1999-2001.**

1995 ☆☆☆☆☆ Star wine of the lineup, from a warmer and drier than average (despite the late rains) growing season. Pale yellow, with green tints. Mouthfilling, very stylish wine, noticeably more delicate than its predecessors, with a beguiling depth of sweet, ripe grapefruit/peach flavours and well-integrated oak adding richness. Not a blockbuster, but very classy. **Drink 1999-2001.**

1994 ☆☆☆☆☆ Full yellow. Still fresh and seemingly in peak condition. Big, richly fruity, mealy, toasty wine, delicious now, with grapefruit/pineapple flavours of great depth, toasty, buttery characters and a soft, long finish. Very harmonious. **Drink 1999-2000.**

1993 ☆☆☆½ From an extremely cool but low-cropping vintage, in which 74 per cent of the wine went through malolactic fermentation. Medium-full yellow. Toasty, slightly honied characters on nose and palate. Strong citrus/peach flavours with firm acidity. Not especially complex and past its best. **Drink ASAP.**

1992 ☆☆☆☆½ Light-medium gold. Fresher than the 1991, with rich citrusy/pineappley flavours, still lively. Mouthfilling and rounded. More delicate than the 1991, with concentrated fruit and toasty, buttery oak giving a quite lush effect. Slightly past its peak. **Drink ASAP.**

1991 ☆☆☆½ From a warm, wet vintage. Deep gold, hint of brown. Big, peachy, toasty wine with sweet fruit characters and loads of flavour, but starting to fall away at the finish and slightly hard. Lacks real delicacy and staying power. **Drink ASAP.**

**Reserve
Chardonnay**
Barrel Fermented

1998

Produced by Clearview Estate
Te Awanga Hawke's Bay
New Zealand

14.5% Alc   750ml

Clearview Estate Reserve Chardonnay

SUPER CLASSIC

If a prize were awarded for New Zealand's most power-packed Chardonnay, Clearview Estate Reserve would romp in. Exceptionally mouthfilling and overflowing with peachy, oaky, mealy flavour, it's a hedonist's delight. Yet despite its grand scale, it is also a wine of delicacy and finesse, ranking among the country's greatest and most memorable dry whites.

"I'm not a winemaker," said Tim Turvey when I asked him how he makes such a brilliant wine. "That is, I'm not a qualified winemaker. What's important is the old *terroir* thing the French talk about – it's this special piece of dirt by the sea."

Turvey is proprietor of the tiny Clearview Estate winery, right on the Hawke's Bay coast, at Te Awanga. The vineyard (an old Vidal block originally planted in 1916) is on a knoll three metres high, with shingle running through the middle. "It's rock hard in summer, but there's enough soil to sustain the vines without irrigation," says Turvey. "The proximity to the sea keeps temperatures up at night, and the lovely, constant air movement means there's normally no disease pressure from *Botrytis*. So we can hold the grapes on the vines until they ripen fully."

Ultra-ripe fruit is the key to the wine's style. The grapes are "golden, honeyish, with an amazingly luscious fruit character," reports Turvey. They are never harvested below 25 brix [sugar], which gives around 14 per cent alcohol, even in cooler years. The 1997 vintage was 14.5 per cent, the 1995 vintage 14.8 per cent alcohol.

Turvey has no interest in making light or restrained Chardonnays. "I want an enormous wine with mid-

palate weight. Anyone can make subtle Chardonnay. Many New Zealand Chardonnays don't have balls. Let's make a statement! People say to me: 'Wow, I've never tasted anything like this.'" Although he has no Burgundian model, Turvey is strongly attracted to the Chardonnays from Kistler Vineyards in California – barrel-fermented, malolactic, toasty heavyweights.

The vines, planted between 1988 and 1991 and all of the Mendoza clone, are pruned for low yields (typically two to three tonnes per acre) and hand-harvested. Half of the juice is given up to six hours skin contact, to give the wine early appeal; the other portion is whole-bunch pressed, producing a delicate juice with a low level of phenolics and pH, which enhances the wine's ability to develop well in the bottle.

Fermentation is in all-new French oak barriques (except for the 1993, when Turvey used a high percentage of American oak). Most of the barrels are cool-fermented for several weeks at 11-12°C; five per cent are fermented hot, at 23-26°C, to "burn off the fruit flavours and give the wine more glycerol and weight". The total time in oak is 10 to 11 months, with weekly stirring of the yeast lees, and about 25 per cent of the final blend undergoes a softening malolactic fermentation.

Clearview Estate Reserve Chardonnay is made in reasonable quantities – over 1000 cases in an average year, sold mainly by mail order at around $30. Turvey suggests cellaring the wine until it is four years old; thereafter, he believes, "it plateaus for another two or three years". The 1994 and subsequent vintages are all outstanding and maturing gracefully.

With its heftiness and exciting flavour concentration, the wine has enjoyed high success on the show circuit, most strikingly at the 1997 Bragato Wine Awards – a show organised by grape growers. Clearview scooped three Chardonnay gold medals (out of a total of eight awarded) with its second-tier Beach-Head Chardonnay 1996 and the 1995 and 1996 Reserve Chardonnays.

I embarked on the vertical tasting (below) wondering whether the wine's upfront style and majestic scale might have been achieved at the price of elegance and an ability to mature well. The doubts proved groundless. Clearview Estate Reserve Chardonnay combines power and finesse in a heady, complex Hawke's Bay style that takes your breath away with its extraordinary explosion of flavour. 🍷

At the basket press: Tim Turvey (right) and vineyard manager Grant Houston.

tasting notes

These notes are mainly from a vertical tasting of the 1993 to 1997 vintages, held at the winery in December 1998. The 1998 vintage was tasted in Auckland in March 1999. (The winery has no stocks remaining of the 1991 and 1992 vintages, labelled Chardonnay Barrel Fermented, but Tim Turvey reports both are "definitely drink up" material.)

1998 ☆☆☆☆☆ Pale lemon-green. Hefty wine (14.5 per cent alcohol) with powerful peach, grapefruit and oak flavours. Quite unevolved and unready, but shows tremendous weight and depth through the palate. Mealy and complex, with a lasting finish. A crime to open before 2000. **Drink 2001-04.**

1997 ☆☆☆☆☆ One of the best yet, offering an enormous amount in its youth. Pale yellow, with a very rich bouquet. Super-bold palate (harbouring 14.5 per cent alcohol), with a bottomless depth of grapefruit, fig and biscuity oak flavours. Excitingly concentrated wine, rivalling the great 1995. **Drink 1999-2003.**

1996 ☆☆☆☆☆ Fractionally overshadowed by the surrounding years, perhaps due to the higher-yielding vintage. Light yellow. Slightly less fragrant than the 1995, but no lack of concentration or delicacy on the palate, which shows lovely, lush, citrusy, figgy fruit flavours coupled with strong biscuity oak. Complex and powerful wine with good acid spine, still opening out. **All in place for 1999-2002.**

1995 ☆☆☆☆☆ Light yellow. A monster of a wine (alcohol 14.5 per cent), with a very creamy texture and thrilling flavour concentration. Astutely balanced citrusy fruit and spicy oak in a muscular, yet beautifully fragrant and very refined style. Absolutely no sign of decline. **Drink 1999-2001.**

1994 ☆☆☆☆☆ Light-medium yellow, slightly green-tinged. Maturing well. A bold, refined wine with intense ripe grapefruit flavours, balanced oak and acidity. Still fresh and vigorous, with a long finish. At peak? **Drink 1999-2000.**

1993 ☆☆☆☆ Medium gold, showing markedly more development than the later vintages. Big, toasty, ripe peach/citrus flavours, slightly honied, with a touch of phenolic hardness (last of the basket press). Good fruit concentration and maturing solidly, but slightly lacks finesse. Still a lot of pleasure to be had, but **drink ASAP.**

Cloudy Bay Chardonnay

Many of New Zealand's leading Chardonnays are hard to find in the shops, their output amounting to only a few hundred cases. Cloudy Bay, by contrast, produces a top class Chardonnay in sufficient volume (currently about 13,000 cases) to market it around the world.

Powerful and authoritative, the Cloudy Bay Chardonnay style reflects the searching, citrusy flavours and high natural acidity of Marlborough grapes. It is a complex wine, utilising a wide range of Burgundian vinification techniques. With its impressive concentration, bold alcohol (typically 14 per cent) and firm acidity, it matures better over the long haul than most New Zealand Chardonnays, and is a classic candidate for the cellar.

The grapes are sourced from both estate vineyards and growers' vineyards, all located within the Wairau Valley. Soils vary from gravelly, clay/silt loams at Fairhall, on the south side of the valley, to stony, sandy/silt loams at Rapaura, all of which are free-draining and require irrigation during typical Marlborough summers. The vines, all of the Mendoza clone, yield an average of 3 to 3.5 tonnes per acre.

"Getting the fruit ripe is not an issue," says winemaker Kevin Judd. "We have no need to chaptalise [supplement the grapes' natural sugars] in most years. The power of the wine comes from ripe fruit and high alcohol." For Judd, the key problem has been high acidity, rather than sugar levels. The first 1986 Cloudy Bay Chardonnay was almost not released, so spiky was its acidity, but Scott Henry trellising and leaf removal around the bunches have since succeeded in reducing the grapes' acid levels.

Machine-harvested, the grapes are transported to the winery, destemmed and crushed directly into tank presses. Most batches are inoculated with *prise de mousse* yeast, but about one-third are allowed to ferment using indigenous yeasts.

About 80 per cent of the juice is fermented in French oak barriques (20 to 25 per cent new); the rest is fermented in stainless steel tanks. All of the wine is then aged in barrels on its yeast lees for a year (with no stirring), protected from the air with a strict regime of sulphur additions. On average, half the final blend goes through malolactic fermentation. All components are blended after 12 months' oak-aging.

Over the years, Judd and his senior oenologist, James Healy, have made two key changes to the way the grapes are handled in the winery. "We didn't use malolactic fermentation at all in 1986," recalls Judd, "but within five years we moved to 50 per cent. It's giving us better acid balance and more savoury characters. In 1992, we introduced a degree of indigenous yeast fermentation, which doesn't give fruitiness or zest, but rather fat, savoury, rich characters."

Priced at around $32, Cloudy Bay Chardonnay improves for at least four years, and top vintages have a proven ability to flourish for a decade. Healy notes that "hand-picking and whole-bunch pressing would give the wine even greater longevity, more like white Burgundy".

Although it is inevitably overshadowed by the all-conquering Sauvignon Blanc, and Cloudy Bay does not enter wine competitions, international acclaim for the Chardonnay has been high. "[New Zealand's] finest Chardonnays, showing balance between oak and fruit, have emerged from Cloudy Bay," declared Robert Parker in the United States, after tasting the 1992. "Yes it's good, yes it's impeccably balanced and yes, it will develop even greater richness and complexity with further time in bottle," enthused *Wine* magazine in the UK, reviewing the 1993 vintage. "Rich, forward, pineappley fruit with a nuance of hazelnuts and a hint of yeastiness on the finish. Grab it while you can."

A world apart from the richly fragrant and vibrantly fruity, softly structured Chardonnays of Gisborne, Cloudy Bay Chardonnay is a taut, slow-developing wine that despite its obvious power can be restrained, even closed, in its youth. At three to four years old, however, it emerges as a sturdy, complex wine that fills the mouth with rich, savoury, steely flavour.

tasting notes
These notes are from a vertical tasting of the 1986 to 1997 vintages, held at the winery in January 1999.

1997 ☆☆☆☆☆ Light yellow. Freshly fragrant, powerful and savoury wine with ripe, citrusy fruit flavours wrapped in nutty, biscuity oak and a creamy texture. Authoritative wine, fairly forward in its appeal. **Drink 2000-05.**

1996 ☆☆☆☆☆ Light yellow. Youthful, savoury, citrusy aromas. A classic vintage – very weighty, with a lovely spread of grapefruit and biscuity oak flavours. Mealy and complex, tightly structured and long. A splendid wine which should have a great future. **Drink 1999-2005.**

1995 ☆☆☆☆ Light-medium yellow. Taut wine, slightly leaner than most vintages. Grapefruit flavours with balanced oak, underpinned by firm acidity. Slightly austere, but still youthful. **Drink 1999-2001.**

1994 ☆☆☆☆☆ Medium yellow. Beautifully constructed wine with rich, well-ripened peach and citrus fruit flavours, strong nutty oak and firm acid. Tight, persistent finish. A top vintage offering great drinking now, but also likely to be long-lived. **Drink 1999-2004.**

1993 ☆☆☆☆ Developed, medium gold colour. A less lush style than usual, slightly green-edged, with tight acidity. Full-flavoured, citrusy and nutty, in a fairly austere style. Maturing well, but clearly reflects the very cool vintage. **Drink 1999-2001.**

1992 ☆☆☆☆½ Full yellow. Maturing gracefully. Slightly leaner and higher in acid than the 1991, but tight and elegant, with excellent depth of citrusy, moderately toasty flavours. Deliciously harmonious. **Drink 1999-2001.**

1991 ☆☆☆☆½ Light gold. Mature, toasty, nutty fragrance. Robust, strapping wine (over 14 per cent alcohol) with rich peachy, citrusy, nutty, slightly honied flavours. High impact wine, slightly less refined than the 1990. **Drink 1999-2001.**

1990 ☆☆☆☆☆ Full yellow. Very smart – fresh, searching citrusy, nutty flavours with great vigour and complexity. Authoritative, weighty, Meursault-like wine with a rich, trailing finish. More youthful than the 1989. **Drink 1999-2002.**

1989 ☆☆☆☆☆ Medium gold. Fresher than the older vintages. Weighty wine with a lush array of toasty, nutty, citrusy flavours. Powerful and slightly creamy, with tremendous depth and power. Outstanding now. **Drink 1999-2001.**

1988 ☆☆☆☆ Medium gold. A less ripe style, but surprisingly good, with tense acidity underpinning very nutty and toasty, slightly honied flavours. Vigorous, persistent, ready. **Drink 1999-2000.**

1987 ☆☆☆☆ Deep gold. Still some vigour here. Slightly green-edged, but very toasty and quite rich, with loads of body and flavour. Firm acid style, but good overall harmony. **Drink 1999-2000.**

1986 ☆☆☆ Deep gold, slightly brown. Dull, slightly oxidised bouquet. Still drinkable, but has lost its fruit character. Looked excellent at five years old, but now well past its best. **Drink ASAP.**

Coopers Creek Swamp Reserve Chardonnay

CLASSIC

What's in a name? Coopers Creek's Hawke's Bay wine was at first called Swamp Road Chardonnay, because the grapes were then grown in Swamp Road, in the Omaranui Valley. After congratulating the winery for its precise labelling, Australian wine writer James Halliday suggested: "Why not change the name of the road?"

Delicious when young, but with a proven ability to mature well for several years, Swamp Reserve Chardonnay is a lush, opulent wine with a finely judged balance of rich, citrusy, peachy fruit flavours and toasty oak. It is not the most multi-faceted New Zealand Chardonnay, but it's certainly one of the most seductive.

Since the 1990 vintage, the grapes have been grown exclusively in Coopers Creek's own vineyard straddling Middle Road, hard up against the hills of Havelock North. "It's a special site," believes the company's co-founder and principal shareholder, Andrew Hendry. "The soils are heavy, with a very high limestone content. The vineyard is sheltered from the southerlies, so it gets very hot."

With the Swamp Reserve Chardonnay, winemaker Kim Crawford, who left recently, set out to produce a wine with mouthfilling body and ripe fruit flavours ("we always get those") but more restraint than the company's Hawke's Bay Chardonnay and Gisborne Chardonnay.

The grapes are machine-harvested on a cool day or in the evening, with no sulphur additions, and transported to Auckland.

Once at the winery, the fermentation kicks off in stainless steel tanks, "to retain the fruit characters in the juice", but is mostly completed in French oak barriques, new and one-year-old. Crawford has been anxious to avoid oak dominance; in some years, part of the final blend is handled entirely in tanks.

A key change in the vinification of the wine over the years has been the mounting use of malolactic fermentation. Only a third of the 1989 vintage, for example, went through the softening, secondary fermentation, but the 1997 and 1998 had full malolactic fermentations. "This is not to make the wines attractive earlier, but to add to their complexity," says Crawford. "I like the rounded mouthfeel you get with malolactic fermentation, but by running the ferments warm, we try to avoid the diacetyl [buttery, butterscotch-like] characters often associated with malolactic."

About 2000 cases of Swamp Reserve Chardonnay are produced each year, retailing at around $27. After "one year in barrel, one year in bottle" is Crawford's suggested optimum time for drinking, although the tasting (below) shows that top vintages can mature well for at least seven years.

The 1986 vintage of Swamp Road Chardonnay got the label off to a great start, winning a gold

Andrew and Cyndy Hendry are the major shareholders in Coopers Creek.

medal at that year's National Wine Competition (although it did not mature well). A more recent success came when Swamp Reserve Chardonnay topped an extensive tasting of 1995 New Zealand Chardonnays organised by *Wine* magazine in 1997.

"It's full-bodied yet elegant," enthused judge Caspar Auchterlonie at the *Wine* magazine tasting in London. "Lovely citrus, grapefruit flavours with super toasty oak." Which sums up Coopers Creek Swamp Reserve Chardonnay perfectly.

tasting notes

Almost all of these notes are from a vertical tasting of most of the 1986 to 1997 vintages, held at the winery in November 1998. (The 1987 and 1990 vintages, not rated highly by Andrew Hendry, were not included. The wine was not produced in 1988, 1991 and 1993.) The 1998 vintage was tasted in Auckland in March 1999.

1998 (Not rated; tasted as a tank sample, blended for bottling.) Succulent wine, with rich, very ripe (23.5 brix) grapefruit, melon and fig flavours and strong mealy and butterscotch characters. Mouthfilling, deep wine with a deliciously soft, creamy texture and tremendous drink-young appeal. **Drink 2000-04.**

1997 ☆☆☆☆☆ Pale yellow. Soft, generous, citrus/fig flavours of lovely depth. A highly seductive wine, slightly more complex than the 1996. Balanced acidity, but real creaminess on the palate, reflecting the 100 per cent malolactic fermentation. **Drink 1999-2003.**

1996 ☆☆☆☆☆ Medium yellow. Mouthfilling wine with sweet, ripe citrusy/fig fruit and good acid spine. Delicate, slightly nutty and toasty flavours in a lush, well-structured wine, still developing. **Drink 1999-2002.**

1995 ☆☆☆☆☆ Full yellow. Refined wine, with ripe grapefruit-like characters shining through and a hint of butterscotch. Superbly delicate flavour – rich, nutty, slightly creamy. Outshines the 1994. Great now. **Drink 1999-2001.**

1994 ☆☆☆☆☆ Pale gold. Very powerful wine, fat and rich, with concentrated, mealy, slightly honied flavours. Good now, but offers slightly less delicacy and finesse than the 1995. **Drink 1999-2000.**

1993 Not made.

1992 ☆☆☆☆☆ From a cool, dry vintage that gave "the best fruit ever", according to Kim Crawford. Full yellow/light gold. Toasty/citrusy bouquet. Lovely palate, with no sign of decline – intense and lively, with concentrated grapefruit and toast flavours and finely tuned acid. Complex, well-integrated wine, now at its peak, but should hold its form for several years. **Drink 1999-2001.**

1991 Not made.

1990 "*Botrytis* year" – Kim Crawford. Not tasted.

1989 ☆☆☆☆ (Labelled as Swamp Road.) Light gold. No delights on the nose, but strong citrusy, toasty flavours. Full-bodied and still alive, with good acid backbone, but now developing a hint of tiredness. **Drink ASAP.**

1988 Not made.

1987 "Weakest of the lot" – Andrew Hendry. Not tasted.

1986 (Labelled as Swamp Road.) Deep gold. Lots of *Botrytis*, slightly sherry-like, oxidised. In its death throes. Not rated.

Corbans Cottage Block Gisborne Chardonnay

CLASSIC

Corbans' top-tier Cottage Block wines are handcrafted by the winemakers in each region, with "total freedom to produce the wines of their choice". In other words, the style of the wine is driven by the winemaker, rather than the marketing staff.

The exceptionally stylish and multi-faceted 1994 Cottage Block Gisborne Chardonnay shot to fame by winning a gold medal, the trophy for champion Chardonnay and the trophy for champion wine of the show at the 1995 Air New Zealand Wine Awards. Tasted in 1999, both the 1994 and 1995 vintages are notably complex wines which have matured superbly. These are nutty, mealy, sturdy yet subtle wines with layers of flavour and lovely harmony and finesse. However, don't rush out to buy the Cottage Block Gisborne Chardonnay – it wasn't produced in the 1996, 1997 or 1998 vintages.

Corbans was a key pioneer of Chardonnay production in New Zealand. From vines planted at Whenuapai, in West Auckland, it made one of the country's first Chardonnays in 1958. Corbans Pinot Chardonnay (as it was labelled for many years) won a gold medal and the trophy for "best table wine, commercial class" at the 1965 Easter Show competition.

In 1971, wine writer Frank Thorpy reported that Corbans Pinot Chardonnay had "excited interest overseas, but supplies as yet are limited." The 1975 vintage, although not barrel-aged, was described by Peter Saunders in 1976 as having "a lovely fruity nose which lives up to itself on the palate – a good clean wine in fine form." The 1980, also unwooded, won the THC trophy for champion wine of the 1981 National Wine Competition (forerunner of the Air New Zealand Wine Awards).

When in 1987 Corbans bought the merged Cooks/McWilliam's wine company, it inherited two distinguished Chardonnay traditions. André Simon, the legendary British wine writer, in 1964 commended the 1958 and 1962 vintages of McWilliam's Pinot Chardonnay, and during the 1970s, McWilliam's was one of the few Chardonnays in the country to be matured in oak. The 1974, 1978 and 1980 vintages all won gold medals. Cooks Chardonnay 1980 also won high acclaim, and the 1982 to 1985 vintages, made from Gisborne fruit, all won gold medals.

For the Cottage Block Gisborne Chardonnay, the grapes (all of the Mendoza clone) are grown in rich, free-draining soils in the Benson vineyard in the Ormond Valley, now owned by Corbans. Dr Richard Smart, the Australian viticultural guru, described it as "a perfect vineyard".

Based on a selection of the vineyard's best fruit, the Cottage Block Gisborne Chardonnay is made by "traditional Burgundian, low-tech methods". The grapes are hand-picked and whole-bunch pressed, and

With few exceptions, Corbans' most memorable Chardonnays have flowed from Gisborne.

the juice is run directly into French oak barriques, where it is fermented with indigenous yeasts and part of the blend undergoes a softening malolactic fermentation. The wine is then barrel-matured, in a much higher proportion of new oak casks than is used for the second-tier Private Bin Gisborne Chardonnay (80 per cent, compared to about 40 per cent). Throughout its 10 months' sojourn in wood, the Chardonnay is lees-stirred on a frequent, weekly basis.

Production of the Cottage Block Gisborne Chardonnay ($30) has ranged from 200 to 1000 cases. The wine matures well; the 1994 and 1995 are currently in commanding form.

Corbans Cottage Block Gisborne Chardonnay is a rare wine. Production is small and infrequent. But the brilliant 1994 and 1995 vintages are among the most memorable Gisborne Chardonnays I have ever tasted. 🍷

tasting notes

These notes are principally from a tasting of the 1994 and 1995 vintages, held in Auckland in April 1999. The debut 1993 vintage was not available for tasting, so I have added my most recent tasting notes, dating from 1994 and 1995.

1995 ☆☆☆☆☆ Full yellow/light gold. Fragrant, mealy, nutty, very complex bouquet. Tight, very elegant wine, with grapefruit-like flavours and a hint of butterscotch. Very nutty and mealy. Layers of flavour. Great mouthfeel. Intense and smooth, with great length. Highly distinguished. **Drink 1999-2001.**

1994 ☆☆☆☆☆ Full yellow/light gold. Fragrant, nutty, mealy bouquet, highly complex. Powerful yet delicate wine, with lovely intensity of ripe citrus/tropical fruit flavours. Nutty, complex and very long, with firmer acidity than many Gisborne Chardonnays. Brilliant wine, maturing superbly. **Drink 1999-2001.**

1993 ☆☆☆☆✩ (This tasting note is from 1995.) Forward, rich and complex. Nutty, mealy bouquet and loads of lemony, slightly limey, savoury, biscuity flavour. The fruit quality is slightly less intense than the best of the 1994s, but the "Burgundian" winemaking techniques referred to on the back label are strongly in evidence. **Open 1996 onwards.**

1993 ☆☆☆☆☆ (This tasting note is from 1994.) Forward. Mouthfilling, very high-flavoured style with strong peach/lemon fruit characters fleshed out with barrel-ferment complexity and underpinned by vigorous acidity. **Enjoy it from 1995 onwards.**

Corbans Private Bin Gisborne Chardonnay

First produced in 1992, this is a consistently delightful wine – always impressive, always charming. Winner of numerous gold medals, it is readily available, and given its top quality, sharply priced at around $23.

The Private Bin is Corbans' second-tier Gisborne Chardonnay (ranked below the Cottage Block), but that doesn't stop it being a superb mouthful. A concentrated wine, it typically offers deep, ripe citrus/melon flavours, well-integrated biscuity oak and a long, creamy finish. For sheer drinkability, it's very hard to beat.

Michael Kluczko, Corbans' wine operations manager, sees the Private Bin Gisborne Chardonnay (there is also a Marlborough version) as "a typical Gisborne style, in the sense of being ripe and rich, but it's also complex and structured. And year to year, it's very consistent."

If you ask Kluczko why the Private Bin wine is so good, he points firstly to the region, then the vineyards. "What is Gisborne's strength? You get very ripe fruit in the good sites, with tropical/citrus flavours, generosity and length."

Kluczko, a widely experienced Australian winemaker who heads Corbans' viticultural and winemaking operations in Gisborne, Hawke's Bay and Marlborough, believes that New Zealand winemakers must put greater emphasis on the ability of each region to grow particular varieties well, "rather than trying to grow every variety in every area. In this way winemaking in this country, already technologically well advanced, will begin to develop

other important characters and personalities."

Kluczko, whose father was a winemaker in the Barossa Valley, was dux of the oenology course at Roseworthy Agricultural College in Adelaide in 1985. After many years with big companies (including being in charge of Southcorp's sparkling wine production), Kluczko worked at Tarrawarra Vineyard in the Yarra Valley, renowned for its slowly evolving Chardonnays and robust, powerful Pinot Noirs, before joining Corbans in late 1997.

The backbone of the Private Bin Gisborne Chardonnay is the Benson vineyard, previously contracted to Corbans but now company-owned. "With good attention to crop levels and leaf removal, it always delivers those flavours," says Kluczko. "The picking date is based on optimum flavour development, not just brix [sugar] levels. You can get carried away in Gisborne with brixes, but you get good flavour development early. We haven't made the mistake of picking the grapes too ripe."

The Mendoza clone vines are vertically shoot positioned, and much work is done with the canopy to promote a consistent, even ripening of the fruit. Harvested by hand, the grapes are whole-bunch pressed and the free-run juice is run straight to barrel. Full barrel fermentation follows, with increasing use of indigenous yeasts.

On average, the wine spends about 10 months in oak (currently all French, new and one-year-old, but in the past American and German too). The wine is matured on its yeast lees, with some stirring, "but we don't overdo that," says Kluczko. "We don't want to lose the fruit characters. We want to keep what the vineyard delivers, and add some winemaker subtleties." The role of malolactic fermentation varies according to the vintage; 30 per cent in 1997, 70 per cent in 1993.

With production running up to 5000 cases per year, Corbans Private Bin Gisborne Chardonnay is usually widely available, although stocks drop dramatically in lesser vintages. Kluczko believes that the best age to drink it is a matter of personal preference. "If you want the impact of citrusy fruit, lees and oak, drink it upon release. But if you're after honied, developed characters, it'll easily go three years-plus." The 1993 is still drinking superbly at six years old.

Corbans Private Bin Gisborne Chardonnay has won a host of top medals. As Kluczko puts it: "Shows reward punchy wine. This is overt Gisborne Chardonnay with complexity, so it gets well rewarded." The 1995 vintage won a gold medal at the 1996 and 1997 Air New Zealand Wine Awards; the 1996 collected golds at the 1997 Air New Zealand Wine Awards and the 1998 International Wine Challenge in London.

Noel Scanlan – Corbans' chief executive since 1991.

Corbans Private Bin Gisborne Chardonnay has swiftly become a regional classic. Deeply scented, with rich, melony, slightly biscuity flavours, it's delicious at 18 months old, but unfolds well for several years. It's a high impact style, but not clumsy – Gisborne Chardonnay at its lush and lovely best.

tasting notes
These notes are from a vertical tasting of the 1992 to 1997 vintages, held at the winery in April 1999.

1997 ☆☆☆☆✦ Light yellow. Slightly lighter than the 1996, but shows the same beguiling harmony of soft, ripe, tropical fruit flavours and oak. Elegant wine with skilfully interwoven melon, fig and butterscotch characters in a creamy, forward style. **Drink 1999-2001.**

1996 ☆☆☆☆☆ Bright, medium-full yellow. Lovely surge of tropical fruit and citrus flavours, fleshed out with biscuity oak. Fresh, mouthfilling and very smooth. Creamy, ripe style, very hard-to-resist. Classic vintage. **Drink 1999-2001.**

1995 ☆☆☆☆☆ Bright, full yellow. Full, elegant wine in a quite fruit-driven style, soft and rich. Lovely now, with ripe tropical fruits to the fore and subtle oak, lees and creamy malolactic fermentation notes. At its peak. **Drink 1999-2000.**

1994 Not tasted.

1993 ☆☆☆☆☆ Light-medium gold. Toasty, nutty bouquet. Still vibrantly fruity. Rich and rounded, with excellent flavour concentration. Fat, peachy and slightly honied with age. Good acid spine. From a very cool year, unexpectedly good, with lovely harmony and a lasting finish. **Drink 1999.**

1992 ☆☆☆☆✦ Bright, deep yellow/light gold. Rich, citrusy, toasty bouquet. Soft and rich on the palate. Mouthfilling (13.5 per cent alcohol), with lush, concentrated fruit and toasty oak. Not hugely complex. Creamy texture. Probably slightly past its best. **Drink 1999.**

Delegat's Proprietors Reserve Chardonnay

CLASSIC

With 15 gold medals and three trophies (including champion wine of the 1996 Liquorland Royal Easter Wine Show) under its belt, Delegat's Proprietors Reserve has been one of New Zealand's most successful Chardonnays on the competition circuit. Yet the 1996 vintage, retailing at around $25, was the last.

"The premium wine market is being redefined," says Jim Delegat, proprietor and managing director of Delegat's. "That market was turned on its head by the success of the Montana Reserve range [at under $20], which is putting pressure on the $25 market." From the 1997 vintage, Delegat's released a lush,

less oak-influenced but richly flavoured Reserve Chardonnay, retailing at $19, to be followed by a "Rolls Royce" label, probably from the 1998 vintage, likely to sell at around $30.

"Richness, fullness and weight" sums up the style of the Proprietors Reserve Chardonnay, says Michael

Jim Delegat and his sister, Rose, who is immersed in marketing.

Ivicevich, who after several years at Delegat's replaced Brent Marris as chief winemaker in 1997. "The goal was always a big, bold Hawke's Bay Chardonnay, but with a harmony between the rich fruit and oak characters."

If you ask Ivicevich about the key factors behind the wine's quality, he points firstly to the fruit. Most of the grapes (between 60 and 100 per cent each year) have come from the company's Vicarage vineyard in Swamp Road, at the entrance to the Dartmoor Valley. "It's a fairly low-vigour site," says Ivicevich, "and with the vines being entirely of the small-berry Mendoza clone, we get excellent flavour concentration in the berries." Yields are low – typically only two or three tonnes per acre.

A high proportion of the fruit is hand-picked and the juice is handled "very carefully", with the pressings kept out of the blend to minimise hard phenolic characters. "And a very important part of the style is the selection of high quality oak. The 1990 is still lively, reflecting the quality of its fruit and oak."

Between 50 and 70 per cent of the wine was barrel fermented, with the rest handled in tanks to preserve its rich, citrus and tropical fruit characters. Subsequently, all the wine was matured on its light yeast lees in French oak barriques (about 50 per cent new). Over the years, Ivicevich recalls the major changes in vinification were "refinements in handling and oak selection. We increased the reductive [non-oxidative] elements, and moved from open-grained to finer-grained oak, which gives a less assertive oak character, more in harmony with the fruit."

Finding a bottle of the Proprietors Reserve Chardonnay was rarely a problem; output ranged up to 6000 cases per year. Ivicevich believes the wine peaks at five to seven years old, but can age even longer; the tasting (below) supports his confidence.

No wine could better sum up the style and achievement of Delegat's Proprietors Reserve Chardonnay than the 1994 vintage, served at the company's fiftieth anniversary dinner in 1997. Golden, with lashings of peachy-ripe, mealy flavour and a delicious creaminess of texture, it was an assertively oaked but arresting wine, magnificently mouthfilling, savoury and rich. ▼

tasting notes

These notes are from a vertical tasting of the 1988 to 1996 vintages, held at the winery in February 1999.

1996 ☆☆☆☆☆ Medium-full yellow. Intense, ripe, almost sweet grapefruit-like flavours, very persistent, and firmer than the 1995. Still developing and quite tight, with rich, delicate flavours in a very refined style. Not a blockbuster, but shows great finesse. **Drink 2000-03.**

1995 ☆☆☆☆✦ Full yellow. Softly structured wine, giving it lots of current appeal. Ripe citrusy fruit and a slightly creamy texture. Slightly lighter than the 1994, but still full and fresh, toasty and rounded. **Drink 1999-2001.**

1994 ☆☆☆☆☆ Winner of four gold medals and two trophies. Light gold. A whopper of a wine, showing enormous body (14 per cent alcohol) and a creamy-soft texture. A hedonist's delight, with highly concentrated grapefruit and toasty oak flavours. The strong wood is now in harmony with the very rich fruit. Oodles of everything – body and flavour. The most heroic wine of the flight. **Drink 1999-2002.**

1993 ☆☆☆☆ Light gold. Lighter than the 1992, but true to the Delegat's Proprietors Reserve style, and one of the better 1993s. Excellent depth of grapefruit and toast flavours, with firm acid spine. Still fresh, lively and tight. **Drink 1999-2001.**

1992 ☆☆☆☆☆ Full yellow. A shining example of the label from a low-crop year, still on its high plateau. Plump, rich, beautifully harmonious wine with very intense flavours of ripe grapefruit and buttery oak. Very complex and persistent. **Great drinking now to 2002.**

1991 ☆☆☆☆☆ Light gold. Still taut and lively. Robust wine with crisp, firm grapefruit and buttery oak flavours, showing excellent concentration. Like a bigger version of the 1990, with impressive power and longevity. **Drink 1999-2001.**

1990 ☆☆☆☆✦ Medium gold, distinctly lighter than the 1989. Still fairly tightly structured. Leaner than the 1989, but maturing very gracefully, with firm acidity threaded through its strong citrusy flavours. Very elegant wine. No rush. **Drink 1999-2002.**

1989 ☆☆☆☆ Deep gold. Mellow, toasty, with ripe and quite rich peach/citrus flavours. Holding well, with a soft finish. **Drink 1999-2000.**

1988 ☆☆☆ Deep gold. From the year of Cyclone Bola. Still faintly alive. Very soft and toasty, buttery and honied. Very respectable for an 1988. **Drink ASAP.**

CHARDONNAY
1997
DRY RIVER
Martinborough

471   Nº 3000
BOTTLED BY DRY RIVER WINES LTD, PURUATANGA RD, MARTINBOROUGH
PRODUCE OF NEW ZEALAND
e 750ml   CONTAINS PRESERVATIVE (1150)   13.8% VOL

Dry River Chardonnay

CLASSIC

If you ask a wine buff which variety he or she thinks of first in connection with Dry River, most say Pinot Gris, followed by Gewürztraminer and Riesling or (increasingly) Pinot Noir. Yet Martinborough winemaker Dr Neil McCallum fashions an aristocratic, long-lived Chardonnay with much of the power and intensity of white Burgundy. "The world is awash with Chardonnay," reflects McCallum. "You can make a brilliant Chardonnay and be passed by."

If you like fat, buttery-soft Chardonnays with lots of drink-young appeal, avoid the Dry River. McCallum's wine is all about subtle power. It's a powerful but restrained wine, tight, savoury and seamless, with rich grapefruit and hazelnut flavours that build in the bottle for several years.

McCallum admits that deciding on his particular Chardonnay style was "a hassle. I won't accept things because they're done traditionally. I had to reach my style from first principles, not because Joe Bloggs did it."

The key challenge was to settle on a style that suited New Zealand – and Martinborough – grapes. "We get a different fruit expression here – more fruit character, but less extract, than in Burgundy. I see Dry River as sitting between Chablis and Meursault. In Chablis, the fruit expression is quite austere. Our recent Chardonnays are mealy and showing increasing richness, yet they're still fairly restrained."

In McCallum's eyes, Chardonnay is the least fussy of all grapes about site. "But exposure of the fruit to sunlight is critical to developing the flavours important to longevity." The vines are grown

principally in the nearby Craighall vineyard, partly owned by Dry River. A further 20 per cent of the fruit, estate-grown, is "later ripening and less gutsy than Craighall's, but more aromatic."

What are the key factors contributing to the quality of Dry River Chardonnay? "Firstly, the yield is automatically limited by having Mendoza vines, which usually crop at below two tonnes an acre. We put great effort into canopy management, to ensure the wines don't develop grassy characters as they age. We hand-harvest, whole-bunch press and pump the juice straight into oak [French, averaging 24 per cent new] for full barrel fermentation."

Over the years, the vinification procedures have changed only a little. McCallum finds that giving the wine a longer time to mature on its lees in barrel (about a year) but with less new oak, "stabilises the flavours and gives better flavour expression". No more than 15 per cent of the final blend has gone through malolactic fermentation. But between the 1994 and 1995 vintages, more *bâtonnage* (lees-stirring) was built into the style, to enhance the mealy characters.

Don't search for Dry River Chardonnay in your local wine shop – only about 400 cases are made each year from 1.5 hectares of vines, and sold principally by mail order at around $30. Recent vintages offer more pleasure in their youth than those of the past, but the wine typically takes three or four years to break into full stride.

Dry River Chardonnay is not a sledgehammer style with bold, upfront flavour. Rather, its key qualities are elegance, restraint and subtle power. It's the sort of classically structured wine you can poke in the cellar for several years, knowing that with maturity it will unfold a rich array of citrusy, mealy, nutty flavours that are highly reminiscent of the great white Burgundies McCallum so openly admires.

Neil McCallum makes a bold Pinot Noir and a tight, savoury Chardonnay with subtle power.

tasting notes

These notes are from a vertical tasting of the 1988 to 1997 vintages, held at the winery in November 1998.

1997 ☆☆☆☆☆ Light yellow. Strong, youthful, beautiful wine, poised and concentrated, with very ripe citrus fruits, harmonious oak and lees-aging characters adding a biscuity, mealy richness. Powerful, mouthfilling wine, and very classy. A great candidate for cellaring. **Drink 2000-05.**

1996 ☆☆☆☆☆ Light yellow. One of the highlights of the flight. A bold (14 per cent alcohol), generous wine with rich, ripe grapefruit characters overlaid with biscuity, nutty complexities. Wonderful poise and tautness of structure. Very similar to the 1991. Powerful, quite Burgundian. A top example of the Dry River style. **Drink 1999-2004.**

1995 ☆☆☆☆☆ Light yellow. Mealy, slightly oxidative nose. Firmly structured and taut. Deep grapefruit and lemon flavours in a slightly austere style with nutty, mealy characters. Lacks the opulence of top vintages, but controlled and complex, with good backbone. **Drink 2000-02.**

1994 ☆☆☆☆☆ Light yellow. Still feels quite youthful. Very stylish wine with rich grapefruit characters and subtle oak and lees influence. Currently slightly restrained, but set for a long life. **Drink 2000-02.**

1993 ☆☆☆☆ Medium-full yellow. Big wine with strong biscuity, citrusy flavours and firm acid spine. Taut wine, lacking a bit of its customary plumpness, and showing good but not great concentration. Fairly complex, with good length. **Drink 1999-2000.**

1992 ☆☆☆☆☆ Medium yellow (deeper than 1991). Complex, biscuity fragrance. Big, firm, well-spined wine with excellent depth of ripe citrus fruits and savoury oak. Slightly less rich than the 1991, but complex, tightly structured and maturing well. **Drink 1999-2000.**

1991 ☆☆☆☆☆ Light-medium yellow. Splendid now, but still evolving. Tight, intense and classy wine in a very Burgundian style. Lovely, deep, mealy, citrusy, biscuity flavours, complex and harmonious, with firm acid structure. Beautifully balanced and controlled. A real stand out. **Drink 1999-2001.**

1990 ☆☆☆☆☆ Bright, medium yellow. Powerful, developed bouquet. Rich, ripe and rounded, with deep grapefruit and oak flavours. Slightly buttery on nose and palate. Fleshy and alive, although slightly less complex than the 1989. Ready. **Drink now.**

1989 ☆☆☆☆☆ (Labelled as Craighall Estate.) Medium yellow. Savoury, much fuller and richer than the 1988, with intense grapefruit/oak flavours and good acid backbone. Fragrant, citrusy, mealy bouquet. Complex, developed, well-integrated wine, holding remarkably well. **Drink now.**

1988 ☆☆☆☆ (Labelled as Craighall Estate.) Two bottles opened. First bottle – light straw in hue, with spiky acid. Big, lemony, toasty, but lacks real flavour richness. Surviving, but no real pleasure. Second bottle – better. More fruit, less austere, still very alive, with citrusy, biscuity flavours, but less rich than the 1989. **Drink now.**

CHARDONNAY
Hawkes Bay
1996

e75cl 13.5%vol
PRODUCED & BOTTLED BY
Esk Valley Estate Limited
Main Road, Bay View, Napier

PRODUCE OF NEW ZEALAND

Esk Valley Reserve Chardonnay

CLASSIC

Esk Valley's top Chardonnay has changed markedly in recent years. The lean, crisp, slightly austere wines of the past have been replaced by a new breed of lusher, riper, more concentrated, softer Chardonnays, possessing much greater immediacy of appeal. The 1994 and subsequent vintages rank among the finest Chardonnays in Hawke's Bay.

"The style has been evolving," agrees winemaker Gordon Russell. "What I'm looking for, along with rich fruit flavours, is texture. Some of the older wines were too acidic; I want a softer mouthfeel. I love the creamy satisfaction that good Chardonnay can give, based on ripe fruit, oak and malolactic fermentation."

The early vintages were grown in vineyards at Hastings, in the Dartmoor Valley and near Fernhill. Since 1994, however, the fruit has all been sourced from a shingly vineyard in Gimblett Road, owned by CJ Pask, where the mature, unirrigated vines are all of the low-bearing Mendoza clone. Future vintages will include clone 15 grapes from Puketapu, which Russell believes will add "perfume, lightness and elegance".

Raised in the Manawatu, Russell studied town planning and then worked in pubs in England before joining Villa Maria in 1988. After rising to chief cellarhand in 1990, he was appointed as assistant winemaker at Esk Valley, and in 1993 he stepped into the top job.

Russell attributes the soaring standard of his premium Chardonnay to changes both in the vineyard and the winery. "The vines are aging and we're manipulating them to achieve low yields and concentrated fruit flavours. We're understanding how to use oak as a supplementary tool, rather than as a dominant influence, and making better use of malolactic fermentation to achieve softness, rather than buttery notes."

The grapes, cropped at around three tonnes per acre, are picked by hand and whole-bunch pressed. The juice (given little if any settling, to preserve its high solids) is fully fermented in oak barrels – all French, 60 per cent new. In his search for complexity, Russell uses warm and cool ferments, cultured and indigenous yeasts. Half of the final blend is lees-stirred for three months.

From the 1995 vintage onwards, Russell has decreased the percentage of new barrels used, but is leaving the wine longer in oak, with greater lees contact. "We're getting fatter, better-textured wines as a result. We're learning as we go."

The degree of malolactic fermentation varies from year to year, depending on the grapes' acidity. "We're using malolactic fermentation more and more, for textural reasons," says Russell, "but using strains of malolactic fermentation culture that don't impart diacetyl [obvious buttery] characters."

About 1000 cases of Esk Valley Reserve Chardonnay are made each year, retailing at $30.

Russell suggests drinking the wine at five years old: "That's when it comes into top form, and hopefully it will plateau for another five years, depending on the vintage and storage." The tasting (below) gave clear evidence of the wine's ability to flourish in the bottle for at least five years.

Esk Valley Reserve Chardonnay is a refined wine with a core of rich, citrus and stone-fruit flavours, enhanced but never swamped by complexities derived from oak maturation, lees-aging and malolactic fermentation. Beautifully crafted, it is not a brash style, but has still won a string of silver medals. The highlight on the show circuit was undoubtedly the gold medal awarded the 1995 vintage at the 1997 Air New Zealand Wine Awards.

Gordon Russell crafts rich, highly refined Chardonnays.

tasting notes

These notes are mainly from a vertical tasting of the 1989 to 1997 vintages, held at the winery in December 1998. The 1998 vintage was tasted in Auckland in April 1999.

1998 ☆☆☆☆☆ (Tasted shortly after bottling.) Light lemon/green, with a rich, savoury, mealy bouquet. Very big and fleshy, with a distinct touch of butterscotch amidst its lovely, deep flavours of grapefruit, melons and figs. Very weighty, rich, complex and rounded. **Drink 2001-05.**

1997 ☆☆☆☆☆ Pale yellow. From a cool year that gave less upfront fruit characters than usual, it shows a slightly stronger malolactic fermentation and lees-stirring influence. Nutty, creamy, slightly less fruit-driven than usual, but still showing quite rich Hawke's Bay citrus/fig flavours. Big, youthful wine, with a firmer finish than the 1996. **Drink 2000-04.**

1996 ☆☆☆☆☆ Light yellow. Spot-on bouquet, featuring intense citrus fruits overlaid with oak/lees-aging complexities. Immaculate, seamless wine with lovely depth of Hawke's Bay citrus and tropical fruit flavours, very rich and and lingering. Ultra-smooth and delicate wine with great texture. **Drink 1999-03.**

1995 ☆☆☆☆☆ Medium yellow. Soft, delicate sweet-fruit flavours. Very ripe style, with tropical/citrus flavours, subtle mealy characters and balanced toasty oak. Very powerful. Complex. Great vintage. **Drink 1999-2002.**

1994 ☆☆☆☆☆ Medium yellow. More absorbing, more multi-faceted bouquet than the older wines (it was given more time in oak and on yeast lees). Wonderful wine, with tremendous depth and complexity. Concentrated citrus, pear and nutty flavours and a creamy-smooth finish. Still developing. **Drink 1999-2002.**

1993 Not made.

1992 ☆☆☆☆☆ Light gold (deeper than 1989 and 1990). Full, stylish, very harmonious. Weighty wine with strong toasty characters from 100 per cent new oak and bottle-age. Citrus and pineapple flavours of excellent depth. Slightly less concentrated than the Ohiti Road Reserve (below). **Drink 1999-2000.**

1992 ☆☆☆☆☆ Reserve Ohiti Road Chardonnay. Gunn vineyard, near Fernhill. Full yellow. Very rich, intense bouquet. Highly concentrated citrusy fruit, with balanced acidity. Still fresh and vigorous. Big, powerful wine, maturing splendidly and now at its peak. **Drink 1999-2000.**

1991 Not tasted.

1990 ☆☆☆☆☆ Full, bright yellow. Similar to the 1989, but less fragrant and revealing higher acidity. Still lively, with quite good depth of citrus fruit and slightly limey flavours. Toasty. **Drink 1999-2000.**

1989 ☆☆☆☆☆ Full, bright yellow. Holding well. Fragrant, rich bouquet of pineapples and toasty oak (100 per cent new). Elegant wine, still very attractive, with mouthfilling body and excellent depth of citrus, pineapple and wood flavours. Firm, crisp finish. **Drink 1999-2000.**

Glazebrook Chardonnay

The top Chardonnay from the smallish Ngatarawa winery in Hawke's Bay is named after the Glazebrook family, partners in the venture, who have owned the site of the present vineyard for over half a century. The wine has always had less success in competitions than with critics; prominent British writer Oz Clarke finds it "very Burgundian and very exciting".

For many years the wine was called Ngatarawa Glazebrook Chardonnay, but winemaker Alwyn Corban now wants the wine to be known simply as Glazebrook Chardonnay. The "Ngatarawa" element on the label is being played down, although not eliminated, due to the pronunciation problems it causes wine lovers in export markets.

Glazebrook is a typical top Hawke's Bay Chardonnay, with concentrated, ripe stone and citrus fruit characters and mouthfilling body. At its best, it is a seductively rich, creamy-soft mouthful, with great harmony and the ability to mature gracefully for five to eight years.

What style of wine is Corban (a great-grandson of Assid Abraham Corban) aiming for? "I'm striving for a rich creamy texture," he says, "which we get from fruit concentration and malolactic fermentation. Also, it's not made as an attractive young wine that soon falls over. It must have the ability to develop in the bottle."

For Corban, ripe fruit is a key quality ingredient. In the past, the grapes were wholly of the relatively shy-bearing Mendoza clone, but since the 1997 vintage some slightly higher-cropping clone 15 Chardonnay has been included. The fruit is typically harvested ripe

Alwyn Corban makes big, lush, softly seductive Chardonnays.

at around 24 brix, with good flavour intensity from an average yield of only 2.5 tonnes per acre.

Between 1987 and 1996 (except for the hail-devastated 1994 vintage) the grapes were all estate-grown at Ngatarawa, but since 1997 other Hawke's Bay fruit has been purchased.

The grapes have in the past been entirely hand-picked and whole-bunch pressed, but in 1997 some machine-harvesting was introduced, and a degree of skin contact to give the wine greater early-drinking appeal.

The juice starts its fermentation in tanks, then about half-way through is transferred into casks (French, all new). A portion also undergoes malolactic fermentation in the barrel.

Once the ferment is over, the wine is racked into both new and one-year-old French oak barriques, where it is matured on its yeast lees (but not lees-stirred; "I haven't felt the need," says Corban) for a year.

Ngatarawa reduced the retail price of its 1997 Glazebrook Chardonnay in 1998 from $27 to $21. Why? "Much of the wine is sold in restaurants, and $21 in a shop equates to $30 to $35 on a wine list," says Corban. There's a lot of pressure on us to meet that price point."

In response to that pressure, from 1997 onwards Glazebrook Chardonnay has been made in a more fruit-driven style, with a reduced influence from barrel fermentation, new oak and malolactic fermentation (20 per cent in 1997). "The wine still all goes into wood," says Corban, "but some of the blend is matured, but not fermented, in oak."

Glazebrook's status as a classic Hawke's Bay Chardonnay – based on its notable flavour concentration, harmony and aging ability – may not survive long term, given the recent price-driven changes. However, the 1997 offered exceptional value, and a new higher-priced Chardonnay, made in 1998, is now in the wings.

tasting notes
These notes are from a vertical tasting of the 1987 to 1997 vintages, held at the winery in December 1998.

1997 ☆☆☆☆☆ Pale yellow. Lush wine with a lovely richness of grapefruit and fig-like flavours, delicately seasoned with oak. Full bodied (over 13 per cent alcohol). Caresses the mouth with its softly seductive texture. Obvious but not dominant malolactic fermentation characters. Long, nutty/buttery finish. Delicious at 18 months old. **Drink 1999-2001.**

1996 ☆☆☆☆✦ Light yellow. Big, very harmonious wine, with deep melon/grapefruit flavours, good acid balance and subtle toasty oak. Quite forward, especially compared to the 1995. **Drink 1999-2001.**

1995 ☆☆☆☆☆ Light lemon/green. Youthful. Quite Burgundian flavour and texture. Creamy, seamless wine with deep, ripe flavours of melons and figs wrapped in biscuity oak. Strong malolactic fermentation influence. Should mature superbly. **Drink 1999-2003.**

1994 ☆☆☆☆☆ (Labelled Glazebrook Reserve. Hawke's Bay fruit, but not estate-grown, due to a hail storm. First vintage handled in barriques, rather than puncheons.) Light-medium yellow. Figgy, nutty bouquet. Big, stylish wine with quite lush stone and citrus fruit flavours and balanced toasty oak. Finely structured, harmonious and long. Best yet. **Drink 1999-2002.**

1993 Labelled Glazebrook Reserve. Not tasted. "Gone" [meaning well past its best] – Alwyn Corban.

1992 ☆☆☆☆☆ (Labelled Glazebrook Reserve.) Light gold. Similar power to the 1991. A big, rich wine with concentrated citrus, peach and toast flavours and firm underlying acidity. Nutty and complex. **Drink 1999-2000.**

1991 ☆☆☆☆☆ (Labelled Glazebrook.) Bright, light yellow. Markedly plumper, richer and softer than the older vintages. Excellent intensity of sweet, ripe grapefruit flavours, nutty oak and mouthfilling body. Maturing superbly. Lovely now, but no rush. **Drink 1999-2000.**

1990 ☆☆☆☆✦ (Labelled Alwyn.) Medium straw hue. Similar style to the 1989 – slightly oxidative, with strong citrus/toast flavours. Complex style – mealy, nutty and slightly flinty. Ready. **Drink 1999.**

1989 ☆☆☆☆✦ Light-medium yellow. Slightly oxidative characters on nose. Mouthfilling wine, holding well, with citrus and toast flavours supported by crisp acidity. Mealy, nutty wine with good vigour. Flinty. **Drink 1999.**

1988 ☆☆✦ Cyclone Bola year. Golden, oxidised and very tired. Avoid.

1987 ☆☆☆ (Labelled Alwyn.) Slightly dull gold. Toasty, very developed nose. Citrusy, pineappley flavours with strong bottle-aged characters. Still alive, but drying out. Very much drink-up time. **Drink ASAP.**

Hunter's Marlborough Chardonnay

CLASSIC

From the start, Hunter's Chardonnay has enjoyed a high profile. In 1986, Hugh Johnson enthused about the first 1985 vintage: "On the scale of a Burgundy *premier cru*; dry and highly charged with flavours waiting to evolve." A year later, the 1986 vintage scooped one of only 12 gold medals awarded to 380 wines in the formal judging at the Sunday Times Wine Show in London, and was also voted best wine of the show at two of the three public tasting sessions. Such early triumphs helped to put Hunter's, Marlborough and New Zealand on the world wine map.

Hunter's Chardonnay is built on the rich, citrusy flavours of Marlborough grapes, enriched but never overpowered by oak. Finesse is the wine's key attribute, rather than upfront power. It evolves gracefully in the bottle; top vintages have the concentration and structure to flourish for many years. Richness, harmony, elegance – these qualities have made the wine a Marlborough classic.

"We've always kept the style fairly fruit-driven," says Jane Hunter. "It can vary from year to year, but it's always along similar lines of not being heavily oaked. We're looking for a rounded, whole wine. We don't want the fruitiest or oakiest or biggest wine in New Zealand; it must be integrated."

For Hunter's long-term consultant oenologist, Australian Dr Tony Jordan (who works closely with winemaker Gary Duke, also an Australian), the Hunter's style reflects the distinctive characters of the Mendoza clone of Chardonnay. "It's very fruity – not necessarily huge, but it's New Zealand and

it's Mendoza. Intrinsically, Chardonnay has a good mid palate, and we seek to optimise that with picking the grapes ripe, and fiddling with malolactic fermentation and lees-stirring to add creaminess."

Like Jane Hunter, Jordan doesn't want to overoak the wine. "But it's hard to escape high alcohols in Marlborough. We don't want a wimp, but we want to avoid loading big oak on big fruit and big alcohol. We start with the Mendoza clone's incredibly strong fruit characters, then use some oxidative handling of the grapes; some solids fermentation; some malolactic fermentation; time on yeast; some barrel fermentation – it's the old blender's game."

Most of the grapes are grown in Hunter's estate vineyard in Rapaura Road, supplemented by small amounts from Wairau Valley growers. The estate-grown grapes ripen relatively early, with ripe flavours and an average crop of three tonnes per acre. This vineyard is currently being replanted with clone 15, which despite its slightly heavier crops than Mendoza, has yielded some high quality wines in New Zealand.

The grapes, all machine-harvested, are partly barrel-fermented and lees-aged – about 45 per cent of the final blend. To avoid "overpowering the fruit" the rest is fermented in stainless steel tanks. However, all of the wine is matured in oak casks (25 to 30 per cent new). "Over the years, we've experimented with more wood influence, but we've always gone back to the same style," says Jane. The percentage of the blend given malolactic fermentation has gone up and down, but now averages about 30 per cent.

Hunter's Chardonnay is a large volume wine – up to 7500 cases are produced each year, retailing at $25. Tony Jordan suggests the wine needs at least two years before it is ready for drinking. "Some vintages start off quietly, and then 18 months to two years later really come up. Others are more upfront. Which raises the issue: when are the fruit, oak and malolactic characters integrated? For Hunter's Chardonnay, it usually takes at least two years." Jane Hunter prefers the wine at three or four years old; so do I.

Recent vintages of Hunter's Chardonnay have not often achieved the gold medal glory of a decade ago. That's not surprising – the wine lacks the upfront characters that are so often rewarded in large comparative tastings. However, at the 1995 InterVin International Wine Competition in North America, the 1992 Chardonnay and two other Hunter's wines won the three gold medals needed to secure the first Black Diamond Award for a New Zealand winery.

tasting notes

These notes are from a vertical tasting of the 1985 to 1997 vintages, held at the winery in January 1999.

1997 ☆☆☆☆✦ Light lemon/green. Very fresh aromas of ripe citrusy fruit and oak. Still a baby. Full-bodied, immaculate wine with deep grapefruit flavours and savoury, mealy characters. Finely balanced, with a slightly creamy texture. **Drink 2000-04.**

1996 ☆☆☆☆☆ Light-medium yellow/green. Lovely, delicate, very harmonious wine with intense lemony flavours and spicy oak. Highly fragrant. Beautifully controlled wine, not a blockbuster, but all style. **Drink 2000-03.**

1995 ☆☆☆✦ Light lemon/green. Quiet nose. Lighter style, lacking its customary fruit intensity. Less ripe than usual, with appley, lemony flavours, but delicate, with a gentle oak seasoning. Reflects the below-average vintage. **Drink 1999-2001.**

1994 ☆☆☆☆☆ Bright, light-medium yellow/green. Immaculate and stylish wine, with deep grapefruit flavours and finely tuned oak, lees and acidity. Controlled, intense wine with a long, lovely finish. A classic vintage, currently in full stride. **Drink 1999-2002.**

1993 ☆☆☆ Light gold. Honied, slightly dull nose. Soft wine, with stronger malolactic fermentation characters than usual. Lacks its customary depth of fruit character. Less vibrant and lively than the 1992. Very toasty and developed. **Drink ASAP.**

1992 ☆☆☆☆☆ Medium yellow. Lovely, generous wine, still fresh and probably at its peak. Powerful surge of grapefruit flavours, balanced toasty oak and firm acid backbone. Very harmonious and complex. A top vintage. **Drink 1999-2001.**

1991 ☆☆☆☆ Bright, medium-full yellow/green. Rich, citrusy, slightly green-edged flavour, crisp and vigorous. Developed, toasty characters. Stylish wine with very good length. **Drink 1999-2000.**

1990 ☆☆☆☆✦ Medium yellow/green. Slightly leaner and less lush than the 1989, but aging impressively, with tight lemon/grapefruit flavours and restrained, deftly judged oak. Firm and elegant style. **Drink 1999-2000.**

1989 ☆☆☆☆☆ Deep gold. Mouthfilling, quite bold wine with rich citrus fruits and toasty oak flavours, long and lovely. Well-balanced acidity and shows power right through the palate. Mellowing, but still lively. **Drink 1999-2000.**

1988 ☆☆☆☆✦ Deep gold. Rich citrus/toast characters, slightly green-edged. Crisply acidic finish. Still reasonably enjoyable, but has reached its "use-by" date. **Drink 1999.**

1987 ☆☆☆☆ Very deep gold. Very toasty bottle-aged characters hold sway. Slightly honied, with some rich citrusy tones. Holding, but mellow. **Drink 1999.**

1986 ☆☆☆ Deep gold. Dull bouquet. Starting to oxidise. Less fruit left than the 1985. Soft and toasty. **Drink ASAP.**

1985 ☆☆☆☆ Deep gold. Fruit starting to dry out, but still alive, with strong honey and toast characters. Mellow wine with citrusy fruit and firm acid. Very harmonious – still a lot of pleasure to be had here. **Drink 1999.**

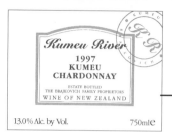

Kumeu River
1997
KUMEU
CHARDONNAY
ESTATE BOTTLED
THE BRAJKOVICH FAMILY PROPRIETORS
WINE OF NEW ZEALAND

13.0% Alc. by Vol.   750ml

Kumeu River Chardonnay

SUPER CLASSIC

It would be hard to exaggerate the importance of this famous wine. Kumeu River Chardonnay played a vital role in the renaissance of winemaking in the Auckland region. The success of the early releases stirred the interest of many other New Zealand winemakers in the traditional white-wine production methods of Burgundy, and the much acclaimed 1987 and subsequent vintages played a crucial role in alerting the American market to the white-wine revolution Down Under.

Yet the launch of the first Kumeu River Chardonnay was surrounded by controversy. As winemaker Michael Brajkovich has written: "In 1985 Kumeu River produced a Chardonnay that underwent a total malolactic fermentation, to the surprise of many, and certainly to the disgust of the wine judges who relegated it to the 'no award' level. The style was totally foreign to that of previous New Zealand Chardonnays; it was the style of Burgundy..." Local critics and the public responded much more enthusiastically, and when the influential American publication, *Wine Spectator*, endorsed the 1987 ("extremely rich ... long and elegant"; 93/100), the label's reputation skyrocketed.

Powerful and rich, with beautifully interwoven flavours and a seductively creamy texture, Kumeu River Chardonnay has distinct stylistic parallels to white Burgundy: Jancis Robinson described the 1989 as "pure Puligny". Brajkovich, New Zealand's first Master of Wine, acknowledges the debt. "In my opinion, the white wines of the Côte de Beaune in Burgundy, with their opulent, peachy fruit aromas and toasted oak, are among the best in the world. At Kumeu River, we have taken the best of the white Burgundy techniques and adapted them to our own situation."

The key to the outstanding quality of the Chardonnay, says Brajkovich, lies in the vineyard. "We manage to get the grapes very ripe. The lyre [U-shaped] trellising system helps to control vigour and increase bunch exposure to the sun – that's where we get the flavour." The fruit, entirely grown in Kumeu (Brajkovich likens the Chardonnay to a "village wine" of Burgundy), comes from three blocks on the top of the hill directly across the road from the winery, supplemented by several other blocks in the district, not all company-owned. The 1989 to 1995 vintages were based entirely on the Mendoza clone, but clone six has been used to add "sweet, beautiful fruit characters" to Mendoza's "nutty weightiness" since 1996, and clone 95, from Burgundy, has also been added recently.

Kumeu River insists on processing only hand-harvested grapes, which ensures the berries are intact and protected from oxidation up to the juice extraction stage. At the winery, the grapes are whole bunch-pressed. After settling, the juice is separated from the sediment and transferred directly to oak barrels for fermentation with indigenous yeasts, which Brajkovich believes "let the vineyard express itself more than selected [cultured] yeasts."

The fermentation temperature is controlled by cooling the air in the cellar; Brajkovich tries to keep it at just below 20°C. In practice, the ferments often peak at 23-24°C, if only for a short time, which allows the development of secondary aromas to complement the primary characters derived directly from the grapes.

Fermented and lees-aged (with weekly lees-stirring) in Burgundy oak barriques (20-25 per cent new each year), the wine also undergoes a full malolactic fermentation, without which Brajkovich believes it would be "unbalanced, with high acidity and a lack of its attractive, soft, milky, cheesy characters."

Looking back, Brajkovich says Kumeu River's changes in production methods since 1985 have been "subtle but significant". The range and quality of barrels has improved, and the methods of inducing malolactic fermentation are now more reliable. A Willmes pneumatic press, which replaced an old mechanical press in 1991, and extracts the juice from the grapes very gently, has given wines with "more finesse and brighter fruit characters".

Produced in large volumes (5000 cases in 1998), Kumeu River Chardonnay is exported principally to the UK and the US, and sells in New Zealand at about $33. Marketing manager Paul Brajkovich suggests drinking it at four to six years old. It typically drinks well at two years old, but (as shown below), the top vintages can mature superbly for at least eight years.

Kumeu River long ago pulled out of local competitions, but the Chardonnay continues to win international applause. In the US, several vintages have been featured in *Wine Spectator*'s annual Top 100, and in the UK, the 1996 was rated equal with Domaine Des Comtes Lafon Montrachet 1991, and ahead of Penfolds Yattarna 1995, in *Wine* magazine's November 1998 article on "The World's Top Chardonnays".

Kumeu River is one of New Zealand's great Chardonnays, with a rock-solid, prestigious reputation. A distinctive wine with notable power and concentration, it is typically lush, harmonious and creamy-smooth – a sheer delight to drink.

tasting notes
These notes are from a vertical tasting of the 1989 to 1998 vintages, held at the winery in March 1999.

1998 ☆☆☆☆☆ Pale lemon/green. Exceptionally good – deeply fragrant, explosively flavoured. Broad, mealy and rich style with lovely, intense fig and grapefruit characters and a deliciously creamy, nutty, rounded finish. Staggeringly good at this stage. **Drink 2000-05.**

1997 ☆☆☆☆¼ Bright, light yellow. Big, mouthfilling, savoury wine with strong grapefruit flavours, rich and rounded. Still evolving, with the power to age well. Slightly more austere than the 1996, and slightly less concentrated than the 1998.

1996 ☆☆☆☆☆ Bright, light yellow. Very classy indeed. Buoyant, concentrated wine, focused on sweet, ripe grapefruit flavours, with barrel fermentation and lees-aging adding smoky, mealy characters. Opulent, weighty wine, with balanced acidity. A star vintage, approaching readiness. **Drink 1999-2002.**

1995 ☆☆☆¼ Light-medium gold. Toasty, developed nose. Flavoursome and nutty, crisp and slightly limey. Forward. Lacks its customary lushness, due to the diluting effect of autumn rain. More advanced than the 1994. **Drink 1999.**

1994 ☆☆☆☆☆ Light gold. Full and complex, with excellent vigour. Toasty, bottle-aged characters with sweet, ripe fruit and a touch of butterscotch. Very nutty, toasty and creamy. A fine example of a mature Kumeu River. Ready. **Drink 1999-2000.**

1993 ☆☆☆☆☆ Bright, medium yellow. Lovely, grapefruit-focused wine, still buoyant, with attractive freshness and power. Slightly leaner than the 1994, but aging very gracefully, with firm acid spine and a very persistent finish. **Drink 1999-2000.**

1992 ☆☆☆ Medium gold. High acid, slightly honied and austere. Clearly a lesser vintage, past its best. **Drink ASAP.**

1991 ☆☆☆☆☆ Bright, full yellow. Lovely, rounded, sweet-fruit characters shining through. Grapefruit, butterscotch and toast flavours, deep and complex. Well structured wine, maturing gracefully and still in full flight. **Drink 1999-2000.**

1990 Not tasted. Paul Brajkovich describes it as "a lesser vintage, past its best".

1989 ☆☆☆☆☆ Mature gold. Fully developed but still very alive. Very nutty, toasty and honied, with rich flavours. Good acid backbone. Mellow. A delicious example of 10-year-old New Zealand Chardonnay.

Kumeu River Maté's Vineyard Chardonnay

CLASSIC

R arer and slightly more expensive than the better known, longer established Kumeu River Chardonnay, Maté's Vineyard is the pinnacle of the West Auckland winery's Chardonnays. Winemaker Michael Brajkovich likens Kumeu River Chardonnay, a blend of grapes from several sites, to "a village wine", and the single-vineyard Maté's Vineyard Chardonnay to "a *premier cru* of the same village".

Destined after another vintage or two to be rated as a Super Classic, Maté's Vineyard Chardonnay is strikingly similar to Kumeu River Chardonnay, but slightly more opulent and concentrated. It offers the same rich and harmonious flavours of grapefruit, peach and butterscotch, but with even greater depth and with a stronger seasoning of new French oak in its youth.

For several years, the Brajkovich family had noted the distinctly defined characteristics of its various vineyard sites, and entertained thoughts of producing limited releases of single-vineyard wines to capture that individuality. Demand for the blended Kumeu River Chardonnay prevented that move, until the launch of the first Maté's Vineyard Chardonnay from 1993.

Maté's Vineyard, with its low-walled entrance, lies straight over the road from the winery at Kumeu, on part of the original property purchased by Mate Brajkovich and his parents in 1944. After the early hybrid vines were uprooted, the land was grazed by cattle until the Brajkoviches decided to redevelop it as a vineyard. After much contouring and drainage work under Maté's direction, planting of the new vineyard was completed in 1990. Mate Brajkovich died in 1992 – a year before the first harvest.

What led the Brajkovich family to choose Maté's

Vineyard as the site for its Rolls Royce Chardonnay? "When we planted it in 1990, we'd been through the learning curve of our earlier vineyards," recalls marketing manager Paul Brajkovich. "For example, we developed a wider U-trellis that is easier to work inside. It's a hot site, and the grapes develop significantly different flavours – sweeter, more akin to pears." The vines are all of the relatively low-yielding Mendoza clone, and each year only the pick of the crop is reserved for the Maté's Vineyard label.

"When we harvested the grapes from Maté's Vineyard in 1993, we knew the wine was going to be something very special," recalls Michael Brajkovich. "Not only was 1993 a beautiful vintage in Kumeu but the vineyard, with its low-yielding Mendoza Chardonnay grafted onto low-vigour rootstocks such as 3309 and 101-14, gave us some lovely fruit aroma characteristics, weight of flavour and length of palate."

At the winery, the hand-picked grapes are handled in almost exactly the same way as the fruit for Kumeu River Chardonnay – whole-bunch pressed; fermented with indigenous yeasts; and given full barrel and malolactic fermentation. However, Maté's Vineyard sees a bit more new oak – 30 per cent, compared to 20-25 per cent for the Kumeu River Chardonnay.

Maté's Vineyard – the source of Kumeu River's premier Chardonnay.

About 1000 cases of Maté's Vineyard Chardonnay are made each year, retailing at around $39 – $6 more than the Kumeu River Chardonnay. Tasted side by side with its stablemate of the same vintage, the Maté's Vineyard tastes more powerful and youthful, suggesting it will have a longer life span. "With its finer, slightly minerally character and extra length and finesse, you'd expect it to," says Paul Brajkovich, "but it's early days yet."

Like Kumeu River Chardonnay, Maté's Vineyard is not entered in shows but has attracted rave reviews overseas. In the UK, Jancis Robinson praised the 1994 vintage as "the finest New Zealand white to have come my way." The 1996, enthused Australian writer James Halliday, "has the longest finish I have encountered in a Chardonnay for many years."

Maté's Vineyard may only be the first of other single-vineyard Chardonnays from Kumeu River. Meanwhile, it ranks among New Zealand's classiest white wines. The 1996 vintage, with its impressive weight and depth of grapefruit, biscuit and hazelnut flavours, reminded me vividly a year ago of a Joseph Drouhin Beaune Clos des Mouches 1995 ($95) I'd opened a few nights earlier.

tasting notes
These notes are from a vertical tasting of the 1993 to 1998 vintages, held at the winery in March 1999.

1998 ☆☆☆☆☆ Light yellow. Super-opulent. Amazingly concentrated flavours of grapefruit, peach and butterscotch, with an almost apricot-like ripeness, intensity and richness. A real conversation piece. **Drink 2000-2005.**

1997 ☆☆☆☆☆ Medium yellow. Biscuity nose. Deep, serious wine, still a bit oak-dominated. Grapefruit and nut flavours, with a hint of butterscotch. Very powerful, mouthfilling and savoury. Already delicious, but best **drinking 2000-02.**

1996 ☆☆☆☆☆ Pale yellow. Still very youthful. Fresh, intense grapefruit flavours, with oak enriching but not dominating. Beautifully poised and elegant. A classic vintage, still ascending. **Drink 2000-03.**

1995 ☆☆☆☆☆ Light-medium yellow. Weighty, although slightly leaner than the 1996 and 1994. Grapefruit and butterscotch flavours, with a suggestion of lime and firm, crisp finish. Developing toasty bottle-aged characters. **Drink 1999-2000.**

1994 ☆☆☆☆☆ Light yellow. Lovely, fresh wine with highly concentrated citrus and nut flavours and firm acid spine. Finely balanced, with great richness and a superbly powerful finish. **Drink 1999-2000.**

1993 ☆☆☆ Full yellow/light gold. Developed but dull nose. Weighty and flavoursome, but slightly oxidised. Based on three-year-old vines and now well past its best. **Drink ASAP.**

Martinborough Vineyard Chardonnay

CLASSIC

A decade ago, 1988 Martinborough Vineyard Chardonnay won not only a gold medal, but the trophy for champion wine of the 1989 Air New Zealand Wine Awards. Several years later, Martinborough Vineyard stopped exhibiting at local competitions, but the wine has remained one of the district's heavyweights.

Notable flavour complexity has always been the hallmark of winemaker Larry McKenna's style. "We've been trying to emulate the complexity of white Burgundy," says McKenna, winemaker at Martinborough Vineyard from 1985 to 1999. "Burgundy is the benchmark. Our fruit is different – higher in acid and with less palate weight, for now – but we want the weight and texture of Burgundy."

Pivotal to the quality of his Chardonnay, says McKenna, has been ripe fruit. "We've learnt a lot about that in the last 10 years. Our vintages have been getting later and later, to get riper fruit." Because Martinborough is a relatively cool grape-growing district, canopy management has been vital to achieve good acid balance in the fruit and reduce disease problems. "Today, the vineyards are far more hand-manipulated. We're creating the canopies we want, to expose the fruit to sunshine and prevent leaf shading."

The vines, currently about half of the Mendoza clone (but also 2/23, RUA-1, clone 6 and clone 15), are all planted on the gravelly, free-draining Martinborough Terrace, in close proximity to the winery. Most of the vines are trained on the Scott Henry system, but some are close-planted with vertical shoot positioning. Crops average three tonnes per acre, and the bunches are all hand-harvested.

McKenna's Chardonnay-making recipe in the winery includes low sulphur levels prior to fermentation ("to let the malolactic fermentation go through quicker"); whole-bunch pressing; 100 per cent barrel fermentation; and about 30 per cent new oak. Since 1997, in the search for greater complexity, indigenous yeasts have been used. "They give what Danny Schuster [of Canterbury] calls 'more corruption', which is a higher level of sulphides," says McKenna, "and the wine seems to be rounder." Extensive lees-aging and lees-stirring imparts yeasty, mealy flavours and improves the wine's mouthfeel and texture.

Key changes over the years are the introduction of *bâtonnage* (lees-stirring) around 1991, whole-bunch pressing around 1992, and fermentation with indigenous yeasts in 1997. "Casks are an ongoing learning curve, in terms of their oak types, levels of toast and so on," says McKenna.

By the district's standards, Martinborough Vineyard Chardonnay ($28) is produced in quite large volumes – about 2000 cases per year, exported to the UK (principally), the United States and Australia. In terms of longevity, McKenna believes most are at their best at around five years: "Complexity takes a while to develop, and it takes a while for the oak to integrate." The tasting (below) confirms that recent vintages have typically matured well for five or six years. Given the changes in vinification, the wines of the mid to late 1990s will probably age more gracefully than their predecessors.

Mouthfilling, peachy, citrusy and mealy, Martinborough Vineyard Chardonnay is typically a powerful and harmonious wine with concentrated flavours, bold alcohol and rich, savoury characters. Complexity has been McKenna's goal, and over the years he has hit the target well. ❦

Larry McKenna produces distinguished Chardonnays – powerful, complex and harmonious.

tasting notes

These notes are mainly from a vertical tasting of the 1984 to 1997 vintages, held at the winery in November 1998. The 1998 vintage was tasted in Auckland in April 1999.

1998 ☆☆☆☆☆ Light lemon/green. Lovely weight, freshness and roundness. Very forward in its appeal, with deep, ripe peach and citrus flavours, a touch of butterscotch and a soft, resounding finish. Beautifully harmonious wine, nutty, mealy and savoury. A top year. **Drink 2000-05.**

1997 ☆☆☆☆☆ Pale lemon. Fragrant, nutty, "malo"-influenced bouquet. Soft, rich and robust, with deep citrus/melon flavours and a mealy, biscuity complexity. Very seductive wine, still developing, with great texture and mouthfeel. **Drink 2000-03.**

1996 ☆☆☆☆☆ Pale lemon. Ripely scented and powerful (14 per cent alcohol) wine with ripe citrus and passionfruit flavours, very pure and delicate. Mealy, slightly buttery and creamy. Lovely harmony and a lasting finish. A classic vintage. **Drink 2000-02.**

1995 ☆☆☆☆☆ Light yellow. Big, chewy and very high-flavoured. Rich citrus fruits and melons, with well integrated oak and lots of mealiness. Less lush than the 1994, but a powerful wine with a tight finish. **Drink 1999-2001.**

1994 ☆☆☆☆☆ Pale lemon hue, still very youthful. Very scented. Very ripe citrus/tropical fruit flavours, delicate and deep. Beautifully overlaid with oak/lees characters. Mouthfilling, finely balanced wine with a creamy texture, delicious now. **Drink 1999-2001.**

1993 ☆☆☆☆☆ Light yellow. Powerful wine, maturing well. Rich citrusy fruit characters, firm acid and mouthfilling body. Impressively weighty and savoury. Now at its peak. Best of the earlier wines for drinking now. **Drink 1999-2000.**

1992 ☆☆☆ Light gold. Slightly honied nose and palate. Weighty, citrusy and crisp, but slightly dull and fading a bit. **Drink ASAP.**

1991 ☆☆☆☆☆ Pale yellow. Powerful, creamy wine, very big in the mouth. Concentrated grapefruit and oak flavours, mealy richness and good acid spine. Very ready, with a hint of oxidation, but has obviously been a superb wine. **Drink ASAP.**

1990 ☆☆☆☆ ⚬ Full yellow. Starting to tire, but still highly enjoyable, with rich citrus flavours wrapped in nutty oak. Complex and savoury, slightly buttery wine, impressively concentrated, but probably at its best around 1996. **Drink ASAP.**

1989 ☆☆ Medium straw. Slightly oxidised nose. Big, mealy, citrusy wine, but a long way past its best. Should have been good five years ago.

1988 ☆ Deep gold. Oxidised nose. Very mouthfilling. Toasty and honied, but also distinctly sherry-like. Gone.

1987 ☆ Full gold. Oxidised nose. Several years past its best. Fading, drying out, no longer pleasant.

1986 ☆☆☆ ⚬ Medium gold, green tinted. Still lively and full-flavoured, with citrusy, slightly honied flavours. Mouthfilling and crisp. Less satisfying than the 1985, but lasting pretty well. **Drink ASAP.**

1985 ☆☆☆☆ Medium gold, slightly green. Still alive! Very toasty bouquet. Surprisingly vigorous and enjoyable, with rich citrus and toast flavours and considerable complexity. Very ready, but not yet over the hill. **Drink 1999-2000.**

1984 ☆ Gold/brown, tired-looking. Oxidised bouquet. Deceased.

GISBORNE

ORMOND ESTATE
CHARDONNAY
1 9 9 6

PRODUCED AND BOTTLED BY MONTANA WINES LTD
LYTTON RD. GISBORNE.
75cl Produce of New Zealand 13.5% Alc/Vol

MONTANA ESTATES

Montana Ormond Estate Chardonnay

POTENTIAL CLASSIC

This is Montana's flagship Gisborne Chardonnay. Packed with well-ripened tropical and citrus fruit flavours, it's a plump, creamy-rich wine with biscuity, mealy complexities and a long, silky finish.

In 1991, Gisborne grapegrowers erected signs alongside the two main roads into the city, proclaiming Gisborne as the "Chardonnay capital of New Zealand". Over 40 per cent of all the region's producing vines in 1999 were Chardonnay. In 2001, when Chardonnay will account for 53 per cent of all bearing vines, Gisborne will be the only region in the country with over half of its planted area devoted to a single variety.

Yet James Millton, of The Millton Vineyard, believes Gisborne's growers are still "scratching the surface in terms of developing quality Chardonnays. There's the ability to produce easy-drinking, cost-effective, commercially excellent Chardonnays, but on the sides of the valleys, with the right clones and sites and careful vine management and reduced yields, there's lots of scope for quality advances."

The Gisborne region produces Chardonnays that are irresistible at one year old (like Montana's own Saints Gisborne Chardonnay), yet Montana's chief winemaker Jeff Clarke sees the style of the Ormond Estate Chardonnay as "quite tight. It's certainly a wine we like to see get some bottle development."

Clarke, an Australian who heads a team of 12 winemakers in Auckland, Gisborne, Hawke's Bay and Marlborough, is constantly on the move, monitoring the company's production in the regions. He previously worked for Penfolds Wines in the Barossa Valley and as chief winemaker at the Tisdall winery in Victoria, and worked the 1989 vintage at Maison Louis Latour in Burgundy, where traditional methods are used to make superlative Chardonnays.

The grapes for Montana's top Gisborne Chardonnay are grown at the company's Ormond Estate, an old, replanted vineyard in the Ormond Valley originally established by Waihirere Wines. The 15-year-old Mendoza vines are established in clay loam soils where "the vigour is not excessive," says Clarke. "They're mature vines yielding small crops of concentrated grapes. The fruit is less aromatic and strongly fruity than some Gisborne Chardonnay, but has tight, subtle, long grapefruit-like flavours that mature well, developing nutty, toasty characters after about four years."

Most of the grapes are hand-harvested and whole-bunch pressed, but some skin contact is allowed to boost the juice's flavour. The wine is fermented with cultured yeasts in French oak barriques (60 per cent new), and matured on its yeast lees, with regular stirring, for 10 months. The degree of malolactic fermentation varies according to the season, but averages about 20 per cent.

Montana Ormond Estate Chardonnay is produced on a fairly large scale - 3000 to 4000

Montana's Ormond Estate at Gisborne yields fleshy, concentrated, creamy-soft Chardonnay.

cases per year. "We've had a great response to it in the UK and the US," says Clarke. The first 1990 vintage was launched in New Zealand at $32, but buyer resistance (to the idea of paying a high price for a big-company wine) has since reduced the price to around $25. By offering superior quality to many boutique wineries' $30 Chardonnays, it's a bargain.

Montana Ormond Estate Chardonnay is softly seductive in its youth, but breaks into full stride at three to five years old. The 1994 vintage won a gold medal at the International Wine Challenge in London; the 1996 won gold medals in the US and Australia. One of Gisborne's classiest Chardonnays, it is fleshy and savoury, delicate, mealy and complex, with tropical fruit flavours shining through and a creamy-soft, lingering finish.

tasting notes

These notes are from a vertical tasting of the 1990 to 1998 vintages, held at the winery in April 1999.

1998 ☆☆☆☆☆ (Tasted one week after bottling.) Pale lemon/green. Still a baby – very fresh and delicate. Lovely, very ripe citrus/melon flavours. Savoury, with lees-aging richness, quality French oak and balanced acidity. Creamy wine, with a hint of butterscotch. It's all there for the future. **Drink 2001-05.**

1997 Not made.

1996 ☆☆☆☆☆ Bright, light-medium yellow. Very rich and smooth. Still youthful, with fresh, deliciously concentrated tropical and citrus flavours and balanced toasty oak. Lovely vigour and harmony. Still ascending. Classic vintage. **Drink 2000-03.**

1995 Not tasted. "Drink up," says Jeff Clarke.

1994 ☆☆☆☆☆ Full yellow/light gold. Fragrant, mature, toasty, nutty bouquet, very inviting. Developed, rich flavours of tropical and citrus fruits, nutty and complex. Weighty and harmonious, with real presence in the mouth. At peak. **Drink 1999-2000.**

1993 Not tasted. "Basically past it," says Jeff Clarke.

1992 ☆☆☆☆ Light gold. Mature, toasty bouquet, with citrus and toasty oak flavours. Firm acidity, reflecting the cool season. Lacks the richness of the later vintages, but still has good concentration and persistence, with a tight finish. **Drink 1999.**

1991 Not made.

1990 ☆☆☆☆☆ Medium gold. Grapefruit and pineapple aromas and flavours, with toasty bottle-aged characters. Mouthfilling and holding well, but fully ready. Slightly minerally character, with a tight finish. **Drink 1999.**

Morton Estate Black Label Chardonnay

SUPER CLASSIC

For 15 years, Morton Estate's flagship has been one of the country's most distinguished Chardonnays. Indivisibly associated with winemaker John Hancock, who crafted the 1984 to 1995 vintages, it is now under the direction of Evan Ward, who formerly headed Corbans' winemaking team in Hawke's Bay.

The Black Label Chardonnay is a justly celebrated Hawke's Bay wine. Refined, weighty and tightly structured, it offers a lovely array of grapefruit and melon-like, mealy, oaky flavours and a long, rich finish. The early vintages were very substantial and huge in flavour, but since 1991 the style has changed, placing greater emphasis on flavour delicacy, tightness and longevity.

The first key step in the Black Label's evolution came in 1981, when John Hancock tasted Louis Latour Corton-Charlemagne 1979. "That mealy, biscuity wine with hazelnut characters was a major revelation," Hancock recalls, "and has figured strongly in the development of my style of New Zealand Chardonnay." That year, at Delegat's, Hancock made his first Chardonnay, employing Australian winemaking techniques, including cold fermentation in stainless steel tanks. Soon after, during a visit to Burgundy, the sight of hand-picked fruit being whole-bunch pressed and the juice going directly to barrels for fermentation "sowed the seeds for a new approach".

The first Morton Estate Black Label Chardonnay flowed in 1984. Although the fruit was still machine-harvested, only the best free-run juice was used and the wine was fermented in oak (100 per cent new)

and matured on its yeast lees for eight months. "The wine was quite radical with unprecedented complexity," recalls Hancock. "I remember saying to [then] winery owner Morton Brown that if the public didn't like the wine, we should drink it all ourselves. They liked it and the Black Label was born!"

Whole-bunch pressing and stirring of the yeast lees were introduced in 1990. Whenever possible, Hancock avoided malolactic fermentation (except when necessary for reducing acidity), preferring to gain "complexity, mouthfeel and integration of oak" from frequent lees-stirring.

By 1991, the company's new Riverview vineyard at Mangatahi, inland from Ngatarawa, began to have a major impact on the wine. "Finally we were getting to where Burgundy was at, with fruit quality matching winemaking." Hancock attributes the much greater finesse evident in the 1991 and later vintages to the quality of Riverview fruit. "We'd previously sourced most of the fruit from a grower in Mere Road. At Riverview we could be far more selective, by using only the best blocks of grapes, and the vineyard gave a different character: more intense grapefruit flavours and better acid balances, eliminating the need for a softening malolactic fermentation in good vintages."

Evan Ward shares Hancock's enthusiasm for Riverview vineyard fruit. "When I first came to Morton Estate, I couldn't believe the quality of the Chardonnay grapes – their level of ripeness and flavour intensity."

At the elevated Riverview site, on terraces of the Ngaruroro River, the vines are cultivated in 40-50 cm of soil over deep shingle. Irrigation is essential. The vines, all the relatively low-yielding Mendoza clone, are mainly trained on the Scott Henry system, which splits the canopy into two curtains, one above the other. Some of the grapes are machine harvested (depending on the condition of the fruit), because the winery is located at the vineyard, thus eliminating the problem of skin contact.

"It's dead simple, mate," says Evan Ward, if you ask him how he makes the Black Label. "The grapes are whole-bunch pressed, or crushed and pressed; the juice is cold-settled and racked into barrels for a cool ferment at 10-12°C; and the wine is stirred weekly until Christmas. There's nothing magical."

Given the Black Label's intense fruit characters, the French oak barriques are 80 per cent new.

The production of Morton Estate Black Label Chardonnay is very variable, reflecting the season. There was no 1997, but in an average year the output is several thousand cases, retailing at around $33. The wine is at its best at three to five years old, while its pure, penetrating fruit characters are still fresh and vibrant.

Morton Estate's Black Label range is no longer entered in local wine competitions (unlike the rest of the company's wines). However, the 1995 vintage (a gold medal winner at the Air New Zealand Wine Awards), later scooped the trophy for champion Chardonnay at the 1997 International Wine Challenge in London.

Morton Estate Black Label is one of the classiest of all New Zealand Chardonnays. It's a powerful wine, robust and awash with flavour, yet highly refined, with beautifully intense fruit characters, firm acid spine and the structure to flourish with age. That London trophy didn't surprise me.

tasting notes

These notes are from a vertical tasting of the 1990 to 1996 vintages, held in Auckland in March 1999.

1998 (Not rated. Pre-bottling sample, tasted April 1999.) Pale lemon/green. Fragrant, toasty oak on the nose. Very mouthfilling, with rich grapefruit and melon flavours and lovely strength through the palate. Elegant, savoury, mealy and tight, with a very long finish. Looks outstanding.

1997 Not made.

1996 ☆☆☆☆☆ Bright, medium yellow. Richly fragrant, fresh and rich, with lovely balance and intensity. Grapefruit and melon flavours, with restrained nutty, mealy characters and lively acidity. Slightly buttery and creamy. Powerful, highly refined wine, still developing. **Drink 1999-2001.**

1995 ☆☆☆☆☆ Full, bright yellow. Richly fragrant and robust (14 per cent alcohol), with intense flavours of grapefruit, fig and buttery oak. Layered with mealy, nutty complexities, but the fruit is the real star – deliciously fresh, ripe and vibrant. Complex wine with lovely weight and richness and a slightly creamy texture. Should be long-lived. **Drink 1999-2000.**

1994 ☆☆☆☆☆ Bright, light gold. Enticingly fragrant, citrusy, mealy bouquet. Rich, integrated flavours of peach, grapefruit and oak. Intense fruit flavours, with slightly more assertive wood than the 1995 or 1996. Fresh, lively and powerful, with fine acidity and a slightly buttery finish. A classic vintage, now

at its peak. **Drink 1999-2000.**

1993 ☆☆☆☆ Deep gold, hint of brown. Very advanced condition. Big wine (14 per cent alcohol) with a honeyish, nutty bouquet and distinctly honied palate. Peachy, nutty and flavoursome, but oak and *Botrytis* dominate. **Drink ASAP.**

1992 ☆☆☆☆ Bright, medium gold. Grapefruit and toasty aromas and flavours. Slightly green-edged, reflecting the very cool season. Has matured well, with rich citrusy fruit and balanced, biscuity oak, but lacks the sheer beauty and class of the 1991. Rounded finish, with the fruit just starting to dry out. **Drink 1999.**

1991 ☆☆☆☆☆ Full yellow/light gold. Riverview fruit. Attractive bouquet of lemons and toast. Very elegant and weighty, with rich, pure tropical/citrus flavours, well judged oak and balanced acidity. Deliciously full-bodied and full-flavoured wine, with finesse, complexity and harmony. Ready. **Drink 1999.**

1990 ☆☆☆☆ Bright, full gold. Very nutty, toasty bouquet. Full, rounded palate with strong citrus fruit, butter and toast flavours. Slightly honied. Strongly oaked wine, with the fruit starting to dry out. Very ready. **Drink 1999.**

Neudorf Moutere Chardonnay

SUPER CLASSIC

The undisputed heavyweight of Nelson wines and the finest Chardonnay to flow from the South Island, Neudorf Moutere Chardonnay is one of New Zealand's greatest wines of all. From their idyllic plot of vines in the blue-green hills of the Upper Moutere, Tim and Judy Finn produce a gloriously rich and multi-faceted Chardonnay that has often been compared to top white Burgundy.

Finn himself only partly accepts the comparison with Burgundy. "Top Chardonnay from New Zealand is always fruitier than white Burgundy. I think it's because our sunlight is more intense. New Zealand's apples are very fruity – all our fruit is fruitier than you find elsewhere. And we get higher levels of acidity in the grapes. But we do get some very similar flavour notes to white Burgundy in our wine," says Finn, who believes those characters are rarely found in other New Zealand Chardonnays, because they don't mature well enough. Anthony Rose, UK wine correspondent for *The Independent*, described the 1997 Neudorf Moutere Chardonnay in December 1998 as "New Zealand's convincing answer to *premier cru* Puligny-Montrachet."

Finn's pursuit of great Chardonnay starts with "quality grapes, and recognising the style parameters set by the fruit. You should run with what your vineyard is producing, rather than try and change it. For instance, if we were growing our wine on [Nelson's] Waimea Plains, we would highlight the grapes' bright fruit flavours. In the Moutere, we get intense, minerally fruit with a limey background that suits a powerful style. We can produce the fruit there for a long-lasting wine; we just add the bells and whistles."

Finn has a clear idea of the style he is after. "I want powerful but not overpowering wine – the world is full of blockbuster Chardonnays. I want to retain finesse and I want the wine to be long-lived."

The grapes are grown in clay soils threaded with gravel in Neudorf's estate vineyard at Upper Moutere. In the typically long, warm summers with cool nights, Finn finds his Chardonnay gets "very ripe, yet retains acidity. So we have the ability to ripen the grapes well, without any blowsiness. And the clay gives us deep, minerally, rather than effervescent, flavours."

The grapes are hand-harvested (sometimes twice, to allow better selection of ripe fruit) and whole-bunch pressed, and after very little settling the juice is run straight into barrels – tight-grained French oak barriques, half new and half one year old. Finn likes Taransaud oak, which he finds imparts "barrel characters without overt, charry oak." To achieve greater vinosity, at the expense of preserving fruit characters, the juice is fermented at high temperatures (up to 26°C) and then barrel-aged for a year on its yeast lees, with regular stirring. Around 70 per cent of the final blend goes through a softening malolactic fermentation.

Looking back, Finn recalls several major changes

in his production techniques since the first 1982 vintage. "Our first big step forward was when we overcame vigour problems by adopting Scott Henry trellising, which gave us more open canopies, less *Botrytis* and riper, richer fruit. We started barrel fermenting in 1986, and around 1989 began whole-bunch pressing and lees-aging. In 1994, we introduced a second label [Neudorf Nelson Chardonnay, a fine wine in its own right, designed for earlier drinking] which provided an outlet for the grapes we didn't require for the top wine. And although we started off using all-new oak, we have found that about 50 per cent new oak provides a better-balanced wine."

Neudorf Moutere Chardonnay ($35) is a rare wine – only about 500 cases are made each year, although new vine plantings will eventually allow production to approach 1000 cases. Tim Finn recommends cellaring the wine for at least three to four years: "That's when the real complexity emerges, and the wine holds up for a minimum of eight years;

perhaps longer." On the evidence of the tasting, the optimal drinking period runs from five to 10 years.

Neudorf Moutere Chardonnay has won important awards in New Zealand, Australia and the UK. The 1991 vintage was champion wine of the 1993 Liquorland Royal Easter Wine Show and headed off all other Chardonnays – including Louis Latour Corton-Charlemagne 1990, at three times the price – in a London tasting of the world's "best wines, regardless of price", published in the June 1993 issue of *Wine* magazine. Finn says, "I like the consistency of the appreciation. Year after year, people are enjoying the wine and they consistently say it's good."

Rich but not overblown, with mouthfilling body and arrestingly intense, peachy, citrusy, nutty flavours threaded with fine acidity, Neudorf Moutere enjoys a reputation second to none among New Zealand Chardonnays. That it is less well known among wine lovers than other such high-fliers as Kumeu River and Te Mata Elston is part of its special appeal for those who have discovered this rare but brilliant gem. 🍷

tasting notes
These notes are from a vertical tasting of the 1990 to 1997 vintages, held in Auckland in March 1999.

1997 ☆☆☆☆☆ Light lemon/green. Rich, powerful wine with intense grapefruit and biscuity oak flavours. More fragrant than the 1996 (reflecting addition of new clones?). Superb concentration, structure and finesse, with fine acidity and great length. At least the equal of 1991 and 1994, and may well prove the greatest vintage yet. Beautifully balanced already. **Drink 2001-07.**

1996 ☆☆☆☆✓ Light lemon/green. Slightly shy on the nose. Stylish, powerful wine that feels weighty yet restrained (it was deliberately made in a "less big" style than the 1994). Nutty, citrusy flavours with a hint of butterscotch from 100 per cent malolactic fermentation and a rich finish. Tight wine, still opening up, but should have an excellent future. **Drink 2001-06.**

1995 Not tasted. From a wet vintage, the wine is past its best.

1994 ☆☆☆☆☆ Light lemon/green. Beguiling bouquet of citrus fruits and hazelnuts. Mouthfilling palate, with very ripe, sweet fruit characters. Robust, with delicate grapefruit/peach flavours and finely integrated oak. A powerful, beautifully balanced wine, it is showing wonderful harmony now, but still developing, with even greater complexity to come. **Drink 1999-2004.**

1993 ☆☆☆☆☆ Light yellow/green. Lush wine with loads of

charm (first vintage with 2/23 clone, giving early appeal). Softer than the older wines, with deep grapefruit and peach flavours, slightly buttery and rounded. Very pretty wine with sweet fruit delights and balanced nutty oak. Delicious now. **Drink 1999-2003.**

1992 ☆☆☆☆☆ Yellow/green, medium depth. Similar to the 1991, but a slightly less ripe style (reflecting the unusually cool summer). Fragrant, citrusy bouquet with biscuity oak. Concentrated grapefruit flavours with a minerally tang, a touch of butterscotch and tight underlying acidity. **Drink 1999-2002.**

1991 ☆☆☆☆☆ Bright, full yellow/green. Very fragrant, oatmealy, nutty bouquet. Fruitier style than the 1990, less oaky, with impressive weight and intense grapefruit/melon characters shining through. Very elegant, firmly structured wine with rich, sweet fruit and balanced wood. A top vintage, maturing very gracefully, it should prove very long-lived. **Drink 1999-2001.**

1990 ☆☆☆☆☆ Light-medium gold. Toasty, minerally nose. Rich, very toasty wine with lovely vigour. Very nutty and concentrated, with a lovely harmony of peachy, toasty, almost honied flavour and finely tuned acid. Slightly woodier style than usual, seemingly at its peak. **Drink 1999-2000.**

MARTINBOROUGH
CHARDONNAY
1997

e750ml   13.5% Vol

PRODUCED AND BOTTLED BY PALLISER ESTATE WINES, KITCHENER STREET, MARTINBOROUGH

WINE OF NEW ZEALAND

Palliser Estate Chardonnay

CLASSIC

Gracefulness, rather than sheer power, is the hallmark of winemaker Allan Johnson's Martinborough wine. A celebration of strong, citrusy fruit flavours, it is gently seasoned with oak, producing a delicious wine with subtle winemaking input and concentrated varietal flavours.

Allan Johnson makes a graceful, citrusy Chardonnay, gently seasoned with oak.

One of the quiet men of the industry, Johnson is a highly talented winemaker, producing top-flight wines from several varieties – Chardonnay, Sauvignon Blanc, Riesling and Pinot Noir. The district's Chardonnay flavours, he believes, are closer to Burgundy than those of other New Zealand regions. "We get riper, richer flavours than in Marlborough, but they're still citrusy, tight and focused."

Trained mainly on the Scott Henry system (which divides the foliage into two vertical curtains, trained upwards and downwards), the vines are almost entirely of the low-yielding Mendoza clone. "Flavour maturity tends to come at high sugar levels," says Johnson, "so the wine often has a high level of alcohol [up to 14 per cent.] Our picking decisions are a balance between achieving flavour ripeness and not allowing the sugar levels to get too high."

In his pursuit of a more complex style, Johnson's approach to Chardonnay in the winery has changed over the years. "Especially since 1997, we've done less pre-ferment settling of the juice. Leaving a much higher level of solids in the juice improves the wine's backbone and texture."

The fermentation gets underway in stainless

steel tanks, then is transferred into French oak barrels. By recently oak-fermenting at warmer temperatures than in the past, Johnson finds he is achieving a wine with "less in the way of pure fruit flavours, but more body and an enhanced vinous character."

Although matured on its yeast lees for nine months, the wine is not lees-stirred. "Nine months gives a lot of lees contact anyway," says Johnson. "I'm not convinced people fully understand what they're doing with lees-stirring."

To produce a style that is not oak-dominated, the percentage of new wood is kept low; an average of 22 per cent. In the past, between a third and a half of the final blend has gone through malolactic fermentation, but that proportion will go higher in the future, in the pursuit of greater softness on the palate.

Palliser Estate is Martinborough's largest winery, and the Chardonnay (retailing at $30) is produced in significant commercial volumes –

around 3000 cases each year. That it does not have an outstanding track record in shows – certainly less glittering than its Sauvignon Blanc, Riesling and Pinot Noir stablemates – is a reflection of its style. In a blind tasting, it can easily be overwhelmed by more assertively wooded wines.

Winery tasting notes on their own wines are hardly an objective guide, yet Palliser Estate's description of its 1996 vintage pinned down the label's style precisely. "A fine fragrant Chardonnay. Aroma and flavour hint at citrus and peaches, with gentle suggestions of sweet, vanilla-like spices imbedded in a silky textured palate. For all its apparent charm, however, this is powerful wine, but its strength never imposes on its balance, leaving the impression of graceful quality."

Gracefulness, delicacy, finesse – these are the key attributes of Palliser Estate Chardonnay.

The wine can cellar well for at least five years, but within three or four years, its charms are fully revealed. 🍇

tasting notes

These notes are mainly from a vertical tasting of the 1990 to 1997 vintages, held at the winery in November 1998. The 1998 vintage was tasted in Auckland in March 1999.

1998 ☆☆☆☆☆ (Tasted soon after bottling.) Light lemon/green. Very youthful and fresh, with beautifully scented, well-ripened fruit. Subtle, mealy, biscuity characters add complexity, but leave the rich, vibrant tropical/citrus fruit flavours holding centre stage. Robust (14 per cent alcohol) wine with finely balanced, delicate flavours, still coming together. **Open 2000-03.**

1997 ☆☆☆☆⚹ Lemon/green hue, medium depth. Rich, ripe fruit aromas and quality oak on the nose. Still very youthful, but stylish and integrated, with sweet fruit characters, tropical/citrus flavours and restrained wood. Mouthfilling, moderately complex, refined. Currently slightly overshadowed by the 1996. **Drink 2000-02.**

1996 ☆☆☆☆☆ Bright lemon/green. Very typical Palliser style, placing its emphasis on refinement rather than obvious power. Ripe, sweet, citrusy fruit, with deft oak handling and malolactic fermentation adding nutty, butterscotch-like characters. Fine acid balance. Lovely delicacy and poise. **Drink 1999-2002.**

1995 ☆☆☆☆ Pale yellow. Elegant wine, less rich than the 1994, but maturing well. Still fresh, with firm acid underpinning ripe citrus fruit flavours, slightly less concentrated than usual. Delicate and finely balanced. **Drink 1999-2001.**

1994 ☆☆☆☆☆ Medium-full yellow. A clear step up in quality and style (small crop, higher percentage of malolactic fermentation). Highly fragrant. Classy, very elegant wine with beautifully rich, ripe, citrusy fruit flavours, biscuity oak and a hint of butterscotch. Incisive and complex, with good acid backbone and a slightly creamy texture. **Drink 1999-2000.**

1993 ☆☆☆⚹ Full yellow. Strong citrusy, slightly toasty characters and firm acidity. Maturing well, but slightly lacks complexity and softness. **Drink 1999.**

1992 Not tasted. "Should be approximately like the 1993," says Allan Johnson.

1991 ☆☆☆☆ Light gold. Toasty bouquet, limey and nutty. Similar to the 1990 – crisp, toasty, nutty, limey, with firm acid. Maturing well, although less rich, ripe and complex than the later vintages. **Drink 1999.**

1990 ☆☆☆☆⚹ (Made by Rob Bower, with a strong new oak influence.) Full yellow/light gold. Toasty, developed nose. Strong, lively palate, citrusy and nutty, with good body and a rounded finish. Very appealing. **Drink 1999.**

PEGASUS BAY

CHARDONNAY
-WHOLE BUNCH PRESSED-

1997

14% Vol   e750ml

GROWN, VINTED & BOTTLED BY IVAN & CHRIS
DONALDSON AND FAMILY. WAIPARA CANTERBURY
NEW ZEALAND. CONTAINS PRESERVATIVE (220)

Pegasus Bay Chardonnay

CLASSIC

This sophisticated, exceptionally powerful and rich Waipara wine is the only consistently brilliant Chardonnay grown south of Marlborough. In Chardonnay – as with several other varieties – the Donaldson family's Pegasus Bay winery has set new standards for North Canterbury wine.

The family is a highly experienced, talented winemaking force headed by Ivan Donaldson, an associate-professor of neurology, wine judge and wine columnist for *The Press*. Ivan's wife, Chris, is the business manager. One son, Edward, is the marketing manager and another son, Matthew, a Roseworthy College graduate, makes the wine with his partner, Lynnette Hudson, who is also a winemaking graduate. Experience counts – Pegasus Bay Chardonnay is a voluptuous wine, muscular and taut, with a seamless array of citrusy, biscuity, complex flavours and great concentration and length.

What style of Chardonnay is Pegasus Bay aiming for? "We don't want sweet, melon-like fruit by itself," says Ivan Donaldson. "We want a concentrated wine, without any rough edges, and with savoury elements."

In Donaldson's eyes, ripe fruit is an essential springboard to quality. "At Waipara, we can ripen the grapes fully and slowly. We aim to pick at around 24 brix, when the grapes are very ripe and concentrated. And we go for low yields. We've never cropped Chardonnay above 2.5 or three tonnes per acre; it's often around two tonnes per acre."

Entirely estate-grown, the grapes are hand-picked and then whole-bunch pressed rather than crushed,

to prevent the extraction of harsh phenolic substances from the stems and skins. At the juice stage, the wine is not heavily protected from oxygen. "Instead of using reductive [anti-oxygen] Australian techniques, we adopt a more Burgundian approach," says Donaldson. "The oxygen 'complexes' with the phenolics; the phenolics precipitate out; and the wine ages better."

The wine is fully fermented in barrels: French oak, about 30 per cent new. Fermentation temperatures are warm – the barrels are allowed to ferment at whatever temperatures they want (up to 25°C). "We don't cool-ferment to preserve fruit flavour, because Chardonnay shouldn't depend just on fruit flavour," says Donaldson. "We get lots of fruit expression in the vineyard anyway, so we're happy to sacrifice some of that."

After the ferment, the wine rests on its lees, but is not lees-stirred. About half of the final blend goes through malolactic fermentation, which occurs naturally with warming the following spring. After about a year, to prevent excessive oakiness the wine is removed from barrels, but before bottling is matured for several more months on its yeast lees in stainless steel tanks, to enhance its complexity and flavour integration.

Pegasus Bay Chardonnay is designed as a cellaring proposition, rather than for immediate consumption. "You can open any of the wines from 1995 onwards, drink half the bottle, leave the rest, and find it'll drink better after a day or two," reports Donaldson. I regretted opening the 1995 vintage at three and a half years old – it was clearly still developing.

Around 2000 cases of Pegasus Bay Chardonnay are made each year, retailing at about $28. That's enough to give the wine national distribution, and at below $30 it offers excellent value.

(Left to right) Edward, Chris and Ivan Donaldson, Lynnette Hudson and Matthew Donaldson.

Although many accolades have flowed from critics, and Ivan Donaldson himself is a vastly experienced wine judge, the family does not enter its extremely classy Chardonnay in competitions. "Some judges have been criticised for entering their own wines. And we're not interested in rushing wines into the bottle to meet show deadlines," says Donaldson. "Our winemaking approach is to do what we think is best for the wine. Also, our styles aren't necessarily the ones that do best in shows."

Strapping yet delicate, richly flavoured yet subtle, Pegasus Bay Chardonnay is a superbly constructed wine. Its core of pure, penetrating, citrus and melon fruit flavours, fresh and appetisingly crisp, is seasoned with complex barrel-ferment and lees-aging characters, creating a beautifully rich and poised wine. A measure of the Donaldson family's achievement is how few vintages it took them to produce a regional classic.

tasting notes

These notes are from a vertical tasting of the 1993 to 1998 vintages, held in Auckland in March 1999.

1998 ☆☆☆☆☆ Light lemon hue. Lovely, mealy, toasty bouquet, complex and rich. Mouthfilling wine, soft and seamless on the palate, with deliciously concentrated grapefruit and nutty oak flavours. Plump, creamy-smooth, and already hard to resist. **Drink 2000-03.**

1997 ☆☆☆☆✧ Light yellow. Big, creamy, savoury wine, still coming together. Mouthfilling body (14 per cent alcohol), with strong grapefruit and peach flavours, quality oak and some butterscotch. Soft finish. Looks very promising, but needs time; **open 2000-03.**

1996 ☆☆☆☆☆ Light yellow, slightly more advanced than 1995. Very fragrant, rich bouquet showing spicy oak and butterscotch. Great weight. Powerful, penetrating palate with lovely grapefruit, hazelnut and mealy flavours. Taut, youthful, beautifully poised wine with lovely harmony, freshness and vigour and tremendous intensity. A classic vintage; perhaps even finer than the 1995. **Drink 2000-02.**

1995 ☆☆☆☆☆ Pale yellow. A clear step up in quality terms. Very fragrant nose of citrus fruits, oak and butterscotch. Sturdy (14 per cent alcohol). Lovely now – refined and poised with intense, sweet grapefruit and melon flavours of great delicacy enriched with mealy, butterscotch characters. Still quite youthful. A top 1995, by any standards, and should be very long-lived. **Drink 1999-2002.**

1994 ☆☆☆☆✧ Light yellow. Rounder, sweeter, riper than the 1993; more vibrantly fruity. Robust wine with cool-climate freshness and structure. Loads of flavour – citrusy, biscuity, mealy. Classy, complex wine with good acid spine and a rich finish. Probably now at its peak. **Drink 1999-2000.**

1993 ☆☆☆ Mature yellow hue, slightly dull. Slightly oxidised nose and lacks freshness on the palate. Mouthfilling, with citrusy, biscuity flavours of some richness and a crisp finish. Still a bit of life left here, but drying out. Faded swiftly in the glass. **Drink ASAP.**

Revington Vineyard Chardonnay

L awyer, double-bass player, vineyard owner – Ross Revington has a varied life, only partly devoted to wine. With an output that has never exceeded 350 cases, his outstanding white wine is one of Gisborne's best-kept secrets. But Revington Vineyard Chardonnay is worth tracking down: the 1988, 1989, 1994 and 1997 vintages have all won gold medals, and the 1989 captured the trophy for champion Chardonnay at the 1990 Air New Zealand Wine Awards.

The Revington Vineyard yields complex, citrusy Chardonnays, classically structured, with the ability to mature well for several years. It's a classy wine with mouthfilling body and superbly rich grapefruit and melon-like flavours.

Revington's goal is a Chardonnay with power and balance. "I don't mean I want a 'knock your socks off' style; I mean power in the sense of strength. A strand of nylon can be as strong as a thick rope. I'm not after a bold, upfront style, but I want the wine to have a certain presence, so that when you drink it, you think: Wow, that was special."

The key factors in the wine's quality, says Revington, are the site, the way the vines are managed, and the winemaking. The small, hill-flanked vineyard in the Ormond Valley, north of the city, in the past supplied the fruit for the award-winning 1980 to 1984 vintages of Cooks Chardonnay, and the trophy-winning Grove Mill Lansdowne Chardonnay 1989.

The Revington Vineyard was first planted by grapegrower Peter Benson in the 1970s and replanted in 1986, just prior to Revington's purchase in 1987. Managed organically, it has been awarded

Ross Revington produces a rare, distinguished Chardonnay.

transitional Bio-Gro status.

What is the key to the vineyard's success? "I don't know the magic ingredient," admits Revington. "We manage the vineyard for quality, but I don't know why the grapes are so intensely flavoured. Kerry Hitchcock, then winemaker for Cooks, used to say 'the fairies live there'."

The Mendoza clone vines are planted in sandy loams overlying clay. "We pay lots of attention to detail," says Revington. "We're very particular about the timing of sprays, keeping the canopy properly trimmed, leaf-plucking." Yields are low, at two to three tonnes per acre, and since 1996 the grapes have all been hand-harvested.

Revington does not own a winery, so the grapes are whole-bunch pressed in Gisborne and then the juice is trucked to Marlborough to be fermented and matured by David Pearce of Grove Mill (who made Revington's first wine in 1988 when he was based at Corbans' Gisborne winery). Fermented with cultured yeasts in all-new French oak barriques, the wine is lees-aged and lees-stirred, and typically undergoes a full, softening malolactic fermentation.

Revington Vineyard Chardonnay ($27) is a rare wine, with an output ranging between 200 and 350 cases per year. The label did not appear in 1995 and, due to rain damage, there will be no 1999 vintage.

Revington recommends drinking his Chardonnay at between one and six years old. The 1994 vintage is currently in top shape, and at a decade old the 1989 still offers magnificent drinking. There is significant vintage variation (as the tasting notes reveal), but at its best, Revington Vineyard Chardonnay is a deliciously weighty and concentrated wine with a seamless array of lush, peachy, complex flavours in a deliciously smooth and powerful style. 🍷

tasting notes

These notes are from a vertical tasting of the 1988 to 1998 vintages, held in Auckland in April 1999.

1998 ☆☆☆☆☆ (Tasted soon after bottling.) Bright, light lemon/green. Plump and rich, with impressively concentrated, sweet fruit characters. Savoury, with deep grapefruit and peach flavours and less obvious "malo" influence than the 1997. Still settling down, but looks extremely promising. **Open 2000-05.**

1997 ☆☆☆☆ Light straw. Fat, soft wine with a strong malolactic fermentation influence. Creamy and slightly cheesy, but lacks the lush fruit shining through such top vintages as the 1994. Weighty, full-flavoured and forward. **Drink 1999-2001.**

1996 ☆☆☆ Light yellow. Mouthfilling, with sweet, grapefruit-like fruit characters, soft and creamy. Strongly malo-influenced. A fat, upfront style, it is less elegant than the 1994, and may not be suitable for long-term cellaring. **Drink 1999-2000.**

1995 Not made.

1994 ☆☆☆☆☆ Medium yellow. Nutty, mealy, complex bouquet. Mouthfilling style (13.5 per cent alcohol), with intense, beautifully poised flavours, delicate and creamy. Floats very smoothly across the palate. Very refined wine, nutty and slightly limey, with subtle, persistent flavours. Still developing. **Drink 1999-2000.**

1993 ☆☆ Dull gold, with a hint of brown. Very honied and dull, and well past its best, with a strong *Botrytis* influence.

1992 ☆☆☆ Gold. Slightly herbaceous, toasty bouquet. Fruity and still lively. Lacks the power of a riper year, but full-bodied. Not highly concentrated. Peachy, nutty, toasty and ready. **Drink ASAP.**

1991 ☆☆☆☆☆ Bright, full yellow. Big (13.5 per cent alcohol) wine with strong, vibrant fruit flavours of pineapples and melons. Mouthfilling wine, still fresh. Offers a shade less complexity than the memorable 1989, but is still a powerful wine, deliciously soft and creamy, and now at its peak. **Drink 1999.**

1990 Not tasted. "Past its best" – Ross Revington.

1989 ☆☆☆☆☆ The star wine of the lineup – the champion Chardonnay at the 1990 Air New Zealand Wine Awards, it is still a magical wine. Light gold. Maturing amazingly well, with deep, ripe tropical fruit and citrus flavours, beautifully poised and complex. Mouthfilling body, with sweet-fruit characters and a long, rounded finish. Still fresh, with balanced toasty oak and mealy, nutty characters, it could easily be taken for five, rather than 10, years old. **Drink 1999.**

1988 ☆☆☆ Deep gold, hint of brown. Very toasty, developed bouquet. Crisp, slightly hollow palate, with peachy, slightly honied flavours. Still just alive, but has lost most of its fruit, with a short finish. On its last legs. **Drink ASAP.**

Tasman Bay Chardonnay

CLASSIC

No other New Zealand Chardonnay has been showered with as many top awards recently as Tasman Bay Chardonnay. Phil Jones made his first vintage in 1994, yet already has a collection of major trophies from competitions around the world – Auckland, Sydney, Hong Kong, San Francisco, London.

Seductively soft, rich and creamy-smooth, Tasman Bay is a hugely drinkable wine in its youth – it is typically irresistible at only 18 months old and peaks within two or three years. Jones, an expatriate Californian, owns the Spencer Hill winery in the Upper Moutere hills of Nelson.

Softness is "so important" to the Tasman Bay style, says Jones. "My goal is to create a Chardonnay that the average drinker will love. I want it to be popular in New Zealand, Hong Kong and San Francisco. And I want it to contribute to a New Zealand style – full of fruit and soft. The wine must come on strongly but end softly, to make you want another glass."

To achieve the rich, soft style of Chardonnay he wants, Jones has certain "must-haves. The grapes must come from heavy loam-clay soils, which contribute to stronger fruit flavours than sandier soils. Secondly, malolactic fermentation gives a beautiful complexity. Higher-acid Chardonnay clones, such as Mendoza and clone 15, allow me to use 100 per cent malolactic fermentation, and achieve perfect acid levels for the concentration of fruit."

The majority of the fruit is grown in Peter and Jim Rose's Brentwood Vineyard in the Rapaura district of Marlborough, supplemented by grapes estate-grown at Upper Moutere. The vines are trained on the two-tier Scott Henry system and are not low-cropping – up to five tonnes per acre.

The mechanically harvested grapes are whole-bunch pressed and the juice is settled overnight before being fermented with a combination of yeasts entirely in stainless steel tanks. Jones prefers hot fermentation temperatures to "blow off the fruit – Mendoza can have too much fruit character".

The winery's fact sheets state that Tasman Bay Chardonnay is "fermented on [rather than in] French and American oak" and the wine "remains on oak for approximately seven months." The significance of this wording is that Tasman Bay Chardonnay is not barrel-aged. Instead, Jones immerses oak staves in his wine.

"Too many premium Chardonnays are over-oaked," Jones believes. "I don't buy a lot of what the academic papers say about barrels. The important thing about staves is to use them for the same time as a barrel. By using staves [often of sweet American oak], we replicate the use of barrels, but gain more control over the oak-aging process. I've been called unconventional; I'd rather be called innovative." Throughout the time in tank, the wine is held on its yeast lees, but little emphasis is placed on lees-stirring.

With an average annual production of 4000 to 5000 cases, Tasman Bay Chardonnay ($23) is exported to the UK, Germany, Belgium, Australia and the US. Jones finds it drinks best at two years old; a conviction supported by the tasting (below).

Of all his show awards (from 1995 to 1998, nine trophies and nine gold medals), Jones finds three particularly satisfying. Tasman Bay Chardonnay 1994 scooped the trophies for champion Chardonnay and reserve (runner-up) wine of the show at the 1996 Air New Zealand Wine Awards. The 1996 vintage won the trophy for champion Chardonnay at the 1997 International Wine and Spirit Competition in London.

If anyone in New Zealand can make Chardonnay taste irresistible at nine months to a year old, it's Phil Jones. The wine does not flourish in the cellar, but holds its form for two or three years, and thereafter appears to lose rather than gain complexity (which may reflect the unorthodox approach to wood-aging). This is a wine to relish in its youth, when it is strikingly rich-flavoured and forward.

Phil Jones makes soft, creamy-rich, trophy-winning Chardonnays.

tasting notes

These notes are from a vertical tasting of the 1994 to 1998 vintages, held in Auckland in February 1999.

1998 ☆☆☆☆☆ Rich, scented bouquet of peaches and butterscotch. Mouthfilling wine, with a powerful surge of tropical fruit flavours and mealy, oaky characters adding richness. Soft and generous, with enormous drinkability. Already highly seductive. Best yet? **Drink 1999-2000.**

1997 ☆☆☆☆☆ Tropical fruit aromas, with buttery "malo" characters. Classic Tasman Bay - deliciously full, rich and rounded, with a beautiful creaminess of texture and very harmonious finish. **Drink 1999.**

1996 ☆☆☆☆☆ Light lemon/green. Highly fragrant, slightly toasty nose. Full and creamy, slightly nutty and buttery, with a delicious balance of tropical/citrus flavours and oak. A classic vintage, at its peak right now. **Drink 1999.**

1995 ☆☆☆☆ (Wet year, with some Gisborne fruit.) Leaner style than usual. Chablis-like, with firm acid and strong citrusy, appley flavours. Still fresh and vigorous. **Drink 1999.**

1994 ☆☆ Deep gold, hint of brown. Slightly oxidised nose. Very developed, with orangey, toasty flavours. Tired. **Drink ASAP.** (A bad bottle, says Phil Jones.)

1994 ☆☆☆☆☆ (Reserve) Full yellow. Weighty and creamy, with concentrated citrus fruits and mealy, oaky richness. Still very alive. Big wine, with good mouthfeel and surprisingly firm acidity on the finish. Ready. **Drink 1999.**

Te Mata Elston Chardonnay

SUPER CLASSIC

F or several years after it was launched in 1984, Elston Chardonnay lived in the shadow of Te Mata's illustrious Cabernet/Merlots, Coleraine and Awatea. Now it is recognised as one of New Zealand's premier Chardonnays – an aristocratic, consistently stylish and intense, slowly evolving Hawke's Bay wine. Its reputation is clearly that of a Super Classic.

At around four years old, Elston Chardonnay is a notably "complete" wine, with rewarding power, richness and subtlety. In its youth it stands out for its substantial body and depth, and then flourishes in the bottle, unfurling savoury, rich flavours of great complexity and length. If you only cellar a select few New Zealand Chardonnays, this should be one of them.

Contrary to widespread belief, Elston is not a single-vineyard wine. The majority of the grapes are grown in two vineyards, Elston and BDM, with "bits" from elsewhere in most vintages.

The Elston vineyard, owned by John Edwards, lies on a north-east facing slope in Te Mata Road, very close to the Te Mata winery. In low-fertility, non-irrigated soils, Mendoza clone vines have been planted, with conventional spacing and trellising. Elston's soils have a high content of calcareous matter. "We wanted this for Chardonnay," says John Buck, Te Mata's co-founder and managing director. "Calcareous [limestone] soils give you 'nervosite' – racy, steely acids." The grapes are usually harvested very ripe, at 23.5 brix or above. Yields are very low, averaging only two tonnes per acre.

The BDM vineyard, which also lies in Te Mata Road, behind the Lombardi winery, is "a brilliant

site, much the same as Elston," says Buck. BDM is an acronym based on the owners' names – Buck, Doug Dewar (chairman of Te Mata since 1974), and Michael Morris (co-founder and part-owner of Te Mata). "It's a classic bit of Havelock North," says Buck. "The richness of the soil doesn't suit reds, but it's ideal for Chardonnay."

Winemaker Peter Cowley describes the fruit as "fat and ripe, with grapefruit flavours, and I don't want to modify that too much. I want to keep that flavour, but add to it, rather than overpower it. In the winery, this means not too much of anything – always checking, tasting, being careful not to lose anything."

The hand-harvested grapes are all whole-bunch pressed (since 1994) and the juice is given a "very rough", quick overnight settling. Fully French oak-fermented since 1989, the wine is now also given a full malolactic fermentation. "With malolactic, you can get a blowsy, buttery wine, or a fine and fruity one," observes Cowley. "The difference is the amount of malic acid you start with. And if you keep the wine on its lees and stir, there's an enzyme in the yeast that will break down the diacetyl [slightly rancid buttery character caused by malolactic fermentation].

About 2500 cases of Elston Chardonnay are

produced each year, retailing at around $33.

Buck suggests cellaring the wine until it's at least three to four years old: "five to six years is the optimum". The tasting (below) confirmed that Elston Chardonnay typically needs at least three years to break into full stride, and then matures well for another three years or so.

Although Te Mata has not entered local wine competitions since the early 1980s, Elston Chardonnay has enjoyed high international acclaim. The most arresting success came at the 1991 International Wine Challenge in London, when the 1989 vintage scooped the trophy for best white wine. The 1997 vintage was ranked equal with Penfolds Yattarna 1995 (dubbed the "White Grange") and Domaine Albert Grivault Meursault Premier Cru Clos Des Perrieres 1996 in a UK tasting of "The World's Top Chardonnays" in the November 1998 issue of *Wine* magazine. James Halliday praised the same vintage in *The Australian* in March 1999 as "without question the best New

Zealand Chardonnay I have ever come across."

Elston is one of the finest of all New Zealand Chardonnays. Making few concessions to drink-young appeal, it is designed to build in the bottle for several years, in the manner of classic white Burgundy. Concentration, complexity, finesse – these are the attributes of great Chardonnay, and Elston has them all. 🍇

Elston masterminds John Buck (left) and Peter Cowley.

tasting notes

These notes are principally from a vertical tasting of the 1989 to 1997 vintages, held at the winery in December 1998. The 1998 vintage was tasted in Auckland in March 1999.

1998 ☆☆☆☆☆ Light lemon/green. Instantly attractive wine, very concentrated and rounded, mouthfilling and delicate, with real power through the palate. Grapefruit and hazelnut flavours, with mealy characters and a hint of butterscotch. Already delicious, with loads of upfront appeal, but also the power to age long term. **Drink 2000-05.**

1997 ☆☆☆☆☆ Pale lemon/green. Infant wine, shier than the 1996, but starting to reveal a lovely richness, delicacy, softness and fullness. Lush, mealy and very harmonious, but needs more time; **open 2001-04.**

1996 ☆☆☆☆☆ Light lemon/green. Lovely, lifted bouquet of grapefruit, fig and oak. Big, open wine, very forthcoming, with beautiful citrus/oak flavours and a distinct butteriness (from 100 per cent malolactic fermentation). Very expressive now. **Drink 1999-2004.**

1995 ☆☆☆☆☆ Light lemon/green. Based on "very ripe" fruit from a dry ripening season; 50 per cent malolactic fermentation. Fresh, robust wine with classic grapefruit-like flavours and biscuity, mealy complexities. Still tight, youthful and developing. An immaculate wine with a crisp, lively finish, it should be long-lived. **Drink 2000-03.**

1994 ☆☆☆☆☆ Light gold. Rich, intense grapefruit, oak and mealy characters in a highly complex style with layers of

flavour. Great drinking now, but the rich, tight finish suggests a strong future. **Drink 1999-2001.**

1993 ☆☆☆☆ Medium gold. Slightly honied nose and palate. Fat, rich peach/citrus flavours, toasty, with tight acidity. Excellent body and flavour depth, with loads of character. Ready; **drink 1999-2000.**

1992 ☆☆☆☆☆ Full yellow. Tight, deep grapefruit flavours threaded with firm acidity. Big wine, fresher than the 1991, showing excellent concentration and a lasting finish. **Drink 1999-2000.**

1991 ☆☆☆☆ ⚹ Full yellow. Big, mealy bouquet, showing a touch of oxidation. Mouthfilling, with strong grapefruit and biscuity oak flavours. Complex, figgy, spicy wine with excellent concentration, but moving past its peak. **Drink 1999.**

1990 ☆☆☆ Medium gold. Slightly dull nose. Tiring. Still some fairly rich grapefruit and toast flavours, but falls away quickly. Clearly past its best. **Drink ASAP.**

1989 ☆☆☆☆☆ Light-medium yellow, surprisingly youthful. (There is some bottle variation, according to Peter Cowley.) Rich, citrusy, mealy bouquet. Holding superbly, with tremendous weight and depth of flavour. Very powerful wine, notably lively and savoury (first vintage to be fully barrel-fermented). **Drink 1999-2000.**

Vavasour Single Vineyard Chardonnay

CLASSIC

F linty and tautly structured, with layers of complex, savoury, grapefruit-like flavours and a sustained, steely finish, Vavasour Single Vineyard is one of Marlborough's most intense and stylish Chardonnays. Grown in the Awatere Valley – east and over the Wither Hills from the Wairau Valley – it was originally called Vavasour Reserve, but since the 1996 vintage has carried a Single Vineyard label.

The pioneer of winemaking in the Awatere Valley, Vavasour sits on the terraced banks of the Awatere River, four kilometres from the sea, with the 2900-metre Mt Tapuaenuku rearing to the south. The immaculate, penetratingly flavoured Chardonnays are consistently top-flight.

Winemaker Glenn Thomas prefers powerful, deeply flavoured, subtle wines, built to last. "I'm after a balanced wine with concentrated yet elegant flavours. I don't want you to taste where the fruit and oak begin; it should be seamless. And its Awatere origin will show as a flinty, minerally character."

Thomas, a Roseworthy College graduate who worked at several Australian wineries and then as winemaker at Corbans Gisborne Winery from 1986 to 1988, has been the winemaker since the first 1989 vintage. The wines are marketed in a three-tiered range, with Vavasour Single Vineyard at the top, followed by Vavasour and Dashwood.

Apart from the 1996 vintage (grown in the Awatere River vineyard, higher up the valley), the Single Vineyard Chardonnays have all been grown in Vavasour's estate vineyard. Here, in a mix of alluvial silt and free-draining gravels, the vines are "well-balanced, with not too much foliage growth and

good exposure of the fruit to sunshine," says Thomas. The vines, all of the Mendoza clone, yield very light crops – typically between one and three tonnes per acre.

The grapes are hand-picked and whole-bunch pressed, and for "complexity of flavour" Thomas ferments the juice with some solids remaining, and temperatures run up to 20°C, which compared with cooler temperatures gives a "softer, less austere" wine.

The Single Vineyard Chardonnay is fully fermented in French oak barriques (currently 20 per cent new, but previously a lot higher), and matured on its yeast lees with very low levels of sulphur dioxide. All of the wine typically has a softening malolactic fermentation and, to add a creamy texture to the mid-palate, throughout its 10 months in oak it is lees-stirred every week.

Over the years, Thomas has gradually decreased his use of new oak barrels. "I find that the wines handled in new oak don't develop as well; we get a toffee-apple, slightly oxidised character." He's also working to reduce the percentage of the wine put through malolactic fermentation, by reducing the natural malic acid

Vavasour viticulturist Allan Croker (left) and long-serving winemaker Glenn Thomas.

levels in the grapes and using lower-acid Chardonnay clones, such as clone 95.

Production of the Single Vineyard and Reserve Chardonnays has ranged between 500 and 1500 cases, sold principally in New Zealand. Thomas recommends drinking it at no less than 18 months and up to four years old. On the tasting (below) I'd say up to five years old.

Splendid power, richness and length are features of Vavasour Single Vineyard Chardonnay. A muscular, vibrantly fruity wine with great depth of citrus and melon-like, nutty, mealy flavours, it is a highly refined wine with a lovely cool-climate freshness, vigour and tautness. 🍇

tasting notes

These notes are from a vertical tasting of the 1992 to 1996 vintages, held at the winery in January 1999.

1998 Not made.

1997 Not made.

1996 ☆☆☆☆☆ (Harvested in the Awatere River vineyard at 24.5 brix.) Lovely wine, fresh and tight, with intense, ripe citrusy flavours and spicy oak. A pure expression of Chardonnay flavour, flattered but not dominated with savoury lees and wood-aging characters. Classy, finely structured wine with layers of flavour and a notably rich finish. **Drink 1999-2003.**

1995 Not made.

1994 ☆☆☆☆☆ (Reserve.) Full yellow. Butter and toast bouquet. A strapping, deliciously intense wine with huge power (14 per cent alcohol). Citrusy fruit flavours wrapped in biscuity,

nutty oak. Very deep and complex, firm yet creamy. Hard to imagine it getting any better. **Drink 1999-2001.**

1993 ☆☆☆☆✦ (Reserve.) Ultra low-cropping year (below one tonne per acre). Medium gold. More advanced and less concentrated than the 1992. Toasty, buttery and slightly green-edged, with toffee-like characters from 100 per cent malolactic fermentation. Ready. **Drink 1999.**

1992 ☆☆☆☆✦ (Reserve.) Medium gold. Exceptionally low-cropping year (0.6 tonnes per acre). Full and toasty, with firm acid underpinning concentrated peach, citrus and slightly limey flavours. Powerful, high-flavoured wine, still lively, with a flinty finish. Ready. **Drink 1999.**

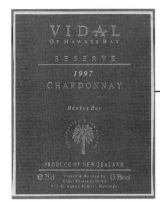

Vidal Reserve Chardonnay

CLASSIC

Vidal Reserve is one of Hawke's Bay's longest-established premium Chardonnays, with a string of vintages stretching back to the mid-1980s. Its show performance peaked with the 1989 to 1991 vintages, which all won gold medals, but the label has remained one of the region's heavyweights.

A mouthfilling wine with layers of stonefruit, citrus and nutty oak flavour, Vidal Reserve is a powerful Chardonnay that demands at least three years to show its best – the 1994 vintage is currently in full flight. "The company philosophy [Vidal is part of the Villa Maria empire] is for the reserve to be simply the finest Chardonnay we can produce," says winemaker Rod McDonald. "It's not driven by volume; we don't drop the quality to achieve volume."

Over the years, the style has changed. "Between 1989 and 1994, there was a definite emphasis on new oak," says McDonald. "We were producing big, bold wines with strong fruit and oak. Beginning in 1995, and especially since 1996, we've shifted to a more complex and layered style."

For the new breed of wines, the fruit must be spotless. "In the past, with higher use of sulphur dioxide, we could get away with lower grape quality. Now we're placing more emphasis on whole-bunch pressing, careful juice handling, some degree of indigenous yeast ferment, greater lees contact, using old as well as new oak. The wines are tighter now in their youth, but they open up with elegance. We're aiming for early appeal plus longevity."

As with the way they are handled, over time the site where the grapes are grown has also changed, as

Vidal winemaker Rod McDonald in a true PR pose.

individual vineyards struck virus and phylloxera problems. Since 1994, the principal source of fruit has been the Simcox vineyard in Omaranui Road, near the golf course at Taradale, where the vines are planted in loose shingle overlying silt and sand. "It's a free-draining site," says McDonald, "but there's enough heavier soil to give the wine guts." The vines here are all clone 15, which McDonald says "does not give a big, oily palate like Mendoza, but lifted aromatics." The Duley vineyard near Puketapu, in the Dartmoor Valley, is also an important source of Mendoza fruit.

The vines, whose yields are restricted to three tonnes per acre, are usually hand-picked (although if bad weather threatens, mechanical harvesters may swing into action). In most years, the juice is run straight from the press to French oak barriques, where it is fermented with some use of indigenous yeasts. To "push the fruit forward more," since 1996 the percentage of new oak has been reduced from 90 per cent to 65 per cent.

The wine is then matured for up to 11 months on its gross yeast lees, with fortnightly stirring of the barrels. The degree of malolactic fermentation varies according to the season – 90 per cent in 1996, 40 per cent in 1997.

Only about 500 to 1200 cases of Vidal Reserve Chardonnay are made each year, mostly sold within New Zealand at around $30. McDonald recommends keeping the wine for up to five years: "The 1995 is standing up fine, and the 1994 is beautiful now."

Robust, peachy and toasty, with excellent staying power, Vidal Reserve Chardonnay is a classic, high-flavoured Hawke's Bay style. The style has evolved during the 1990s, as the winery has placed more and more emphasis on delicacy and finesse. The 1994 and subsequent vintages promise to be the finest and most long-lived yet.

tasting notes

These notes are mainly from a vertical tasting of the 1989 to 1997 vintages, held at the winery in December 1998. The 1998 vintage was tasted in Auckland in April 1999.

1998 ☆☆☆☆☆ (Tasted soon after bottling.) Light lemon/green. Crisp and savoury, with rich, persistent flavours of tropical fruit, grapefruit and butterscotch. Mouthfilling, very ripe wine, firm and long, but still very youthful and unevolved. **Drink 2001-04.**

1997 ☆☆☆☆☆ Pale lemon/green. Fresh, citrusy, mealy bouquet, very fragrant indeed (reflecting the clone 15 influence). A baby. Sweet fruit flavours of grapefruit and melon, with mealy lees-aging characters and quality oak. Finely balanced, classy wine, but not quite as concentrated as the 1995 or 1996. **Drink 2000-02.**

1996 ☆☆☆☆☆ Light lemon/green. Powerful wine with a rich array of grapefruit, melon and fig flavours and a soft finish. Excellent concentration. A more forward style, with more buttery malolactic influence, than the 1995, but still developing. **Drink 1999-2001.**

1995 ☆☆☆☆☆ Light lemon/green. Highly fragrant, very ripe bouquet (the fruit was all harvested prior to the wet autumn). Lovely, immaculate wine, robust (14 per cent alcohol), with deep grapefruit/fig flavours and well-spined acidity. A class act, for the long haul. **Drink 1999-2001.**

1994 ☆☆☆☆☆ Light-medium yellow/green. Very stylish and satisfying. Rich aromas and flavours of grapefruits, fig and oak. Soft and mealy, with a creamy texture and very concentrated fruit. Beautiful now, with real delicacy and finesse. **Drink 1999-2000.**

1993 ☆☆☆☆☆ Bright, medium yellow. Full wine, with markedly higher acidity than usual. Rich citrusy flavours, still quite fresh, and balanced oak. Mouthfilling, concentrated. Maturing very gracefully. **Drink 1999-2000.**

1992 ☆☆ First bottle – dark and oxidised. Second bottle – medium gold, toasty, very developed, firm acid. Lost its freshness. Past it. An unexpected failure from a good Chardonnay vintage. **Drink ASAP.**

1991 ☆☆☆☆☆ Light-medium gold. More fruity and lively than the 1990, with rich flavours of citrus fruits and toasty. A lush, deep, very high-flavoured mouthful with good acid backbone. Still very satisfying. Ready. **Drink 1999.**

1990 ☆☆☆ Medium gold, much darker than the 1989. Lyons vineyard. Mouthfilling. Still solid, but a bit clumsy and falls away on the back palate. Honied, very toasty flavours. Losing its fruit. Lacks real delicacy and finesse. **Drink 1999.**

1989 ☆☆☆☆☆ (Gimblett Road) Pask/Chittick vineyard. Bright, light-medium yellow/green colour, very youthful. Mature, slightly earthy bouquet, citrusy and toasty. Lovely ripe fruit flavours still shining through – melons, grapefruits, pineapples. Balanced oak. Still very alive and maturing very gracefully. No rush at all. **Drink 1999-2001.**

1989 (The standard Reserve Chardonnay, not labelled as Gimblett Road.) Not tasted, but winemaker Rod McDonald reports it is not maturing as well as the 1989 Reserve Gimblett Road.

Villa Maria Reserve Barrique Fermented Chardonnay

SUPER CLASSIC

T he only Super Classic Chardonnay from the big four wine firms (Montana, Corbans, Villa Maria and Nobilo), Villa Maria Reserve Barrique Fermented is a high impact style, sturdy and drenched with flavour. From the start, it was "a big, bold, in your face style," says Michelle Richardson, Villa Maria's chief winemaker. "People simply hadn't seen a Chardonnay like it, and it quickly won a cult following."

Villa Maria's two premier Chardonnays, the Reserve Barrique Fermented and Reserve Marlborough, afford a clear style contrast. An elegant style, the Reserve Marlborough showcases its rich, vibrant fruit flavours, whereas the Barrique Fermented Chardonnay was designed from the start as a weighty, high extract style with a powerful new oak influence. Richardson is carrying on but modifying the early tradition. "We still want a big wine, but not so uncouth. It's more reined-in now, tighter, less clumsy."

The early vintages were based on Gisborne grapes, but the wine's region of origin now varies according to the season. The 1998 vintage was made solely from Gisborne fruit; the 1997 was sourced predominantly from Marlborough; the 1996 was a blend of Hawke's Bay (60 per cent) and Marlborough. "When we're blending the wine, we put the different regions out of our heads," says Richardson. "We taste blind, and the uppermost consideration is style, not region."

Strikingly powerful, mealy, creamy and rich, the Reserve Barrique Fermented Chardonnay is a strongly winemaker-influenced style, based on very

Michelle Richardson joined Villa Maria for three months – in 1992.

ripe fruit from low-yielding vines. Hand-harvested and whole-bunch-pressed since 1994, it is run straight from the press to barrel, with no juice settling, and fermented partly with indigenous yeasts. New oak is a vital ingredient in the recipe (currently averaging 80 per cent; 100 per cent in the past). The wine is matured on its yeast lees in French oak barriques for 10 months, with some lees stirring. The percentage of the final blend put through malolactic fermentation varies, but does not exceed 50 per cent.

Only moderate amounts of the Reserve Barrique Fermented Chardonnay are made each year – between 500 and 1500 cases. Richardson recommends drinking the wine at between two and five years old, but points out that "the goal posts are moving. With changing viticultural and winemaking techniques, we're getting greater longevity; five years now is conservative." Despite their drink-young appeal, some of the early vintages matured unexpectedly well; the 1986 opened in 1994 with an almost Burgundian complexity and richness.

A powerful, upfront style of Chardonnay like the Reserve Barrique Fermented is perfectly suited to the demands of large comparative tastings, and Villa Maria is a keen supporter of competitions. As former chief winemaker, Kym Milne, put it: "We spend very little on advertising. Wine shows are really our advertising expenditure."

Every vintage of the Reserve Barrique Fermented Chardonnay ($35), with the exception of the 1995, has won at least one gold medal or five-star award. The 1996 vintage won gold at the 1998 Air New Zealand Wine Awards; the 1997 won gold at the 1998 Liquorland Royal Easter Wine Show; and the 1998 won gold at the 1999 Liquorland Royal Easter Wine Show.

Villa Maria Reserve Barrique Fermented Chardonnay offers layers of citrusy, figgy, mealy, buttery flavour, strikingly concentrated, rich and creamy. For sheer drinking pleasure, it's hard to beat. 🌿

tasting notes

These notes are from a vertical tasting of the 1989 to 1998 vintages, held at the winery in April 1999.

1998 ☆☆☆☆☆ (100 per cent Gisborne fruit.) Light lemon/green. Lovely, lifted tropical fruit aromas. Soft and full of charm. Voluptuous style, rich and creamy, lush and vibrantly fruity. Deliciously deep and harmonious. Quite forward. **Drink 2000-03.**

1997 ☆☆☆☆☆ (85 per cent Marlborough, 15 per cent Hawke's Bay.) Light yellow/green. Soft, succulent wine, very delicate, with exceptional flavour depth. Very mouthfilling. Beautifully integrated and already gorgeous. **Drink 1999-2002.**

1996 ☆☆☆☆☆ (60 per cent Hawke's Bay, 40 per cent Marlborough.) Light yellow/green. Robust wine (14 per cent alcohol), savoury and complex, with great weight and persistence. Lush grapefruit and oak flavours, notably rich and persistent. Lovely now. **Drink 1999-2001.**

1995 ☆☆☆☆ (100 per cent Gisborne.) Full yellow/light gold. Toasty bouquet of moderate intensity. A more forward wine than the top 1995s from Hawke's Bay, with deep tropical/citrus flavours, rounded and developed. Big, toasty wine, now ready. **Drink 1999.**

1994 ☆☆☆☆☆ (Gisborne mainly, with some Hawke's Bay and Marlborough fruit.) Bright, medium-full yellow. Splendid now. High impact style with rich grapefruit flavours and good acidity, wrapped in toasty oak. Still fresh and lively. Succulent wine with a rich, mealy finish. Top vintage. **Drink 1999-2000.**

1993 ☆☆☆☆☆ (Mangere, Auckland.) Full yellow/light gold. Tense wine with strong grapefruit and toast characters and firm acidity. Slightly buttery. Holding well. Fairly complex. Ready. **Drink 1999.**

1992 ☆☆☆☆☆ (100 per cent Gisborne.) Full yellow/light gold. Toasty nose. Powerful (14 per cent alcohol) with great depth of grapefruit and toast flavours. Showing lots of bottle-age, but still vigorous, with lovely richness. A classic year. **Drink 1999.**

1991 ☆☆☆ – ☆☆☆☆☆ (100 per cent Gisborne.) Two bottles tasted. (1) Mature, medium gold. Slightly dull nose. Soft and toasty, but a bit tired. (2) [Magnum] Bright, medium yellow. Surprisingly youthful, with concentrated citrusy flavours and savoury oak. Fresh and vigorous, with plenty of life ahead.

1990 ☆☆☆☆ (Hawke's Bay and Gisborne.) Light gold. Taut and complex, with very toasty, slightly green-edged flavours and firm acidity. Full-bodied and full-flavoured, but just starting to dry out. Very ready. **Drink 1999.**

1989 ☆☆☆☆☆ (100 per cent Gisborne.) Medium gold. Very toasty and springy, with concentrated grapefruit and lime flavours, still crisp and lively. Lots of interest here. Excellent for 10 years old. Ready. **Drink 1999.**

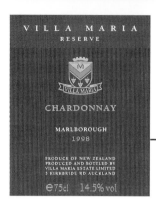

Villa Maria Reserve Marlborough Chardonnay

CLASSIC

F or several years, this wine lived in the shadow of its more opulent stablemate, Villa Maria Reserve Barrique Fermented Chardonnay. Since the trophy-winning 1996 vintage, it has really hit its straps, emerging as a consistently stylish and distinguished wine in its own right.

Kym Milne, then Villa Maria's chief winemaker, in 1992 described the style of the Reserve Marlborough Chardonnay as "almost at opposite ends of the scale" to the weighty, rich, strongly new oak-influenced Reserve Barrique Fermented Chardonnay. "With the Reserve Marlborough wine, we are aiming at a much more elegant, fruit-driven sort of style, with less new oak and a shorter period of barrel-aging."

Seven years later, chief winemaker Michelle Richardson is determined to "let the regional fruit characters speak, without making the wine too clean. We want to add something. And we've recently moved to a lower-acid style. If the pH is right, you don't need high acidity for the wine to age."

If you ask Richardson about the key factors in the wine's quality, she sums up succinctly: "We've got the right sites, the right vineyard management, the right yields and the right winemaking." Gradually coming to understand the characteristics of individual vineyards has been important. "Some of the fruit suits malolactic fermentation, but some doesn't. Some of the vineyards produce juice that is best left to speak for itself; others suit barrel-aging."

Owner George Fistonich is the driving-force behind Villa Maria.

Over the years, the Waldron and Fletcher vineyards in the Wairau Valley have been the major sources of fruit, now supplemented by grapes from Seddon Vineyards in the Awatere Valley. A range of Chardonnay clones contributes to the wine – Mendoza and clones one and 15. The vines' yields do not exceed 3.5 tonnes per acre, and are often around 2.5 tonnes per acre. Harvesting is entirely by hand, "which lets me control the degree of skin contact, rather than the truck driver," says Richardson.

At the winery, the grapes are whole-bunch pressed and the juice is fermented at around 14°C in French oak barriques. In the past, 20 per cent of the blend was tank-fermented "to retain its natural fruit flavours", but since 1996 the wine has been fully barrel-fermented. In Richardson's view, the fruit characters are "robust and quite grunty", so the wine is typically given 60 per cent new oak. The lees-aging period is gradually getting longer (currently up to nine months) and the degree of malolactic fermentation varies, depending on the high-acid or low-acid nature of the crop.

With an annual output of 2500 cases, the Reserve Marlborough Chardonnay ($26) is more widely available than its Reserve Barrique Fermented stablemate and almost $10 cheaper. The 1991, 1992, 1996 and 1997 vintages have all won gold medals. Richardson was especially delighted by the trophy for champion Chardonnay awarded to the 1996 vintage at the 1999 Liquorland Royal Easter Wine Show. "It's nice when an older vintage does well, because with age many New Zealand Chardonnays reveal big hollows on the palate and a high-acid finish. The 1996 is still tight and elegant – that's good for the future of New Zealand Chardonnay."

Villa Maria Reserve Marlborough Chardonnay displays a beautiful balance between fruit and winemaking influences, giving it great elegance. The 1996 and subsequent vintages have been seductive in their youth, but the wine blossoms in the bottle for several years. A marriage of intense, ripe Marlborough fruit with premium French oak, it is clearly one of the region's finest Chardonnays.

tasting notes

These notes are from a vertical tasting of the 1990 to 1998 vintages, held at the winery in April 1999.

1998 ☆☆☆☆☆ Bright, light lemon/green. Stylish bouquet of fresh, ripe fruit aromas and oak. Soft initial impression in the mouth. Very robust (14.5 per cent alcohol). Grapefruit and tropical fruit flavours, mealy and slightly buttery. An unusually rounded, forward vintage. **Drink 2000-04.**

1997 ☆☆☆☆☆ Light yellow/green. Pure, vibrant fruit characters to the fore, ripe and rounded. Quite fat (14 per cent alcohol), with cool-climate freshness. Immaculate wine, already delicious, with lovely harmony. Bigger, softer, more forward than some past vintages. **Drink 1999-2002.**

1996 ☆☆☆☆☆ Bright, light yellow/green. Strikingly harmonious wine, big and fresh, with lovely depth of grapefruit/apple flavours seasoned with toasty oak and a slightly creamy texture. Gorgeously scented and finely balanced. **Drink 1999-2001.**

1995 ☆☆☆✮ Light-medium yellow/green. Slightly musty nose. Full wine with a touch of butterscotch amidst its slightly green-edged, grapefruit-like flavours. Some savoury complexity and a rounded finish. Very solid, but clearly reflects the difficult (very wet) year. **Drink 1999-2000.**

1994 ☆☆☆☆☆ Bright yellow/green. Attractive, pineappley, slightly toasty bouquet. Weighty and rich, with deep, ripe citrus and tropical fruit flavours, subtle oak and mealy characters and a sustained, well-rounded finish. Delicious now, and probably at its peak. **Drink 1999-2000.**

1993 ☆☆☆☆ Full yellow/light gold. Quiet nose. Tense acidity, reflecting the very cool ripening season. Lemony, appley, minerally flavours, with good depth and vigour and developed, toasty bottle-aged characters. Holding well. **Drink 1999-2000.**

1992 ☆☆☆☆☆ Full yellow/green. Mouthfilling and still fresh, with a lovely harmony of rich grapefruit and toast, slightly buttery flavours. Concentrated and powerful, with firm underlying acidity and a very persistent finish. Should live for ages, but lovely now. **Drink 1999-2000.**

1991 ☆☆☆☆ ✮ Bright, light gold. Very toasty and developed, but still lively. Flinty style, with excellent flavour intensity and a crisp, tight finish. Very good, but slightly overshadowed by the 1992. Ready. **Drink 1999.**

1990 ☆☆☆ ✮ Deep gold. Slightly tired nose. Very toasty, with green-edged flavour. Still alive, with a tense, high-acid finish.

MARLBOROUGH

Wither Hills

WINEMAKERS

1998
CHARDONNAY

Brent Marris

WINEMAKERS

750 ML   WITHER HILLS VINEYARDS MARLBOROUGH, LIMITED   13.5% VOL.

WINE OF NEW ZEALAND

Wither Hills Chardonnay

CLASSIC

Many top winemakers avoid the show circuit. Not Brent Marris. A senior wine judge himself, he enjoyed notable competition success during his past spell as Delegat's winemaker. Now Marris's own wines under the Wither Hills label are building an illustrious track record in shows – the first four vintages of Wither Hills Chardonnay scooped nine gold medals in New Zealand, Australia and the UK.

Classy and very full-bodied, Wither Hills Chardonnay displays lush, concentrated fruit flavours, a mealy, biscuity complexity from cask fermentation and lees-aging, and a deliciously long, creamy finish. A powerful wine, it overflows with the intense fruit flavours of Marlborough fruit.

The son of John Marris, a prominent grapegrower, Brent Marris named his venture after the ranges that form the southern flanks of the Wairau Valley. The Wither Hills winery will eventually be built in Marlborough, but in the meantime Marris is based at Pleasant Valley in West Auckland, where he is the consultant winemaker. The grapes for the Wither Hills label are dejuiced in Marlborough and the juice is sent to Henderson to be fermented and matured.

"The catch-phrase for Wither Hills is 'created in the vineyard'," says Marris, who lives in Auckland but was raised in Marlborough. "With all our wines, I identify the different blocks of land. As each season progresses, I manage the vines' health and balance to get clean, *Botrytis*-free fruit and maximise the grapes' flavours. From the various blocks, I take a parcel of fruit right

through to completed wine, by fermenting it separately, which then gives great opportunities for blending."

Marris, New Zealand's first Marlborough-born and raised qualified winemaker, believes the key benefit of working with top-grade fruit is "being able to adopt a policy of minimal intervention ... I adopt a nurturing approach to winemaking, designed to complement the naturally rich, intense fruit characters of Marlborough and reflect each season's sunlight and rainfall."

In crafting his Chardonnay, Marris allows Marlborough's glorious fruit flavours to hold centre stage. "I want a full-bodied Chardonnay that highlights the strong tropical fruit characters and depth of flavour that Marlborough can so easily produce. The fruit is the hero, and I don't bastardise it with heaps of malolactic fermentation. I want a big wine with a long, soft palate – high in extract, with concentrated fruit, but no phenolic hardness."

The grapes, all of the low-bearing Mendoza clone, are entirely hand-picked and whole-bunch pressed. Fermentation is entirely in French oak barriques, typically 60 per cent new, which Marris finds gives "mealiness and integrated rather than aggressive oak characters". The wine is lees-stirred for 12 months, and "to add layers of complexity", between 15 and 35 per cent of the final blend goes through a softening malolactic fermentation.

Volumes are rising fast. Only 250 cases were made of the debut 1992 vintage, but production climbed to 3500 cases in 1998. Marris aims the wine to drink well upon release, but also believes it benefits from three to four years' cellaring. The tasting (below) indicates it holds its form well for at least six years.

To cater for soaring export demand, in 1999 Brent Marris merged Wither Hills with his father's business interests. The new company's 125 hectares of land, produces Chardonnay, Sauvignon Blanc and Pinot Noir grapes for the Wither Hills brand.

Wither Hills Chardonnay is always an exciting mouthful – burly and crammed with fresh, ripe tropical fruit flavours. There's typically plenty of oak, but plenty of everything else too, creating a lush, powerful style with striking overall intensity.

Brent Marris was born and raised in Marlborough.

tasting notes

These notes are mostly from a vertical tasting of the 1992 to 1997 vintages, held in Auckland in November 1998. The 1998 vintage was tasted in March 1999.

1998 ☆☆☆☆☆ (Tasted soon after bottling.) Big, seamless wine, bursting with superbly ripe tropical fruit characters. Impressive delicacy of flavour, with softer acidity than usual. Mouthfilling and slightly creamy, with a hint of butterscotch. Very harmonious already. **Drink 2000-04.**

1997 ☆☆☆☆☆ Pale yellow/green. Slightly closed bouquet. Still very youthful, but highly approachable, with a powerful surge of vibrant, ripe citrus/melon flavours and a deliciously creamy texture. Complex and mealy, with a hint of butterscotch. Mouthfilling wine with a powerful finish, but needs another year to fully unfold. **Drink 2000-03.**

1996 ☆☆☆☆☆ Pale yellow/green. Gorgeous wine, robust and ripely scented. Fills the mouth with very pure and delicate tropical/citrus flavours, enriched but not overwhelmed by mealy, nutty characters. Very complete and harmonious wine. The best yet. Magnificent drinking from now onwards. **Drink 1999-2002.**

1995 ☆☆☆☆☆ Medium yellow. Very classy wine (especially for a 1995 Marlborough Chardonnay). More refined, less oaky than the 1994; less of a blockbuster. Beautifully balanced, harmonious wine with rich, still fresh citrus fruit flavours to the fore and a subtle oak and lees-aging influence. Absolutely classic structure. **Drink 1999-2000.**

1994 ☆☆☆☆☆ Deep yellow/light gold. Lush, strapping wine with an intense, biscuity, toasty fragrance. Exuberantly oaked wine with strapping body and concentrated citrus, peach and toast flavours. Good acid spine. Bigger wine than the 1992. A hedonist's delight. **Drink 1999-2000.**

1993 Not made.

1992 ☆☆☆☆☆ Golden. Rich, toasty, nutty bouquet. Excellent drinking now, with rich citrusy flavours and buttery, mealy, toasty complexities. Weighty, concentrated wine with good acid structure, integrated and ready. **Drink 1999.**

Chenin Blanc

Chenin Blanc's potential in New Zealand has yet to be fully explored. The great grape of Vouvray, in France's Loire Valley, is naturally high in acidity and has yielded many austere, sharp wines in New Zealand, lacking ripeness and richness.

Many growers, put off by Chenin Blanc's late-ripening nature and the susceptibility of its tight bunches to *Botrytis* rot, have uprooted their vines. Plantings have plummeted from 372 hectares in 1983 to only 133 hectares of bearing vines in 1999.

Only a few producers – including Collards and Esk Valley – have produced a consistently satisfying Chenin Blanc. Other growers are starting to plant Chenin Blanc in warm, sunny sites with devigorating soils, where its canopy can be controlled and yields reduced. Rich and full of character, for well over a decade Millton Barrel Fermented Chenin Blanc has shown what can be done.

Gewürztraminer

New Zealand Gewürztraminers have attracted international praise, but few can stand close comparison with the benchmark wines of Alsace. Many lack concentration, relying on sweetness to fill out the palate and skin contact to boost their flavour (at the price of delicacy and aging ability).

For many growers in the past, Gewürztraminer proved too susceptible to adverse weather at flowering, which can dramatically cut yields. Between 1983 and 1996, plantings dropped by almost two-thirds, but are now starting to expand again as more and more producers explore this classic grape's fine-wine potential.

Pinot Gris

Pinot Gris is gradually coming to prominence in New Zealand as a robust, richly flavoured dry wine that makes an ideal alternative to Chardonnay. Between 1998 and 2001, the area of bearing vines will more than double – from 61 to 129 hectares. Only Dry River in Martinborough, however, can point to a consistent record of excellence with this aristocratic Alsatian variety.

chenin blanc

gewürztraminer

pinot gris

Millton Barrel Fermented Chenin Blanc

CLASSIC

Full of personality and with the ability to flourish in the cellar for at least a decade, James Millton's Gisborne Chenin Blanc is New Zealand's top example of the variety. Intensely varietal, from one year to the next it offers a compelling richness and individuality, reflecting Millton's passion for the noble grape of Vouvray.

"I'm one of the few people in the country who have tasted the glory of a 1949 Vouvray," says Millton. "During my visits to the Loire Valley [in 1989 and 1995], my drinking experiences intensified my belief that Chenin Blanc is a classic variety. Much of New Zealand's Chenin Blanc was planted around 1980 to help overcome the ban on wine-watering. Its true potential here hasn't been explored."

In Millton's view, too many New Zealand Chenin Blancs are Chardonnay look-alikes: "We're definitely not looking for that. The style of our wine varies, depending on whether the growing season is hot or cool, dry or moist, but we want vinosity and texture, and a Chenin Blanc that will age. I want honey and acidity and almond flavours."

In his pursuit of great Chenin Blanc, James Millton sees soil and locality as of pivotal importance. "Our vineyard at Manutuke is within five kilometres of the coast, so we get cooling sea breezes, which keeps up the acidity. Chenin Blanc needs that acidity for spine and longevity. And our soils are high in calcium, which Chenin Blanc likes. The calcium gives the wine backbone – like our skeleton – and upon that the acidity is built."

In the vineyard, Millton adopts an aggressive approach to the challenge of controlling Chenin Blanc's natural tendency to grow and crop abundantly. "It's renowned for over-cropping. So we lay down few buds, head-thin the water shoots, and fruit-thin." The average crop is between two and four tonnes per acre.

The grapes are hand-picked over a month at three different stages of ripening, culminating in the final harvest of *Botrytis*-affected fruit. "We pick some of the grapes when they're still green and malic, for their acidity. Then we pick ripe and fruity grapes, at around 20 to 23 brix, for texture. Finally – and it's in the lap of the gods – we pick for noble rot, which increases the wine's vinosity."

Fermentation is partly in large, 620-litre French oak casks called *demi-muis*, used in the Loire for Chenin Blanc. Millton prefers these to the much smaller (225-litre) barriques, because "the volume of wine to the wood's surface area is greater, so we get less pick-up of wood flavour". About 50 per cent of the final blend is oak-fermented, but all of the wine is barrel-aged for three to nine months. Lees-aging is optional, depending on the fruit condition.

Unlike most other wineries, which treat Chenin Blanc as a minor part of their range or as a useful blender, Millton sees it as a "mainstay. We pulled out our Sauvignon Blanc vines, and wisely or unwisely have hung our hat on Chenin Blanc". The annual output of up to 2000 cases accounts for about 20 per cent of Millton's entire production. Tesco, the giant UK supermarket chain, listed the 1998 vintage at £8.

The 1985 Chenin Blanc, currently drinking superbly, was "kicked out" of shows, but other vintages have enjoyed greater competition success. The 1987, 1988 and 1994 vintages all claimed the trophy for "champion other white wine" (reserved for less popular varieties) at the Air New Zealand Wine Awards.

Millton suggests drinking his wine at about four years old, but his commitment to organic viticulture and winemaking means the wine's often deep colour requires understanding. "We were growing organically in 1984," he recalls, "but not working to a certified standard. Since we joined the New Zealand Biological Producers Council in 1990, we have only been able to use half the legal amount of sulphur dioxide as an anti-oxidant. Hence the wine's deeper colours since 1990." Will the 1990 and later vintages live as longer as the older wines? "Yes. Don't be put off by the colour."

Richness and personality are the two key attributes of Millton Barrel Fermented Chenin Blanc. An intensely varietal wine with concentrated, fresh, vibrant fruit flavours to the fore in one vintage, nectareous scents and flavours the next, it vividly reflects James Millton's long love affair with one of the country's most neglected classic varieties.

tasting notes

These notes are from a vertical tasting of the 1984 to 1998 vintages, held in Auckland in March 1999.

1998 ☆☆☆☆☆ Light lemon. Still very youthful, with lovely freshness and ripeness. Mouthfilling wine with no obvious *Botrytis* character. Very rich and pure citrus and pear flavours, very refined and delicate. Crisp, dry finish. **Drink 2000-06.**

1997 ☆☆☆☆☆ Full yellow/light gold. Honied wine with a clear *Botrytis* influence. Full, slightly sweet and full of character. Citrusy, slightly nutty flavours with good acid spine. Lovely harmony. **Drink 1999-2003.**

1996 ☆☆☆☆ Bright, medium-full yellow. Crisp, slightly toasty. No *Botrytis* showing. Pineapple and grapefruit characters and good vigour. Still developing. Slightly limey. **Drink 1999-2004.**

1995 Not made.

1994 ☆☆☆☆ Deep gold. Strong honey and toast characters. Good acid. Rich, slightly sweet finish. Full of character, but very advanced. **Drink 1999-2000.**

1993 ☆☆☆ɣ Deep gold/amber. From a very cool season with significant *Botrytis*. Very honied and toasty. Crisp. Distinct splash of sweetness (8.7 grams/litre). Real sweet-and-sour stuff. Very developed. **Drink 1999-2000.**

1992 ☆☆☆☆☆ Light gold. Dry style, weighty, vibrantly fruity and toasty. Powerful, richly flavoured and sturdy, with intense varietal character. Peach and grapefruit flavours, faintly nutty and honied. A classic vintage, now in full stride. **Drink 1999-2001.**

1992 ☆☆☆☆☆ (May Harvest) Selected bunches picked in late May with 50 per cent *Botrytis* infection. 54 grams per litre residual sugar. Deep gold/amber. Treacly, apricot-like bouquet. Lush, lovely, with an oily texture and concentrated flavours of peach, apricot and honey, sweet and harmonious. **Drink 1999-2001.**

1991 ☆☆☆☆ Full yellow/light gold. No *Botrytis* influence. A dry style. Very tight, lemony and toasty, with a crisp, persistent but fractionally hard finish. Wearing its age well and should live for ages.

1990 ☆☆☆ɣ Deep gold/amber. Honey and toast flavours, oranges too, even tea. Dry wine with a hint of honey. Full bodied and high flavoured, but starting to dry out. **Drink 1999-2000.**

1989 ☆☆☆☆☆ Very youthful, bright, light yellow. Very tightly structured indeed. Lemon and grapefruit, slightly toasty flavours. Intense, not honied, but amazingly well-preserved, with a slightly sweet, flinty finish. **Drink 1999-2001.**

1988 ☆☆☆☆ Cyclone Bola – but you'd never know it. Full yellow/light gold. Lemony, citrusy, slightly sweet and honied. Still fresh, lively and poised. Holding unexpectedly well. **Drink 1999-2000.**

1987 Not tasted.

1986 ☆☆☆☆☆ (May Harvest) Deep gold/green. Deliciously sweet and full. Grapefruit and lime flavours with honey characters adding interest without dominating. In great shape; will probably live for decades. **Drink 1999-2002.**

1985 ☆☆☆☆☆ Bright, medium yellow. Still lively. Lovely lemon and toast scents and flavours. Citrusy and gently honied. Beautifully balanced, with a dry finish. Not dramatic, but very seductive. **Drink 1999-2000.**

1984 ☆☆☆☆☆ Medium gold. Sweet, full and persistent. Grapefruit, toast and honey flavours, with good vigour and acidity. Lovely harmony. Rich and powerful wine. Great finale to the flight. **Drink 1999-2000.**

Dry River Gewürztraminer

SUPER CLASSIC

"Gewürztraminer is a variety we do take seriously," wrote Martinborough winemaker Neil McCallum to his mail-order customers. A notably powerful, ripe style with deliciously deep flavour, Dry River has emerged since the mid 1980s as the country's greatest Gewürztraminer.

Bone-dry in some vintages but medium-dry in most, in top years the wine shows a power and richness comparable to Alsace's *vendange tardive* (late harvest) wines. McCallum also produces outstanding dessert wines from Gewürztraminer (see under Dry River in the Sweet White Wines section).

Neil McCallum, a former scientist with a distinguished academic record which culminated in an Oxford doctorate in chemistry, planted his first vines in 1979. He was the first of the "gang of four" (which by 1980 included Clive Paton of Ata Rangi, Stan Chifney and Derek Milne of Martinborough Vineyard) to pioneer the planting of commercial vineyards in Martinborough.

Right from the start, McCallum was careful to distance his wine from those made further north. "Your experience with Gisborne-sourced Gewürztraminers is not applicable to cool-climate Gewürztraminers such as this," he advised his customers in 1986. "In general, the fertile Gisborne situation produces strong varietal characters from the extra growth but increased potassium uptake also produces higher pHs in the wine. The net effect is that the Gisborne wines tend to be big in flavour but for drinking in the short term. Wines such as ours can

Dry River is clearly the pick of New Zealand's Gewürztraminers.

be more subtle and they require more bottle-age, ending up with a distinctive palate structure and developed character."

Crucial to achieving fine quality Gewürztraminer, McCallum believes, are low crop levels and well-exposed fruit. "Richness and concentration are essential, and you get that from beautifully ripe grapes, when the flavours have moved from floral characters to ripe fruits and spice." And skin contact to add aroma and flavour to the wine when it is young (a common practice) should be avoided. "Lack of skin contact provides a more fine-grained and less obvious wine to which bottle development is more important, finally resulting in a rounder wine with purer Traminer character."

In the vineyard, leaf-plucking is crucial. "Research shows that by increasing the fruit's exposure to sunshine, you don't help the new wine flavours, but do get the flavour terpenes that are released with bottle-age." In the winery, despite their high levels of extract, McCallum finds his Gewürztraminer grapes need "delicate, cautious handling to get the flavour nuances. I'm more protective [from oxygen] now than I used to be, although I'm not neurotic about it."

Dry River Gewürztraminer is a rare wine. Based on a half-hectare plot of vines, the annual production has ranged from 70 to 200 cases. "It's not economic," McCallum admits, "but I like Gewürztraminer."

The tasting (below) showed that the wine is at its peak at between two and four years old. McCallum agrees: "It loses its lovely freshness over time."

Power and finesse are key attributes of Dry River Gewürztraminer. Always rich in alcohol and exceptionally full-flavoured, it is also very delicate and finely balanced, with lifted orange-peel, citrus and gently spiced aromas and a tight, concentrated, highly refined palate. The 1997 vintage, at $32 the country's most expensive Gewürztraminer, sold out in a few days.

tasting notes

Most of these notes are from a vertical tasting of the 1986 to 1997 vintages, held at the winery in November 1998. The 1998 vintage was tasted in Auckland in March 1998.

1998 ☆☆☆☆☆ Powerful wine, harvested at about 25.5 brix and fermented to 13.5 per cent alcohol. Light lemon/green. Lovely, rich wine, soft and slightly sweet, with highly delicate, citrusy, spicy flavours. Beautifully aromatic, with great weight. Already delicious, but power to age long-term. **Drink 1999-2004.**

1997 ☆☆☆☆☆ Light yellow. Scented bouquet of citrus fruits and spice. Rich, slightly sweet flavour of lemons and spices, with luscious intensity. Fresh, powerful yet delicate wine, highly refined. Already delicious. **Drink 1999-2002.**

1996 ☆☆☆☆☆ A top year. Light lemon/green. Still freshly scented. Powerful, robust wine (13.7 per cent alcohol) with a rich surge of lemon and spice flavours in a lush, medium-dry style. Impression of great depth and great delicacy. Intensely varietal and should mature splendidly. **Drink 1999-2002.**

1995 Not made.

1994 ☆☆☆☆✦ Pale lemon, very light for its age. Big wine, less forthcoming than the 1996, with citrusy, appley, well-spiced flavours and a slightly sweet finish. Developing slight minerally characters on nose and palate. **Drink 1999-2000.**

1993 Not made.

1992 ☆☆☆☆☆ Developed, light gold. Gently honied nose. Mouthfilling, with rich flavours of lemons, spice, honey and ginger. Slightly sweet, with a clear *Botrytis* influence. A lush mouthful with loads of character, excellent now. **Drink 1999-2000.**

1991 ☆☆☆☆☆ Light lemon/green, showing little development for its age. Delicate lemon/spice perfume. Restrained but very stylish wine in a tight style with powerful body and immaculate, intense, lemony, well-spiced flavours, crisp and long. Great staying power. **Drink 1999-2000.**

1990 Not tasted.

1989 ☆☆☆☆ Medium yellow. Developed, minerally nose. Mouthfilling (13.5 per cent alcohol), with citrusy flavours to the fore and moderate spiciness. Crisp, firm finish. Tastes fully developed. **Drink 1999.**

1988 ☆☆☆☆☆ Bright, medium-full yellow. Substantial wine (13.5 per cent alcohol) with deep, peppery, gingery flavours and great vigour. Intensely varietal, dry and firm. A standout, showing great longevity. **Drink 1999-2000.**

1987 ☆☆☆☆ Light gold. Honeyish, spicy, slightly earthy bouquet. Still lively on the palate, with crisp, gingery flavours developing strong bottle-aged characters. Holding well, but very ready. **Drink 1999.** ("Cellar at least one year", suggests the label.)

1986 ☆☆☆☆✦ Medium yellow. Starting to lose a bit of fruit, but still offers plenty of lemony, spicy, slightly earthy flavour, crisp and lively. Has matured gracefully. **Drink 1999.**

PATUTAHI ESTATE
GEWÜRZTRAMINER
1998

PRODUCED AND BOTTLED BY MONTANA WINES LTD
171 PILKINGTON ROAD, AUCKLAND 6.
75cl Produce of New Zealand 13.0% Alc/Vol

MONTANA ESTATES

Montana Patutahi Estate Gewürztraminer

POTENTIAL CLASSIC

Gewürztraminer has long been grown in New Zealand, but its wines, although pleasant, have rarely been memorable. This lush Gisborne beauty is one of the few distinguished Gewürztraminers to emerge. The 1996 vintage won the trophy for champion aromatic white at the 1998 Sydney International Wine Competition, ahead of 104 other wines, including many Australian Rieslings.

Alsace is the benchmark for Gewürztraminer, and Montana wants a style that "is close to Alsace," says chief winemaker Jeff Clarke. "We want full-on flavour from ripe fruit – a high alcohol, full-bodied style with development potential and a touch of *Botrytis* for complexity." Due to the slight bitterness derived from the skins of Gewürztraminer berries, the wine consistently harbours a touch of sweetness.

The Gisborne region does not enjoy the international profile of Marlborough or Hawke's Bay, but the recent emergence of top wines like Montana Patutahi Estate Gewürztraminer is boosting the area's fine-wine reputation. Past doubts over grape quality centred on the fact that the highly fertile soils and plentiful autumn rains combine to produce dense vine foliage growth and bumper crops. However, by using devigorating rootstocks; planting new and improved clones and virus-free vines; leaf-plucking to reduce fruit shading; later harvesting; and a range of other approaches, Gisborne's viticulturists have of late been exploring more fully their region's fine-wine potential.

At its best, Montana Patutahi Estate Gewürztraminer is a notably mouthfilling wine with an ebullient, musky, gingery perfume and intense pepper and lychees-like flavours, delicate, ripe and lush. It is grown at the company's Patutahi Estate, hard against the hills inland from the city of Gisborne. "It's a relatively low rainfall site, protected from the southerlies," says Clarke, "with very free-draining loams that dry out and crack during summer."

Many of the vines are more than 10 years old and Montana finds it is not difficult to ripen the grapes fully, to around 22.5 brix. "Gewürztraminer is a better corporate grape than grower's variety," says Clarke, noting that the vines crop at an average of only three tonnes per acre. A degree of 'hen and chicken' (large and small berries) gives especially concentrated, sweet berries. Some *Botrytis*-affected, nobly rotten grapes are also picked at a super-ripe 28 to 30 brix, imparting an apricot-like intensity and lusciousness to the final blend.

Both machine-harvested and hand-picked, the juice is held in contact with its skins for up to 12 hours prior to the ferment, to boost its flavour concentration. Such skin contact, to produce a more upfront style, can give the wine a shorter life, but as Clarke puts it: "We're not after a wine that takes 10 years to mature."

The Gewürztraminer is fermented at cool temperatures with a neutral yeast, to retain its natural grape flavours. Oak and lees-aging play no part in the vinification. "After the fermentation, we blend the late harvest with the earlier-pick material, clean the wine up and bottle it," says Clarke. The vertical tasting suggests it reaches its peak at about three years old.

With its annual production of around 2000 cases, there is enough of the Patutahi Estate Gewürztraminer ($22) to be exported. It's proving popular in the US, and with few other comparable wines produced internationally, Clarke believes the wine has a good opportunity "in the premium restaurants of the world".

Full of character, Montana Patutahi Estate Gewürztraminer has excellent mouthfeel and texture, with a lovely richness of citrus/spice flavours, very concentrated and long. Over the years, many of the country's best Gewürztraminers have flowed from the Gisborne region – a tradition Montana is doing more than anyone else to preserve. 🍇

Montana's Patutahi Estate at Gisborne yields powerful, intensely varietal Gewürztraminer.

tasting notes
These notes are from a vertical tasting of the 1995 to 1998 vintages, held at the winery in April 1999.

1998 ☆☆☆☆☆ Light yellow. Fresh, delicate rose petal and spice aromas. Weighty and crisp, with deep flavours of citrus fruits, lychees and spice. Still very youthful, but shows lovely delicacy and impressive body. Very refined and powerful – could be the best yet. **Drink 2000-03.**

1997 ☆☆☆☆☆ Light-medium yellow. Robust (13.5 per cent alcohol), high-flavoured wine with balanced acidity and strong ginger, orange and spice characters. Slightly less delicacy and finesse than the 1996 or 1998. **Drink 1999-2000.**

1996 ☆☆☆☆☆ Full yellow/light gold. Lush and lovely, with a touch of sweetness and beautiful intensity of ripe, citrusy, well-spiced flavour. Weighty and rich. Benchmark stuff. Starting to round out, and sheer delight now. **Drink 1999-2000.**

1995 ☆☆☆☆ Developed, full gold. Very mature palate – toasty, gingery and slightly honied. Weighty and mellow, with lots of flavour, but starting to lose its freshness and dry out. **Drink 1999.**

PINOT GRIS
1998

DRY RIVER
Dry River Estate

No. 1002
BOTTLED BY DRY RIVER WINES LTD, PURUATANGA RD, MARTINBOROUGH
e 750ml   PRODUCE OF NEW ZEALAND   13.5% VOL
CONTAINS PRESERVATIVE (230)

Dry River
Pinot Gris

SUPER CLASSIC

"People are getting tired of drinking Chardonnay all the time," says Dr Neil McCallum, producer of New Zealand's first outstanding Pinot Gris. "And it's a superb food wine."

Since its first vintage in 1986, Dry River has towered above other New Zealand Pinot Gris, by virtue of its exceptional body, flavour richness and longevity. "There was a time when people only wanted to taste our Pinot Gris," recalls McCallum, who produces several other top-flight Martinborough wines. "But the price [\$30 for the 1998 vintage] keeps it as a niche wine."

What does Dry River Pinot Gris taste like? The first impression is of a satisfying sturdiness, from its high levels of alcohol and extract. The flavours are typically attractive but restrained in its youth, with peachy, slightly spicy and earthy characters that can develop great subtlety and richness with maturity.

McCallum, who sourced his vines from Mission Vineyards, believes them to be an old Alsace clone, imported into New Zealand in 1886, that belongs to the low-yielding clonal class called *Tokay à petit grain* (small berry Pinot Gris). "We follow the Alsace tradition, which places so much emphasis on ripeness and quality of fruit. The vines mustn't be cropped too heavily; the people in Alsace go on about the necessity of having the small berry clone." If in any vintage he harvests over two tonnes per acre of Pinot

Neil McCallum - the first New Zealand winemaker to make outstanding Pinot Gris.

Gris, McCallum thinks he's lucky.

McCallum picks Pinot Gris around the end of April (when he's harvesting the last of his Pinot Noir). "It is critical to achieve physiological ripeness [mature skin colour, berry texture, flavour, phenolic changes, etc], not just the right brix level. If you don't get that right, the first thing you lose is weight and richness."

By holding the grapes on the vine until they start to fall off, McCallum gives buyers of his Pinot Gris a late harvest wine in disguise. Acid loss isn't a problem, because Pinot Gris has such good weight and alcohol. Sometimes the fruit hangs on the vines until May to produce Dry River Selection Pinot Gris, a bold, sweet, late harvest style equivalent to an Alsace *vendange tardive*.

In the winery, McCallum finds Pinot Gris easy to work with. "The wine's made at the time you pick the grapes. We handle it like Chardonnay, favouring a reductive [non-oxidative] approach, although we are able to handle it less reductively than our other whites, because it's so robust. It's got awkward phenolics [Pinot Gris wine often shows a slight tannic hardness], so we whole bunch press." Fermentation is relatively warm, at around 18°C. McCallum doesn't mature it in oak, to avoid any loss of varietal flavours: "Pinot Gris doesn't take wood easily."

Dry River Pinot Gris drinks splendidly at five years old and the tasting (below) shows that although lesser years dip earlier, the top vintages look good for a decade. The Germans have no doubts about the grape's longevity, believing that Pinot Gris should be consumed when it has "grey hairs".

Like all Dry River wines, the Pinot Gris is rare, with an average annual output of 200 cases. It's worth getting on the winery's mailing list. At a Pinot Gris blind tasting held in Auckland in early 1992, the two top wines on my scoresheet were from Alsace – Zind-Humbrecht Rotenberg 1988, followed by Marcel Deiss 1989. In third place came Dry River 1986. Fourth equal were Dry River 1991 and another representative of Alsace, Hugel Cuvée Tradition 1986. Inspired by the classic Pinot Gris of Alsace, McCallum has succeeded in creating a Martinborough wine of comparable power and class.

tasting notes

These notes are mainly from a vertical tasting of the 1989 to 1997 vintages, held at the winery in November 1998. The 1998 vintage was tasted in Auckland in March 1999.

1998 ☆☆☆☆☆ Light lemon hue. A baby. Powerful wine (13.5 per cent alcohol) with mouthfilling body and crisp citrus/peach flavours. Lovely freshness, delicacy and finesse, with deliciously ripe, sweet fruit characters and a sustained finish. A classic vintage. **Drink 2001-08.**

1997 ☆☆☆☆☆ Light lemon/green. Very robust and concentrated, with rich flavours of citrus fruits and spice and balanced acidity. Immaculate and long, with great mouthfeel. Already quite expressive, but still youthful. **Drink 2001-07.**

1996 ☆☆☆☆☆ (Selection). *Vendange tardive* style, harvested in early May at 29 brix, with a small amount of *Botrytis* and natural shrivelling. Light lemon/green. An extraordinary wine with great richness and ultra-ripe flavours of lemons, spices, pears and lychees. Excitingly powerful and intense, it harbours 65 grams/litre of residual sugar, but due to its tremendous weight is not overtly sweet. **Drink 2000-10.**

1995 ☆☆☆☆☆ Light lemon/green. Alcohol 14 per cent. Taut, crisp wine with plenty of spicy, slightly appley flavour. Very robust palate, but lacks the opulence of a top vintage. **Drink 2000-02.**

1994 ☆☆☆☆☆ Light yellow. Still evolving. Fresh and tight, with concentrated peach/spice flavours and firm acidity. Big dry wine with classic varietal characters. Should mature well for a decade; even longer. **Drink 2000-04.**

1993 ☆☆☆☆ Light lemon/green. Plenty of crisp, lemony, slightly spicy flavour, but lacks richness of a top year. Big body, firm acid. Taut. **Drink 1999-2001.**

1992 ☆☆☆☆☆ Light lemon/green. Generous, lush wine, slightly sweet, with intense peachy, lemony flavours and overtones of earthiness and spice. Beautifully structured. Classic vintage. Should be very long-lived. **Drink 1999-2002.**

1991 ☆☆☆☆☆ Light lemon/green. Bold, rich wine, still very vigorous and fresh, with firm acid and lovely peach, lemon and spice flavours. Still developing. Poised, controlled, classic. **Drink 1999-2001.**

1990 ☆☆☆☆ Medium yellow. Toasty, developed bouquet. Starting to tire. Lemony, very toasty flavours and firm acidity, but losing its fruit. **Drink 1999.**

1989 ☆☆ Slightly dull gold. Oxidised nose. Dried out palate. Gone.

Ridiculously out of fashion in New Zealand until the early 1990s, Riesling has since won greater – although still limited – recognition as the source of some of this country's finest and most ravishingly beautiful white wines. The supreme grape of Germany and Alsace has found a natural antipodean home in New Zealand, where the top wines display the inimitable perfume and mouth-wateringly crisp, incisive flavour of classic cool-climate Riesling.

Despite isolated successes in Gisborne and Hawke's Bay, Riesling flourishes in New Zealand's cooler wine regions, where the slower ripening conditions imbue the grapes with the most magical scents and flavours. Over half the vines are clustered in Marlborough.

Most of the wines are made fractionally sweet, to balance Riesling's high natural acidity, but styles range from bone dry to honey-sweet (see Sweet White Wines). Of all New Zealand's top white varieties, Riesling is the strongest performer in the cellar, with a proven ability to mature well for at least a decade.

riesling

Collards Queen Charlotte Marlborough Riesling

CLASSIC

The small to medium-sized Collards winery in West Auckland has played a key role in the slow emergence of Riesling in New Zealand. "When we planted Riesling at Henderson in the early 1970s, we were greeted with derision by many winemakers," recalls Lionel Collard. "In Auckland, you made port and sherry." The critics fell silent when Collards scooped the country's first Riesling gold medal with its Rhine Riesling 1978.

Lionel Collard celebrated his 50th vintage in 1996: "My mother always said I had the obstinacy of the weak-minded," he chuckles. Collard, who still oversees the firm's administration and sales, is a fiercely independent perfectionist. The Collard family does not promote its wines aggressively, but its Chardonnays, Chenin Blancs and Rieslings are always of high quality.

The Collard holding in Lincoln Road, which was originally 25 hectares, has contracted to only two hectares under severe urban pressure, but the family also owns the 15-hectare Rothesay Vineyard in the Waikoukou Valley, near Matua Valley, and about half the company's grapes are purchased from growers in Hawke's Bay, Te Kauwhata and Marlborough.

For many years, Collards has made two Rieslings: the off-dry Marlborough Riesling and a slightly sweeter wine, labelled Rhine Riesling, typically a three-way regional blend of Auckland, Hawke's Bay and Marlborough fruit. Both are classy, but in recent vintages the Marlborough model (since 1996 called Queen Charlotte Marlborough Riesling) has been the most

impressive. Always immaculate and exquisitely balanced, in top years it has a beguiling fragrance and delicious flavour intensity.

After working for three years in the Mosel, Geoffrey Collard (Lionel's son) made a major contribution to the Collards' Riesling style. "He emphasised the importance of balancing the fruit flavours, acidity and sweetness," says Lionel. "It's what Hugh Johnson calls 'a glorious symphony' of flavours."

In Lionel Collards' view, climate, soils and vineyard practice are key factors in producing a superior Riesling. "In Marlborough, the soils are not over-rich, so the vines don't grow madly. Canopy management – including leaf trimming – is also critical, to allow the sun, air and sprays to penetrate the fruit zone."

Up to and including the 1996 vintage, the grapes were grown in The Corners Vineyard, owned by David Barnsley, in Hammerichs Road. Since 1997, however, the fruit has been drawn from Simon Mathews' vineyard in Jacksons Road. The average grape crop is between three and four tonnes per acre.

There are no secrets involved in producing a

fine quality Riesling, insists Lionel Collard. "It's basically all about good grapes, but in the winery [where his other son, Bruce, oversees production] we do give careful attention to the details, such as avoiding ullages [exposure to air] by gas blanketing. Those details count, because Riesling is a gentle grape variety and must be handled gently. Over the years, we've waged a war on astringency in Riesling."

With an annual production ranging from 750 to 2000 cases, the Queen Charlotte Riesling ($17) is in good commercial supply. Lionel Collard recommends cellaring the wine until it's at least three or four years old, and then drinking it over the next several years. The tasting (below) indicated that most vintages are at their best between three and seven years old.

Collards no longer enters wine shows, so its early stream of gold medals for Riesling has dried up. But the Collards are proven masters of this delectable variety. Top vintages of Queen Charlotte Riesling are simply exquisite, with a ravishing scentedness, intensity and harmony.

Lionel Collard produced New Zealand's first gold medal Riesling.

tasting notes
These notes are from a vertical tasting of the 1991 to 1998 vintages, held in Auckland in March 1999.

1998 ☆☆☆☆☆ (Tasted soon after bottling.) Light yellow/green. Soaring bouquet of tropical and citrus fruits, slightly honied. Youthful but lovely palate, with strong passionfruit and lemon flavours and perfect sugar/acid balance. Very refined. **Drink 2000-05.**

1997 ☆☆☆☆ Pale lemon/green. Leaner and more austere than the 1998 or 1996. Strong lemon and apple flavours, slightly sweet and cut with fresh acidity. Some developed, toasty characters emerging. **Drink 2000-02.**

1996 ☆☆☆☆☆ Medium yellow/green. Highly attractive floral/honey scents. Rich, intense wine with a lovely harmony of ripe citrusy fruit and honey characters, a touch of sweetness and long finish. Developed, but still crisp and lively. A classic vintage. Ready; no rush. **Drink 1999-2003.**

1995 Not made.

1994 ☆☆☆☆ (Labelled as Collards Marlborough Riesling.) Full

yellow. Toasty, springy lemon/lime flavours. Firm acidity. Gently honied. Attractive wine, but less concentrated than the 1996. Probably now at its peak. **Drink 1999-2000.**

1993 ☆☆☆☆½ Light gold. Honied bouquet. Very elegant wine, still vigorous, with intense lemon/honey flavours, threaded with invigorating acidity. Slightly limey, with toasty bottle-aged characters. Maturing well. **Drink 1999-2001.**

1992 ☆☆☆☆ Developed gold colour. Mature bouquet, limey and very toasty. Tense, high acid style, slightly austere, with strong lemon/lime flavours and a hint of honey. Full of character. **Drink 1999-2000.**

1991 ☆☆☆☆ Golden, developed colour. Minerally, mature bouquet. Full bodied wine, losing a bit of freshness, but still showing good concentration of citrusy fruit characters and a distinct honeyishness. Firm, long finish. Ready. **Drink 1999-2000.**

Coopers Creek Hawke's Bay Riesling

In the relatively warm Hawke's Bay region, few growers have managed to coax the most magical scents and flavours from Riesling, a classic cool-climate variety. Over the past decade, Coopers Creek has been the most consistently successful.

At its best ravishingly fragrant, the Hawke's Bay Riesling is a fractionally off-dry style with fresh, piercing lemon/lime flavours, a touch of honey and good, tart acidity. Always immaculate, it is scented, delicate and vibrantly fruity, with notable intensity and vigour. Why is it so good?

"It's partly the site," says managing director and principal shareholder, Andrew Hendry. "The grapes are grown in Jim Scotland's vineyard near Clive. Good air movement close to the sea reduces the risk of disease, allowing us to hang the fruit out late. The grapes don't get wildly ripe, but they build up intense flavours. And we leave part of the block unsprayed to encourage *Botrytis*."

Scotland's vineyard lies four kilometres from the coast in Lawn Road, between Clive and Haumoana. Cooled by the regular afternoon sea breezes, the grapes benefit from a long, flavour-intensifying

Coopers Creek produces one of the few impressive Hawke's Bay Rieslings.

period of ripening. The fruit, grown on the Scott Henry trellising system, is typically harvested at around 21.5 brix, two weeks later than most other Riesling in the Bay.

Kim Crawford, Coopers Creek's winemaker between 1989 and 1998, believes the style of the Hawke's Bay Riesling has "defined itself. It's made just off-dry, but dries out with age. I don't see it as a delicate, aromatic style like Marlborough's. Since it's from Hawke's Bay, it's got more weight. And it's more citrusy than the Marlborough wines."

The grapes are machine-harvested at night, with no sulphur dioxide additions, and trucked overnight to the winery in West Auckland. After crushing, draining and pressing, the juice is cold-settled and then cool-fermented in stainless steel tanks with an aromatic yeast. The fermentation is stopped at around seven grams per litre of residual sugar, and the wine is bottled early.

For a variety commonly regarded in New Zealand as difficult to sell, Coopers Creek make plenty of the Hawke's Bay Riesling – 3000 cases per year. Crawford believes the wine shows marked vintage variation. "Botrytis-affected years like 1990 can be attractive young, but they colour up early. The best years are cool and dry, like 1991, 1994 and 1996." The 1994 is currently in devastating form.

Among the many accolades awarded to Coopers Creek for its Hawke's Bay Riesling are the trophies for champion Riesling won by the 1991 and 1996 vintages at the Air New Zealand Wine Awards. The 1994 also won the trophy for champion Riesling at the 1995 Liquorland Royal Easter Wine Show.

Finely scented and penetratingly flavoured, in its youth the Hawke's Bay Riesling is an attractively fresh and tangy mouthful, but top vintages are also an ideal candidate for cellaring. At $15, this is one of the most affordable of the country's wine classics.

tasting notes

These notes are from a vertical tasting of the 1985 to 1998 vintages, held at the winery in November 1998.

1998 ☆☆☆☆☆ Pale lemon/green. Lovely, lifted pear/citrus aromas. Mouthfilling (from the ripest-ever vintage), lively and powerful, with fresh, rich lemon/lime flavours, slightly rounder than usual. Should cellar for a decade. **Drink 2000-08.**

1997 ☆☆☆☆☆ Light lemon/green. Still very youthful, with good concentration of lemon/lime flavour, fresh, crisp and slightly appley. Beautifully balanced, but less aromatic than the 1996. A slow developer. **Drink 2000-04.**

1996 ☆☆☆☆☆ Very light lemon/green. Richly fragrant bouquet of pears and honey. Fleshy and slightly sweet, with deep, ripe citrus flavours and firm acidity. Big wine (13 per cent alcohol), worth cellaring. **Drink 1999-2005.**

1995 ☆☆☆☆ Light lemon/green. Honeysuckle scents. Fresh and crisp, with delicate, springy lemon/apple flavours. Less rich than the 1994, but very good for a 1995. **Drink 1999-2002.**

1994 ☆☆☆☆☆ Classic aged Riesling. Bright, light yellow/green. Superbly fragrant, pungent, minerally bouquet. Rich, concentrated citrus/lime flavours, delicate, toasty, steely and long. A standout vintage. **Drink 1999-2004.**

1993 ☆☆☆☆☆ Pale lemon/green. Slightly under-ripe style (picked at 18 brix) from a very cool vintage. Strong appley flavours with high acidity. Austere, but incisive and lively.

1992 ☆☆☆☆☆ Bright, light yellow/green. Still very tight. Fleshy wine with strong lemon/lime flavours, toasty bottle-aged characters and firm acid spine. **Drink 1999-2001.**

1991 ☆☆☆☆☆ Bright yellow/green. Surprisingly youthful. Mouthfilling, clean and fresh. Lovely poise and intensity, with incisive citrus/lime characters. A top vintage, drinking superbly now. **Drink 1999-2001.**

1990 ☆☆☆ Developed, deep gold. Honied, limey flavours, crisp and toasty, with some Botrytis (noble rot) showing. **Drink ASAP.**

1989 ☆☆☆☆☆ Yellow/green, medium depth. Attractive lemon/lime scents. Still fresh and vigorous, with a strong surge of lemon/lime flavour and balanced acidity. By far the best of the early wines. **Drink 1999-2000.**

1988 ☆☆☆ Pale gold. (Picked after cyclone Bola at a very low 16.5 brix.) A flinty middleweight with lively lemon/lime flavours and high acidity. Not intense, but solid. **Drink ASAP.**

1987 Not tasted. (Bottling was spread over two days. One batch re-fermented in the bottle, report Coopers Creek.)

1986 ☆☆☆ Deep gold. Dull nose. Noble rot gives a honeyish character, but the wine lacks fruit flavour. Can still be drunk. **Drink ASAP.**

1985 ☆☆☆☆ Light gold. Developed, minerally, toasty bouquet. Still alive, with appley, toasty, slightly honied flavours, but falling away on the back palate. **Drink ASAP.**

Corbans Private Bin Amberley Riesling

CLASSIC

Canterbury's first classic wine was called Robard & Butler Amberley Riesling for its first eight vintages, but in 1993 was relabelled Corbans Private Bin. It is grown at Waipara, rather than Amberley, in North Canterbury. The story goes that when the wine was first released in the mid 1980s, the name Waipara failed to find favour with the company's marketing boffins, who plumped instead for the name of a small town to the south – Amberley.

Half way through the vertical tasting, I considered dropping this wine from the book, on the grounds that the older vintages were not maturing impressively over the long haul. But the most recent releases are setting a new standard for the label.

Michael Kluczko, Corbans' wine operations manager, accepts the criticism of the older vintages. "*Botrytis* previously gave the wine a lot of upfront appeal. Now we're putting emphasis on picking the grapes riper, with less *Botrytis* influence, so the wine will live longer."

Corbans Private Bin Amberley Riesling is a single-vineyard wine, grown by John Corbett at Waipara. Kluczko sees it as a "pretty good site, with free-draining soils and a bit of limestone washed down off the hills." Corbett grows only Riesling, exclusively for Corbans.

Most of the vineyards at Waipara - including John Corbett's - are draped over flat to gently sloping terrain, four kilometres north of the township of Waipara, near the Picton- Christchurch highway. This is Chardonnay, Pinot Noir, Sauvignon Blanc and Riesling country. John McCaskey of the Glenmark winery - who pioneered viticulture in North Canterbury in the early 1980s - stresses that the hot, dry nor'westers dictate Waipara's weather: "The trees, even the power poles, lean with the winds." The vineyards are sheltered from cooling coastal breezes by the Teviotdale Hills to the east.

Limey flavours and a tight structure are the key attributes Kluczko finds in the Amberley Riesling. The grapes are harvested by machine and trucked to the Corbans winery in Marlborough. "It's standard processing," says Kluczko. "Very protective [of the juice against air], technically correct winemaking, with cool ferments."

Production of Corbans Private Bin Amberley Riesling ($17) has ranged from 200 to 1500 cases per year. When discussing the best time to drink the wine, Kluczko draws a clear distinction between the most recent and older vintages. "If you open a wine from the early 1990s, you may be disappointed. But with their mouthfeel and length, the most recent years may live longer than our Stoneleigh Vineyard Riesling." With its fresh, penetrating lemon/lime flavours and dry, steely finish, in a blind tasting the 1996 vintage could easily be taken for a top Australian Riesling.

During the mid to late 1980s and early 1990s,

90

the wine won many top awards, although its show performance has tapered off in recent years. Rich and spicy, with *Botrytis*-affected flavours, it was a honeyish, highly individual wine that drank well for several years – but not a decade, as top Rieslings usually do. The new breed of cleaner, tighter and more delicate Corbans PB Amberley Riesling (exemplified by the 1996 vintage) is more restrained in its youth, but should attain a much higher quality peak. ⚥

Michael Kluczko (left), Corbans' wine operations manager, and viticulturist Dr Damian Martin.

tasting notes

These notes are from a vertical tasting of the 1989 to 1996 vintages, held at the winery in April 1999.

1996 ☆☆☆☆☆ Youthful, light lemon/green. Very youthful, fresh and springy. Robust and immaculate, with delicate, dry lemon/lime flavours and no obvious *Botrytis* influence. Excellent intensity and vigour. Looks like a top vintage. **Drink 2001-2005.**

1995 ☆☆☆☆☆ Medium yellow. Lovely, lifted, scented bouquet, slightly honied. Fresh, rich palate, lemony and poised, with good acid drive. Intense, vigorous and long. Developing superbly. **Drink 2000-04.**

1994 ☆☆☆☆☆ Full yellow. Concentrated and finely balanced. Rich, springy, citrusy fruit, developing minerally, complex characters with age. Firm acid spine. Loads of character – a classic year. **Drink 1999-2003.**

1993 ☆☆☆☆ ⚥ Bright yellow. Aging gracefully. Slightly minerally bouquet, with strong lemony flavours threaded with firm acidity. Tastes bone-dry. Tight-knit, very clean wine, likely to be long-lived. **Drink 1999-2002.**

1992 ☆☆☆☆ (Robard & Butler) Full yellow/light gold. Tense, high acid style with developed lemony, toasty characters. Plenty of spring, but slightly austere, with a fractionally hard finish. **Drink 1999.**

1991 ☆☆☆☆ (Robard & Butler) Full gold. Very honied and toasty. The fruit is still alive, but the wine is fully developed. Limey and tangy, with an almost fully dry finish. **Drink ASAP.**

1990 ☆☆☆ ⚥ (Robard & Butler) Deep gold/amber. Very toasty bouquet. Dry style with very mature apricot and toast flavours. Past its best. **Drink ASAP.**

1989 ☆☆☆☆ (Robard & Butler) Deep gold. Very mellow. Flavoursome, spicy and slightly honied, but losing its vigour. Toasty, minerally and still full of character, but past its best. **Drink ASAP.**

Dry River Craighall Riesling

SUPER CLASSIC

When I first tasted Neil McCallum's striking 1998 Craighall "Amaranth" Riesling, I wanted to rush out and buy a case. Stephen Bennett, a young Master of Wine, praised it as "the finest white wine ever made in New Zealand". That's the sort of passion aroused by Dry River Craighall – the country's only Super Classic Riesling.

Craighall Riesling is a wine of exceptional purity, delicacy and depth. An intensely varietal Martinborough wine, it is always immaculate and highly concentrated, with a proven ability to flourish in the cellar for many years. McCallum believes that, in quality terms, Riesling is at least the equal of Pinot Noir in Martinborough.

The key factors contributing to the splendid quality of Craighall Riesling, says McCallum, are "primarily the fruit and then very gentle handling, including whole-bunch pressing. It must be handled anaerobically [without oxygen], to preserve the essential varietal flavours."

In terms of style, he's certainly not aiming for a blockbuster. "Riesling can be lean – it shouldn't show obvious extract – but the fruit must express itself. Riesling depends on grace, elegance and flavour intensity. I don't like high alcohol Rieslings; alcohol makes them sturdy but Riesling is all about delicacy and detail. It should never be burly."

The grapes are grown in the nearby Craighall vineyard, now part-owned by Dry River (although most of the fruit for the 1998 "Martinborough Riesling" came from the local Canning vineyard). McCallum sees a strong correlation between crop

levels and wine quality. "Young Riesling may conceal flavour dilution. But limiting the crop to below three tonnes per acre shows up over time." When the vines flower in the Craighall vineyard, some of the flowers are "pinched out", and at *veraison* the bunches are green-thinned, to limit yields to an average of 2.5 tonnes per acre.

The fruit is hand-harvested as late as possible each year. Hanging the grapes on the vines for two or three weeks after their sugar levels have stopped climbing can achieve major advances in flavour, and "maximises any *Botrytis* [noble rot] for complexity and texture in the wine as it develops."

In the winery, McCallum reports he does "nothing especially different. We've always been very anaerobic. Processing the grapes is done as gently as possible to preserve the purity of flavours".

Like all Dry River wines, the Craighall Riesling ($20) is rare – the single hectare of vines yield 300 to 400 cases of wine. It's a prime candidate for cellaring – none of the 11 wines in the vertical tasting was tired. "The 1989 will be the shortest-lived we've made," says McCallum. "Provided the corks are good and the wines are well cellared, they'll be 10 to 15-year wines. It's not smart to drink them at less than five years old."

Dry River Craighall Riesling is not entered in local competitions, but with its small supply and regular rave reviews, doesn't suffer any lack of demand. McCallum is confident about the quality of his wine, and rightly so. "I've seen the 1992 alongside Wehlener Sonnenuhr [the great Mosel, famous for its fruit and finesse] and it holds its own easily. It's clearly there, in terms of intensity and style."

Although initially acclaimed for his magnificent Pinot Gris, and lately for a Pinot Noir of great power, McCallum is deeply devoted to Riesling and regards Craighall Riesling as "something of a flagship" for Dry River. Given its splendid quality throughout the past decade, this is clearly New Zealand's most illustrious Riesling. 🍇

Exquisitely perfumed and intense Rieslings trickle from Dry River.

tasting notes

These notes are from a vertical tasting of the 1989 to 1998 vintages, held at the winery in November 1998.

1998 ☆☆☆☆☆ (Labelled "Amaranth") Light yellow. Fully dry. Minerally rather than floral, on nose and palate. Very intense grapefruit/lemon flavours, with a hint of marmalade. Well-spined. Poised, complex wine, highly refined and extremely long. Carries the dry style effortlessly – not at all austere. Already stunning. Arguably the greatest Riesling yet made in New Zealand. **Drink 2000-13.**

1998 ☆☆☆☆☆ (Labelled "Martinborough") Predominantly from Strat Canning's vineyard, with a small percentage of Dry River fruit. Light yellow. Juicy and very ripe. A medium-dry style with deep lemony, limey flavours and lively acid. Concentrated wine, immaculate, with real backbone. Already approachable. **Drink 2000-10.**

1997 ☆☆☆☆☆ Beautifully fragrant. Tight, rich grapefruit/lime flavours, lively, immaculate and piercing. Slightly sweet, with fresh, appetising acidity and a distinct touch of *Botrytis*-derived honeyishness. **Drink 2000-05.**

1996 ☆☆☆☆ʒ (Craighall Dry) Pale straw. Dry, minerally and taut. Intense, vigorous wine with highish acidity in a fairly austere style. More advanced than the 1995. **Drink 1999-2002.**

1995 ☆☆☆☆☆ (Craighall Dry) Pale lemon/green. Lifted, minerally nose. Intense, pure lemon/lime flavours, cut with mouth-watering acidity. Very tightly structured and long. Still very fresh and maturing well. Should be long-lived. **Drink 2000-05.**

1994 ☆☆☆☆☆ (Craighall Estate Dry) Bright, light lemon/green. Bell-clear flavours of lemons and limes, gently overlaid with toasty bottle-aged characters. Tight-knit. Enlivened by fresh acidity and beautifully balanced. A top vintage, built for the long haul. **Drink 2000-04.**

1993 ☆☆☆☆ʒ (Craighall Estate Dry) Bright lemon/green. Slightly honied nose and palate. Elegant wine with deep lemony, slightly toasty flavours and balanced acidity. From a very cool year but not austere. Aging well. **Drink 1999-2003.**

1992 ☆☆☆☆☆ (Craighall Estate) Medium yellow. Strong harmony of lemon, honey and toast flavours. Beautiful now. Very elegant wine, slightly sweet and notably complex. Riesling at its mature (or maturing) best. Absolutely classic. **Drink 1999-2002.**

1991 ☆☆☆☆☆ (Craighall Estate) Medium-full yellow. Rich bouquet of citrus fruits and toast. Medium style, slightly honied. Very richly flavoured. Sweeter than most in the lineup. Intense, slightly minerally and complex. Very impressive. Ready; no rush. **Drink 1999-2001.**

1990 Not tasted. "Like the 1989, with stuffing" – Neil McCallum.

1989 ☆☆☆☆☆ (Craighall Estate) Light-medium yellow, still youthful. Very minerally bouquet. Slender but concentrated and full of character. Strong but delicate lemon/lime flavours, slightly off-dry. Finely poised and long. Lighter-bodied than most in the lineup, but exquisitely proportioned. Delightful now. **Drink 1999-2000.**

Grove Mill Marlborough Riesling

CLASSIC

"Riesling is a much more aristocratic grape variety than Sauvignon Blanc," believes David Pearce, winemaker at Grove Mill, whose company sells 2500 cases of Riesling per year, compared to 18,000 cases of Sauvignon Blanc. Pearce's Rieslings are consistently immaculate, with fresh, penetrating, slightly honied flavours and lovely harmony and vigour.

Riesling has always been important at Grove Mill. Grove Mill's grower-shareholders had Riesling planted in the late 1980s – and Pearce was itching to make it. "I've always loved Mosel-style Rieslings, with their lightness and flavour persistence. Our wine isn't like a Mosel, but what remained with me was the knowledge that the sugar/acid balance is crucial."

Pearce describes the Riesling flavours he is after as "floral, spice and musk". Sugar is a key part of the recipe. The Grove Mill typically harbours over 20 grams per litre of residual sugar – twice as sweet as most of the region's Rieslings. "That's what the marketing department want," reports Pearce. "It sells." The sweetness is finely balanced with the wine's lush, intense fruit characters and appetising acidity. "The emphasis is always on balance," says Pearce. "Balance between sugar, acid, alcohol and fruit flavours."

Born in Christchurch, as a child David Pearce made cider at home and before leaving school had decided to be a winemaker. After working as a cellarhand and laboratory technician at Corbans in Henderson, he gained a food technology degree from Massey University and rejoined Corbans,

where he worked his way up to the senior post of Gisborne winemaker. In 1988, Pearce went south to join Grove Mill.

In Pearce's view, Marlborough has the potential to be a great Riesling region. Over the years, much of the fruit has come from the Framingham vineyard at Renwick, but this source is now being replaced by grapes from an adjoining property owned by Peter Johansen. Two other vineyards in the Wairau Valley supply Riesling fruit. "The precise location of the vineyard is less important than that the vines must be cultivated in fairly water-stressed ground," says Pearce.

To achieve flavour concentration, the vines' crops are restricted to between three and four tonnes per acre. Some *Botrytis* has been present in every vintage except 1994, adding "weight and glycerol" to the finished wine.

The juice is fermented at low temperatures with a slow-fermenting yeast, Assmanshausen, known for producing spicy characters in the wine. Sweetness is achieved by arresting the fermentation, rather than backblending. Unusually for New Zealand, since 1995 Pearce has put about half of the final Riesling blend through malolactic fermentation, "not to modify acidity but to enhance the wine's texture".

Although past vintages of Grove Mill Marlborough Riesling have won gold medals and the 1991 vintage was the first Riesling to be offered on Air New Zealand's first class service, Pearce reports that Americans are more accepting of the wine than domestic consumers. "New Zealanders have a sweetness hang-up, but in the US the *Wine Spectator* has rated both the 1997 and 1998 highly."

At its best ravishingly perfumed, with intense lemon/lime flavours and power right through the palate, Grove Mill Marlborough Riesling ($16) is typically an exquisitely well-balanced wine. Although delicious young, it breaks into full stride at three to four years old. Its quality over the past decade certainly vindicates Pearce's early faith in Marlborough's potential for the great grape of Germany.

David Pearce's Rieslings are awash with zingy lemon/lime flavour.

tasting notes

These notes are from a vertical tasting of the 1988 to 1998 vintages, held at the winery in January 1999.

1998 ☆☆☆☆☆ Light lemon/green. Powerful and tight, with rich tropical/passionfruit flavours. Robust wine (13 per cent alcohol) with appetising acidity and a hint of honey. Built for the long haul. **Drink 1999-2005.**

1997 ☆☆☆☆☆ Light lemon/green. Lifted, floral, citrusy, slightly honied bouquet. Big, rich wine with a lovely array of grapefruit, lime and honey flavours, lively and long. Powerful and concentrated. **Drink 1999-2004.**

1996 ☆☆☆☆☆ Light-medium yellow/green. Lovely, poised wine, still fresh, with a delicious harmony of strong lemony flavour, sweetness and acidity, plus some ripe, passionfruit-like characters and a hint of honey. Top vintage. **Drink 1999-2003.**

1995 ☆☆☆ Light gold. Slightly dull, kerosene-like bouquet, lacking floral characters and charm. The palate lacks freshness, revealing austere, lemony, toasty flavours. Lacks concentration. Won't last much longer. **Drink ASAP.**

1994 ☆☆☆☆☆ Pale lemon/green. Stands out in the lineup, due to the absence of *Botrytis*. Slightly toasty, lemony, appley bouquet. Very refined and intense. Classic, poised Riesling, aging splendidly. Perfect sugar/acid balance. Should live for a decade, or longer. **Drink 1999-2002.**

1993 ☆☆☆ Full yellow/light gold. Austere style from a very cool season, with slightly honied, limey flavours and a high-acid finish. Lacks the richness and charm of a warmer, riper year. **Drink 1999-2000.**

1992 ☆☆☆ᵠ Full yellow/light gold. Slightly dull nose. Grapefruit and honey flavours, quite developed, with firm acid backbone. Very solid, but lacks the exquisite nature of the 1991. **Drink 1999-2000.**

1991 ☆☆☆☆☆ Full yellow/light gold. Lovely now – deep honeyish, slightly toasty flavours threaded with firm acidity. *Botrytis* adds richness and personality, without dominating. Good weight. Obvious sweetness. Now in full flight. **Drink 1999-2000.**

1990 ☆☆☆ᵠ Medium yellow/green. Lifted, limey, minerally bouquet. Tightly structured wine with citrusy, minerally characters on the palate. A bit lean and high-acid, and lacks its customary length. **Drink 1999.**

1989 ☆☆☆ Bright, full yellow/green. Bigger than the 1988, with *Botrytis*-derived honey characters. Rounded, with quite good flavour depth. Mellow. Very solid, but no real excitement here. **Drink 1999.**

1988 ☆☆☆ᵠ Medium lemon/green. Developed, toasty, limey bouquet. Elegant, medium-bodied wine with classic, citrusy, toasty, aged Riesling characters, not intense but true. No rush. **Drink 1999.**

Millton Opou Vineyard Riesling

Riesling is a rarity in Gisborne, accounting for just one per cent of the region's vines. As a classic cool-climate variety, the great German grape has tended to perform best in the South Island, or at least from the Wairarapa south. Yet for many years Gisborne winemaker James Millton has pursued his ardent love affair with Riesling.

After working in the Rheinhessen, James Millton is passionate about Riesling.

Millton's Opou Vineyard Rieslings are typically opulent and honeyish, in a softer, less racy style than the classic Marlborough wines. Perfumed and slightly sweet, with lovely poise and concentration, they are highly characterful wines with a proven ability to flourish long-term in the cellar.

"I'm passionate about Riesling," says Millton, who in his youth worked on a small estate in the Rheinhessen, "working and tasting a raft of wines. The extraordinary thing is we grow Riesling without any chemical crutch [despite Gisborne's warm, moist climate, Millton practises organic viticulture], yet the critics say we're successful. There's a parallel there to a person with cancer, ignoring chemotherapy and pursuing natural remedies."

Millton is currently planting citrus trees among his Riesling vines, to harbour beneficial insects such as ladybirds. "The trees flower at the same time as the vines, so perhaps there'll be some transfer of citrus aromas."

Millton has modelled his Opou Vineyard Riesling on the classic *spatlesen* (late-harvested wines) of Germany. Its residual sugar level, typically between 15 and 25 grams per litre, making it a truly medium style, varies each year according to the wine's natural acidity, which is not adjusted. "Sometimes the ferment stops by itself; sometimes we help it stop," says Millton.

The grapes are grown in the original, loam-clay Opou vineyard at Manutuke, a couple of kilometres from the winery, where the vines are trained on the German *halb-bogen* (half heart) system, which Millton finds gives "better fruit positioning and better air and sunlight penetration". The berries are hand-harvested over a month at three stages of ripening, culminating in a final pick of *Botrytis*-affected fruit.

At the winery, Millton handles Riesling more reductively (protecting the juice and wine from air) than any other variety, to retain its lovely fragrance. "But I'm not a technocrat," he says. "Some people comment on oxidative characters in the wine. Rather than locking in every aromatic compound, we bring

the wine to its maturity [sometimes partly in oak barrels], and then we bottle it."

Millton Opou Vineyard Riesling ($20) is made in substantial volumes – about 2000 cases per year. James Millton suggests drinking the wine at "four years old and onwards, when you get greater complexity. But there's a lot of variation – it's very vintage-dependent."

The tasting (below) shows the wine generally has excellent cellaring potential.

The 1985, 1986 and 1987 vintages all won gold medals, as did the 1994, and the 1998 at the 1999 Liquorland Royal Easter Wine Show. Typically ravishingly perfumed, with a delicious surge of lemony, honeyish flavour, Millton Opou Vineyard is the country's northernmost classic Riesling. ⚕

tasting notes
These notes are from a vertical tasting of the 1985 to 1998 vintages, held in Auckland in March 1999.

1998 ☆☆☆☆☆ Pale lemon/green. Beautifully scented, with very ripe, pure fruit aromas. Meticulous wine with lovely, concentrated, very delicate lemon/grapefruit flavours in a medium style with fresh acidity. Big wine, perfectly balanced. A great vintage. **Drink 2000-08.**

1997 ☆☆☆☆☆ Light-medium yellow. Floral, lemony scents. Rich, medium style with grapefruit, honey and marmalade characters. Good concentration, with some *Botrytis* showing. Slightly musky. Forward, but will live. **Drink 2000-05.**

1996 ☆☆☆☆☆ Light yellow. Deep lemon/lime flavours, very lightly tinged with honey. Lovely balance of sweetness and acidity. Delicate, yet rich and firmly structured, and should really honey up with age. **Drink 1999-06.**

1995 Not made.

1994 ☆☆☆☆ Deep gold. Very developed, with gingery, toasty characters. Distinctly medium style. Drying out and slightly hard. **Drink 1999.**

1993 ☆☆☆☆ Medium-full gold. Very honied nose. Full, medium style with a strong *Botrytis* influence and plenty of fruit. Grapefruit and ginger flavours, harmonious and ready. **Drink 1999-2000.**

1992 ☆☆☆☆☆ Full yellow. Lovely, delicate wine with rich grapefruit flavours, ripe and rounded. Gentle *Botrytis* influence. Very elegant, finely balanced wine with good body (12 per cent alcohol.) Classic vintage. **Drink 1999-2002.**

1991 Not tasted.

1990 ☆☆☆☆ Deep gold/light amber. Heavily *botrytised* style, with apricot and ginger flavours. Quite good depth, but perhaps starting to fade, with a slightly weak, soft finish. **Drink 1999.**

1989 ☆☆☆☆☆ Bright, full yellow/light gold. Toasty, limey, developed nose. Lovely, mature Riesling, still very lively and harmonious, with gently honied, toasty flavours, now rounding out. Delicious now. **Drink 1999.**

1988 ☆☆☆☆☆ Deep gold. Toasty, honied, developed nose. Hint of kerosene. Gingery, honeyish flavours, holding quite well, but very ready. **Drink ASAP.**

1987 ☆☆☆☆☆ (Late Harvest) 750 ml bottle. Gold/amber. Rich, mellow and concentrated, with honey and grapefruit flavours and plentiful sweetness (88 grams per litre). Very developed but very intense, with a slightly nutty, softening, powerful finish. A mellow masterpiece, delicious now. **Drink 1999.**

1986 ☆☆☆☆ (Late Harvest) 750 ml bottle. Amber-hued. Honied and toasty, with good acid spine and plenty of residual sugar (70 grams per litre). Still characterful and delicious, although less exquisite than the 1987. **Drink 1999.**

1985 ☆☆☆☆☆ (Late Harvest) 375 ml bottle. Amber/green. Rich and treacly, with flavours of apricots, honey and nuts. Concentrated wine with firm acidity and considerable sweetness (70 grams per litre). Has certainly matured well. **Drink 1999.**

Palliser Estate Riesling

Martinborough winemaker Allan Johnson produces top wines from several grape varieties. As the architect of one of the country's most compelling Rieslings, he has crystal-clear ideas about how to achieve quality.

Palliser Estate Riesling is typically beautifully scented, with intense, slightly sweet lemon and lime flavours and a long, racy finish. Garden-fresh, fruity and zesty, it bursts with varietal character.

"The fruit is the key quality factor," says Johnson. "Riesling is very much a wine that is a transformation of the fruit, through careful handling. You need good fruit from good sites, picked at the right points of flavour development and acid balance."

Johnson prefers a slightly off-dry Riesling, stop-fermented at around six grams per litre of sugar. "That's an important point – it's not artificially sweetened." His goal is a fine Riesling, which avoids harsh phenolics by gentle crushing and pressing of the fruit. The style varies slightly from year to year: "We let the vintage speak, in terms of its varying alcohol, acidity and flavour. Flavour-wise, we want complexity, with lemon blossom, grapefruit and often honied notes. Quite a few of the wines have had a small degree of *Botrytis*, which is a positive contribution."

Palliser Estate produces a piercingly flavoured and ravishingly scented Riesling.

The grapes are grown in two company-owned vineyards, one on heavier soils than the other, but in Johnson's view climate is the major factor. "We're at a similar latitude to Marlborough, but slightly more continental. We don't get the cooling sea breezes they get in the Wairau Valley. So compared to Marlborough, we get a slightly richer style of Riesling."

The vines, all trained on the two-tier Scott Henry system, are leaf-plucked by hand, not so much for flavour development, but to control the degree of *Botrytis* infection. Johnson finds Riesling quite elastic. "We get more concentration at moderate to low yields, but have won gold medals in higher-cropping years." Crops average four tonnes per acre.

At Palliser Estate, Riesling is the last variety to ripen – in some years it hasn't been picked until the second week of May. "It's difficult to over-ripen Riesling in Martinborough," says Johnson, "but in most years we get an ideal balance of flavours and acidity."

At the winery, the fruit is crushed lightly and pressed quickly, to minimise contact between the juice and skins. The juice is then cold-settled for three days before the ferment, to achieve a high degree of clarity. Throughout the vinification process, handling is minimal and reductive (to exclude oxygen).

Palliser Estate Riesling ($17) is only made in moderate volumes (about 1200 cases per year), but in Johnson's view, it matures the best of all his wines. He enjoys drinking it at three years old, when "the fruit flavours are strong and bottle-aged characters are adding complexity". The vertical tasting (below) revealed that top vintages blossom for at least eight years in the cellar – and probably much more.

Several vintages of Palliser Estate Riesling have won gold medals, most recently the 1998 at the 1999 Liquorland Royal Easter Wine Show. The most notable award went to the 1993 vintage, which scooped the trophy for champion Riesling at the Australia National Wine Show in Canberra.

Explosively flavoured, with a beguiling perfume and great vigour, Palliser Estate Riesling is one of Martinborough's top white wines and (with Dry River) one of its two leading Rieslings. At its best, it's a truly exciting mouthful. ▸

tasting notes

These notes are from a vertical tasting of the 1990 to 1998 vintages, held at the winery in November 1998.

1998 ☆☆☆☆☆ Pale lemon/green. Highly aromatic. Powerful (13 per cent alcohol) and broad palate, very ripely flavoured, with citrus and passionfruit flavours and balanced acidity. Lovely poise and length. Accessible early, but power to age. **Drink 2000-08.**

1997 ☆☆☆☆☆ Light lemon/green. Ripely fragrant bouquet of lemon blossom and honey. Rich wine with very intense flavours of passionfruit and limes and invigorating acidity. Currently more enjoyable than the 1996. **Drink 2000-07.**

1996 ☆☆☆☆✫ Light lemon/green. Perfumed, citrusy bouquet. Youthful wine with strong lemon/lime flavours, lively acidity and a hint of toastiness. Tense wine, currently a bit disjointed. Needs more time, and should be a stayer. **Drink 2000-06.**

1995 ☆☆☆☆ Light lemon/green. Appley, slightly green-edged aromas. Very fresh and frisky. A less ripe style than usual. Slightly austere, but very clean, with good flavour length and a freshly acidic finish. **Drink 1999-2002.**

1994 ☆☆☆☆☆ (45 per cent Marlborough fruit.) Light lemon/green. Beautiful, enticing bouquet – citrusy, limey,

toasty, slightly honied. Big, immaculate wine, exquisitely balanced, with rich, ripe flavours and lively, tangy acidity. A top vintage. Should be long-lived. **Drink 1999-2004.**

1993 ☆☆☆☆ Light gold. Highly toasty, quite developed nose. Strong, minerally, honeyish flavours, threaded with firm acid. Toasty, dry flavours, with a slight dip at the finish. **Drink 1999-2000.** (Allan Johnson reports other bottles have looked less developed.)

1992 ☆☆☆☆☆ (88 per cent Marlborough and 12 per cent Martinborough fruit.) Bright, medium yellow/green. Very juicy and slightly honied, with a clear *Botrytis* influence. Strong lemon/lime flavours and a high acid finish. If the 1991 is an Australian style, this is Germanic. **Drink 1999-2002.**

1991 ☆☆☆☆☆ (Labelled Rhine Riesling.) Light lemon/green, showing very little development. Lovely, rich lemon and lime, slightly toasty flavours, still very fresh and vigorous. An absolute classic – dryish, piercing and long. An exceptional wine of great intensity, that could perhaps live 20 years. **Drink 1999-2005.**

1990 Not tasted. "Holding up reasonably well" – Allan Johnson.

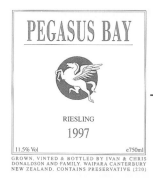

RIESLING
1997

11.5% Vol   e750ml

GROWN, VINTED & BOTTLED BY IVAN & CHRIS
DONALDSON AND FAMILY, WAIPARA CANTERBURY
NEW ZEALAND. CONTAINS PRESERVATIVE (220)

Pegasus Bay Riesling

POTENTIAL CLASSIC

With its stunning 1995 vintage, Pegasus Bay announced its arrival as an important Riesling producer. The exciting quality of the 1995 and subsequent releases has added weight to the evidence, initially provided by Corbans Private Bin Amberley Riesling, that North Canterbury is well suited to Riesling.

"Riesling is a regionally sensitive grape," believes Ivan Donaldson, an associate-professor of neurology, wine judge and wine columnist for *The Press*, and the driving force behind Pegasus Bay. "You need to achieve full ripeness over a prolonged ripening period, with warm days and cool nights, so that the grapes don't ripen too quickly. It certainly performs best overseas under those conditions."

Pegasus Bay Riesling is very classy. Grown at Waipara, at its best it is richly fragrant and thrillingly intense, with searching, concentrated flavours of citrus fruits and honey, complex and luscious.

Despite the fashion for bone-dry wines, Donaldson is adamant that Pegasus Bay Riesling should be slightly sweet. "When you get the grapes fully ripe, they have quite a phenolic structure that's not there in greener fruit. That gives the wine more weight, but it can also add harshness, and if you make the wine fully dry, it can be hard and steely. We believe you need some sweetness, which dries out in time." A small proportion of nobly rotten fruit adds another flavour dimension. (Pegasus Bay also makes a sweeter, late harvest Riesling, labelled Aria, comparable to an Alsatian *vendange tardive*.)

Estate-grown in stony soils, ideal for achieving advanced ripeness, the Riesling vines are fully netted,

which lets Pegasus Bay's winemakers decide when to harvest, "rather than our feathered friends". Donaldson believes that yields are a less critical quality factor in Riesling than with some other varieties. "We're not tremendously low or high. But you can't afford to over-crop, because then the fruit wouldn't ripen and we don't de-acidify; we want to retain natural acidity."

The hand-harvested grapes are whole-bunch pressed (to keep the phenolic levels down), and the juice is cold-settled prior to the fermentation, which proceeds slowly under cool conditions, sometimes not finishing until after Christmas. The wine then has prolonged aging on its yeast lees to develop mid-palate weight, texture and creaminess.

Pegasus Bay is determined not to rush its Riesling onto the market too early. "We want some aged characters showing in the wine," says Donaldson. "Sauvignon Blanc and Gewürztraminer show their character instantly, but Riesling character comes mainly from terpenes, which with age change hugely in aroma and flavour. Our aim is to bottle the wine at one year old, and before release give it a further six months in the bottle."

Pegasus Bay Riesling ($18) is made in sufficient volumes (1000 to 2000 cases per year) to achieve

Pegasus Bay is emerging as the foremost Riesling producer in North Canterbury.

national distribution. Donaldson advises keeping the wine until it's three to four years old, and believes it will "hang in for at least 10 years". The 1995 vintage certainly looks good for a decade.

Pegasus Bay does not enter wine competitions, but Donaldson has been thrilled by the reception to the wine in Australia. "Despite having so many Rieslings of their own, they're interested in ours. We've had very good press in Australia – and it's selling."

Hugh Johnson, the great English wine writer, visited Pegasus Bay in late 1995 and was reportedly highly impressed with the Riesling.

Clearly one of Waipara's finest wines, the Pegasus Bay is also an emerging star of New Zealand Riesling. Watch out for the winged horse.

tasting notes

These notes are from a vertical tasting of the 1994 to 1998 vintages, held in Auckland in March 1999.

1998 ☆☆☆☆☆ Light lemon/green. Strikingly rich, musky fragrance, leading into a very lush and intense palate. A medium style with gorgeous depth of very ripe, slightly honied flavour and rounded acidity. Very classy and already extremely enjoyable. **Drink 2000-05.**

1997 ☆☆☆☆☆ Light yellow. Rich lemon and honey scents. Full, fresh, very concentrated palate, with a lovely intensity of lively lemon/lime flavours, a hint of honey, and notable harmony and length. A medium style, beautifully poised and already irresistible. **Drink 1999-2007.**

1996 ☆☆☆ ☆ Medium-full yellow. Bouquet lacks excitement – slightly dull. Weighty, with good depth of ripe, citrusy, slightly honied flavours and firm acidity, but lacks the structure, intensity and zing of the 1995. **Drink 1999-2000.**

1995 ☆☆☆☆☆ Full yellow/light gold. Gorgeous, floral, honied bouquet. Classic bottle-aged Riesling, powerful, with very intense, toasty, lemon/lime flavours, overlaid with *Botrytis*/marmalade characters. Developing great richness and complexity with age. **Drink 1999-2005.**

1994 ☆☆☆☆ Pale yellow. More subdued bouquet than the 1995 or 1997. Palate is the highlight – flinty and persistent, with good acid drive. Punchy, citrusy, slightly sweet wine, full of character. Builds to a powerful finish. **Drink 1999-2001.**

Classic Wines of New Zealand

Stoneleigh Vineyard Marlborough Riesling

CLASSIC

How many other top-flight, regular award winners can you buy at any corner wine store at a low price? Of Corbans' four-label range of Stoneleigh Vineyard Marlborough wines, in quality terms the Riesling is the standout success. At the 1998 Air New Zealand Wine Awards, the trophy for the champion wine of the show went to Stoneleigh Vineyard Marlborough Riesling 1996. The wine had previously been available throughout the country at about $13.

Deliciously fragrant in its youth, Stoneleigh Vineyard Riesling is typically a refined wine with good body, excellent depth of lemony, slightly sweet flavour and a crisp, slightly honied, impressively long finish.

Highly expressive in its youth, it also has a proven ability to flourish for several years in the cellar.

Michael Kluczko, Corbans' wine operations manager, believes the warm, shingly nature of

Corbans' Stoneleigh Vineyard yields deliciously fresh, rich and racy Riesling.

Stoneleigh Vineyard, in the Jacksons Road/Rapaura Road area of the Wairau Valley, is a key quality factor in the wine. When builders dug the foundations of Corbans Marlborough Winery, adjacent to the Stoneleigh Vineyard, they went down six metres – and it was all stones. "It's one of the best sites in Marlborough," says Kluczko. "It's the most free-draining part of the valley, so you can ripen the grapes earlier and get better flavour development."

The wine's style is evolving. As with the company's Private Bin Amberley Riesling, Kluczko is keen for future vintages of Stoneleigh Vineyard Riesling to display more sheer varietal character, less sweetness and less *Botrytis*. "The 1998, with no *Botrytis*, could be the best ever," he says. "*Botrytis* is OK as a complexing, rather than dominating, character, but it can take the wine over. I want the wine to be fruit-driven at the point of bottling, and to let the complexity develop later."

Much vineyard work - crop thinning, shoot removal, leaf removal - is done in an effort to get ripe, clean fruit, disease-free and evenly ripened. The vines have an average yield of three to four tonnes per acre: "The bigger the crop, the more you delay ripening and the higher the risk of *Botrytis*," says Kluczko.

The grapes are mechanically harvested and given "classic Riesling handling. That means cool fermentation in stainless steel tanks with yeasts that will enhance the wine's aromas, but no oak and no malolactic fermentation. We want pristine fruit flavours, so don't fiddle around. It's very reductive [non-oxidative] winemaking." Arresting the fermentation at about eight grams per litre of residual sugar (11 to 12 grams prior to the 1996 vintage) leaves the wine with a gentle touch of sweetness.

As the style of Stoneleigh Vineyard Riesling becomes drier and less *Botrytis*-influenced, Kluczko is confident its international appeal will grow. Production is currently running at about 5000 cases per year.

The best time to broach the wine is a matter of personal style preference. Fresh, aromatic and crisp upon release, the wine develops minerally, toasty complexities at two or three years old.

Richly scented and vibrantly fruity, with piercing citrus/lime flavours, a sliver of sweetness and a crisp, racy finish, Stoneleigh Vineyard Riesling is a Marlborough classic. Given its consistently impressive quality and low price, it deserves a place in every wine lover's cellar. 🍷

tasting notes
These tasting notes are from a vertical tasting of the 1992 to 1998 vintages, held at the winery in April 1999.

1998 ☆☆☆☆☆ Pale lemon/green. Fresh lemon/apple scents, with no sign of *Botrytis*. Still very youthful. A style departure, with excellent weight and power in a rather Australian style, markedly drier than in the past. Strong lemony, limey flavours, taut and very persistent. Should mature well for many years. **Drink 2001-07.**

1997 ☆☆☆☆☆ Light-medium yellow. Lovely, full wine with obvious sweetness. Rich, ripe flavours, lemony and slightly honied. Mouthfilling (13 per cent alcohol) and still youthful. Powerful wine, with good acid spine. **Drink 2000-05.**

1996 ☆☆☆☆☆ Medium-full yellow. Complex wine, with great depth and persistence. Rich, ripe flavours, with slight sweetness and finely balanced acidity. Lovely freshness and vigour. Some mineral characters starting to unfold. Great now onwards. **Drink 1999-2006.**

1995 ☆☆☆ Gold, slightly dull. Minerally, honied nose. Very advanced for its age, with high acidity and strong *Botrytis*-derived apricot and honey flavours. Plenty of character, but tastes 10, not four, years old. **Drink 1999.**

1994 ☆☆☆☆☆ Bright, medium yellow. Richly scented, with a lovely harmony of lemony, slightly honied flavour. Slightly sweet finish, with good acid drive. Starting to acquire attractive, toasty, bottle-aged characters. Superb now but still developing. **Drink 1999-2004.**

1993 ☆☆☆ Amber/gold, very advanced. Dull. Some obvious *Botrytis* characters (honey and apricot). Lacks richness and freshness. Past its best. **Drink ASAP.**

1992 ☆☆☆☆☆ Full, bright yellow/light gold. Poised wine, aging very gracefully. Intense and vigorous lemony flavours, with good sugar/acid balance and a hint of honey. Classic Riesling richness and harmony. **Drink 1999-2002.**

Sauvignon Blanc (or more precisely, Marlborough Sauvignon Blanc) is the classic wine style of New Zealand, in the eyes of the world. Nowhere else does this traditional grape of the Loire Valley and Bordeaux yield wine of such breathtaking pungency, crammed with crisply herbaceous, garden-fresh flavour.

New Zealand's second most widely planted variety (after Chardonnay), Sauvignon Blanc accounted for almost 22 per cent of the producing vineyard in 1999. Over two-thirds of the vines are concentrated in Marlborough, with other important clusters in Hawke's Bay and Gisborne.

Sauvignon Blanc's strong grassy characters in New Zealand stem from the unusually high concentration in the grapes (three times higher than in Australia) of an organic compound that is much easier to drink than it is to pronounce – methoxypyrazine. The variety's penetrating, green capsicum-like flavours (well-ripened examples also display tropical fruit characters) are not necessarily flattered by oak, and in fact the majority of New Zealand Sauvignon Blancs are

fermented in stainless steel tanks, placing their accent squarely on their fresh, assertive varietal character.

Sometimes a minor part of the final blend (five to 10 per cent) is handled in oak, to add a subtle extra dimension. Only Sauvignon Blancs based on very ripe fruit with relatively non-herbaceous flavours and rounded acidity suit the degree of oak handling typically associated with Chardonnay.

Most Marlborough winemakers believe their Sauvignon Blancs drink best in their first 18 months, although the top wood-aged wines from the North Island can develop well for three years. However, provided you are prepared to accept the asparagus and canned peas characters that typically emerge after a couple of years in Marlborough Sauvignon Blanc, on the evidence of the tastings in this book, the wines can mature well for many years, replacing their youthful, vibrant fruit flavours with interesting limey, toasty characters.

sauvignon blanc

Cloudy Bay Sauvignon Blanc

SUPER CLASSIC

S ome of the classics featured in this book are rare, with an annual production of about 200 cases. Not Cloudy Bay Sauvignon Blanc. New Zealand's most internationally acclaimed wine is on sale around the world. Its production level of 40,000 cases is approximately double the total annual output of such wineries as Kumeu River and Collards.

A striking Marlborough wine that overflows with fresh, ripely herbaceous and zingy flavour, in the glass Cloudy Bay Sauvignon Blanc fully lives up to its illustrious reputation. Aromatic and zesty, with arresting flavour depth, it's irresistible in its youth, yet can also mature gracefully for up to a decade – even beyond.

Winemaker Kevin Judd seeks to produce Sauvignon Blanc having "a lively gooseberries and lychees – rather than green peas – fruit character and a touch of oak complexity. It should have intense varietal character, but not be too herbaceous, with succulent, juicy, tropical characters and fresh acidity."

Climate and vineyard management are the two key factors that explain the roaring success of Cloudy Bay Sauvignon Blanc, believes Judd. "Climate gives the flavours. By ripening the fruit in cool but dry, sunny conditions, we retain lots of varietal character. Here, it's not too hot or too cold." By managing the vines' irrigation systems to get well-balanced grapes, and using the Scott Henry (two-tier) trellising system and leaf-plucking to expose the ripening grapes to air movement and sunshine, in an average year Cloudy Bay can get the combination of tropical and herbaceous flavours it wants.

Sourced entirely from the Wairau Valley, the

grapes are grown in the company-owned vineyards encircling the winery in Jacksons Road and by other growers on long-term contracts. The vines yield an average crop of 3.5 to 4 tonnes per acre and are entirely machine-harvested. Most years, the blend includes five to 10 per cent Sémillon, but in Judd's view this has very little impact on the wine.

Little has changed over the years in the way the grapes are handled in the winery. Most of the juice is cool-fermented in stainless steel tanks with a neutral yeast. About five per cent barrel fermentation gives "a subliminal dimension, something extra, but it's hard to taste oak in the wine". The technique of giving the juice overnight skin contact was abandoned in 1989, after the Cloudy Bay winemakers concluded it was increasing the tannin in the wine without any gains.

As Cloudy Bay's founder, David Hohnen, has put it: "Our Sauvignon Blanc winemaking is modern babysitting. It's very different to making a Chardonnay, when you're *inducing* things like malolactic fermentation and yeast autolysis. By contrast, Sauvignon Blanc is early release; it's very straightforward, do-it-by-numbers winemaking to retain fruit characters."

When is the best time to drink New Zealand's most fashionable Sauvignon Blanc? If you love its exuberant fruit characters, open it at six to 18 months old. As Judd puts it: "When the new season's wine is released, it always looks better than the previous vintage." Yet the vertical tasting revealed that the wine can retain its freshness, intensity and vigour for many years, losing its initial explosiveness but softening and acquiring considerable complexity.

At $24, New Zealand's most famous wine is still affordably priced. Although not entered in local competitions (what would there be to gain?) it has been lauded in *Punch* as "New Zealand's finest export since Sir Richard Hadlee", and praised in Melbourne's *Sun Herald* as "like hearing Glenn Gould playing the Goldberg variations, or seeing Niki Lauda at full tilt".

Mouthfilling, with an arresting intensity of gooseberry and green capsicum-like flavours, a touch of complexity and a rich, trailing finish, Cloudy Bay Sauvignon Blanc is an exciting mouthful. That it has retained its stunning quality while being built into sufficient volumes to be exported around the world is the greatest achievement of Hohnen, Judd and the Cloudy Bay team.

tasting notes

These notes are from a vertical tasting of the 1985 to 1998 vintages, held at the winery in January 1999.

1998 ☆☆☆☆☆ Pale lemon/green. Lifted passionfruit and lime aromas. Notable weight and sweetness of fruit, reflecting the hot, dry season. Very ripe tropical/passionfruit flavours, enlivened by fresh acidity. Long. Rounder than usual, but very recognisably Cloudy Bay. **Drink 1999-2008.**

1997 ☆☆☆☆☆ Light lemon/green. Richly scented. Lively, with sweet-fruit delights and a touch of complexity. Classic vintage, well-structured and slightly flinty, with a very long finish. **Drink 1999-2007.**

1996 ☆☆☆☆☆ Light lemon/green. Classic – full and zingy, with rich, ripe flavours of gooseberries and limes. Slightly rounder than the 1997. Benchmark Cloudy Bay, with the intensity and structure to age well. **Drink 1999-2006.**

1995 ☆☆☆☆ Light lemon/green. A top 1995 – fresh, lively and incisive. Lighter, greener than the 1994, but no sign of rot characters from the exceptionally wet vintage. Quite good length. **Drink 1999-2001.**

1994 ☆☆☆☆☆ Light-medium yellow/green. Plump wine with sweet, ripe fruit, still very lively. Delicious now, with a touch of complexity and good acid spine. Ripe, rounded feel and a very persistent finish. Still in full flight. **Drink 1999-2004.**

1993 ☆☆☆☆ Light lemon/green. Lively, crisp, green-edged flavours with good vigour. High-acid year, but not too austere, with good complexity, structure and length. **Drink 1999-2001.**

1992 ☆☆☆ ⚬ Light-medium yellow. More herbaceous style, quite green-edged. Some canned peas character showing. Good acidity. Lacks a bit of richness. **Drink 1999-2000.**

1991 ☆☆☆☆☆ Light-medium yellow. A star vintage. Fresh and strong, with lively acid and considerable complexity. Good body and tremendous vigour for its age. A classic year, maturing superbly. **Drink 1999-2001.**

1990 ☆☆☆☆☆ Full yellow. Strong lime/toast aromas and flavours. Some Riesling characters (from a warm but frost-shortened season). Lovely firm structure, intensity and length. Real enjoyment and presence in the mouth. **Drink 1999-2000.**

1989 ☆☆☆☆ Full yellow/light gold. (Warm year.) Generous, mouthfilling wine with toasty bottle-aged characters coupled with sweet, ripe fruit. High-flavoured, but slightly lacks finesse, and drying out on the finish. **Drink 1999.**

1988 ☆☆☆ Deep gold. (*Botrytis*-affected year – cyclone Bola.) Toasty, very mature nose and palate. Fruit dried out. Losing its varietal character. **Drink ASAP.**

1987 ☆☆☆☆ Two bottles opened. (1) Very toasty, crisp and lean, but with good flavour depth. More developed than the 1986, less vibrantly fruity, but still enjoyable. (2) Slightly fresher and more attractive than the first bottle, with good zip and length. **Drink 1999.**

1986 ☆☆☆☆☆ Medium-full yellow/green. Richly flavoured, still crisp and lively, with clearly herbaceous, toasty characters. Sweet, ripe fruit. Weighty and long. Maturing superbly. **Drink 1999-2000.**

1985 ☆☆☆☆ ⚬ Looked good five years ago, but now very tired. Full yellow/light gold. Toasty and very "peasy", developed flavours. Firm acid. Two bottles opened, of varying vigour. **Drink ASAP.**

Goldwater Dog Point Marlborough Sauvignon Blanc

POTENTIAL CLASSIC

The name Goldwater is indivisibly linked in most New Zealanders' minds with Waiheke Island's first great red. Yet Goldwater's white-wine production far outstrips its reds. Only 500 to 1000 cases of the famous Cabernet Sauvignon/Merlot are made each year, whereas in 1999 the Goldwaters made over 17,000 cases of their outstanding Marlborough Sauvignon Blanc.

Why is a long-established Waiheke Island winery, acclaimed for its red wine, producing a Marlborough Sauvignon Blanc? Kim and Jeanette Goldwater found that you can't make a decent living from an output of less than 1000 cases per year of red wine, even if you can sell it at $50 per bottle. And Goldwaters' overseas agents were crying out for a Marlborough Sauvignon Blanc.

Kim Goldwater makes a powerful, rich Waiheke red – and his preference for bold, deeply flavoured wine is clearly evident in the Dog Point Marlborough Sauvignon Blanc. "I want balance, first and foremost," he says, "together with structure, finesse and concentration. I don't want herbaceous characters at all. I want the sort of wine where you wouldn't switch away from it and say: 'I'd rather have a Chardonnay.' "

Goldwater Dog Point Sauvignon Blanc is a notably weighty wine, very powerful and ripe, with concentrated tropical fruit flavours, balanced acidity and a long, rich finish. It's a distinctive style – much bigger, riper and rounder than most of the region's Sauvignon Blancs, yet still very fresh and lively.

Up to and including the 1992 vintage, the Goldwaters made a Sauvignon Blanc Fumé using Waiheke fruit, but the island's warm climate produced a robust dry white with subdued varietal character. The first Marlborough wine flowed in 1995.

The grapes are grown principally in the Dog Point vineyard at Brancott, owned by Ivan Sutherland, who is also the full-time viticulturist for Cloudy Bay. In a block Sutherland planted specifically for the Goldwaters, the vines are trained on the two-tier Scott Henry system, shoot-thinned and leaf-plucked by hand. Crops are kept to a maximum of 3.5 tonnes per acre, and the grapes are harvested mechanically at a very high brix level – typically 23 to 23.5 brix. Since 1998, grapes have also been drawn from David Rose's vineyard in St Leonard's Road, in the heart of the Wairau Valley.

The wine is made to Kim Goldwater's specifications at the Rapaura Vintners contract facility in Marlborough. Most of the final blend is cool-fermented with neutral yeasts in stainless steel tanks, and matured on its gross lees "to add to the wine's body and mouthfeel". A minor proportion (five to 10 per cent) is fermented and lees-aged in seasoned oak casks.

The biggest market for Goldwater Dog Point Sauvignon Blanc is the eastern seaboard of the

United States where, Kim Goldwater enthuses, its "fruit concentration and acidity blow them away". The *Wine Spectator* recently gave the 1998 vintage 90 points out of 100. Michael Franz, of the *Washington Post*, praised the 1996 as "one of the half-dozen greatest Sauvignons I've ever tasted, with an uncanny combination of broad, generous fruit and laser-sharp focus."

Many Marlborough Sauvignon Blancs are medium-bodied, with crisp, grassy, strongly herbaceous flavours. The Goldwater bears little resemblance to those wines. Bold and weighty, with a striking intensity of ripe, pineapple and passionfruit-like flavour, enlivened with fresh acidity, Goldwater Dog Point is an exceptionally power-packed Sauvignon Blanc – the sort that would even force a diehard Chardonnay fan to sit up and pay attention. ￼

Based on Waiheke Island (above), Goldwater Estate produces a memorable Marlborough Sauvignon Blanc.

tasting notes

These notes are from a vertical tasting of the 1996 to 1998 vintages, held at the winery in April 1999.

1998 ☆☆☆☆☆ Light lemon/green. Richly scented and robust (14 per cent alcohol), with intense, superbly ripe tropical fruit flavours, fresh and lively. Notably weighty, with lovely concentration of flavour and a distinct touch of oak/lees complexity. One of the top 1998s. **Drink 1999-2001.**

1997 ☆☆☆☆☆ Light lemon/green. Maturing bouquet. Big, tropical fruit style with very sweet-tasting, pineappley-ripe fruit characters. Powerful (over 14 per cent alcohol), with impressive depth right through the palate and a long, rounding finish. **Drink 1999-2000.**

1996 ☆☆☆☆☆ Light-medium yellow. Big, fleshy, pineappley wine with balanced acidity. Weighty and succulent, with loads of flavour, developing toasty, honied characters with age. Ready. **Drink 1999.**

1995 Not tasted.

MARLBOROUGH
SAUVIGNON BLANC
1998

PRODUCED AND BOTTLED BY   750ML   ALCOHOL BY VOLUME 13.5%
GROVE MILL WINE COMPANY LIMITED, WAIHOPAI VALLEY ROAD, MARLBOROUGH, NEW ZEALAND.

Grove Mill Marlborough Sauvignon Blanc

CLASSIC

With a shower of awards around the world in the past three years, this label has emerged as a regional classic. When Grove Mill Marlborough Sauvignon Blanc 1996 scooped the trophy for champion wine of the 1997 Liquorland Royal Easter Wine Show, it was the first time in New Zealand that a Sauvignon Blanc had been chosen as the champion wine of a competition.

Deliciously weighty and richly flavoured, the wine is typically intensely aromatic, with deep gooseberry/capsicum flavours, power right through the palate and a very rich, sustained finish. The 1996 and subsequent vintages have been especially memorable.

For winemaker David Pearce, the style of the wine is basically set by its varietal and regional characteristics. "On top of that comes the way I like wine, with a degree of opulence, in terms of ripe fruit and weight."

Pearce delights in each year producing a markedly different Sauvignon Blanc. "I want to maximise the individuality of each vintage. You get some style continuity from having the same vineyards, equipment and winemaker, but I don't care about variations in acidity or alcohol. For example, when we're blending the new season's Sauvignon Blanc, you'll never see the previous year's wine on the bench, because it has nothing to do with the new wine."

The cool 1997 vintage yielded fruit with intense herbal characters. "It wasn't opulent, so you couldn't build in too much other stuff like oak or malolactic fermentation, to bulk it up in terms of fatness. It was better to preserve its beautiful, finely structured fruit

Grove Mill Sauvignon Blanc is attracting strong international acclaim.

by being light-handed and not competing with its clear, crisp flavours."

The 1998 vintage was the opposite – a very ripe year in which the grapes developed lots of flavour, muscle and weight. "So we leaf-plucked one side of the row, rather than both, to achieve ripeness but preserve some herbaceous characters. And when setting the harvest date, we put less emphasis on brix [sugar] levels, and more on pH and acid."

The grapes are drawn from eight vineyards scattered across the Wairau Valley, mostly not company-owned but on long-term supply contracts. This spread of vineyard sites reduces the risks of frost and hail damage, and contributes a variety of flavours to the blend, which in most years includes minor proportions of Sémillon and (unusually) Chardonnay – which adds "ripeness and weight". Yields average four to five tonnes per acre, and the grapes are machine-harvested.

The ferment is long and cool – up to six weeks at 10 to 14°C. The wine spends a couple of days in oak during the ferment, although Pearce acknowledges he isn't quite sure what that achieves. "And since 1995 there's always been a component, around 20 per cent, put through malolactic fermentation. No one ever picks it. It's not used to modify acidity, but to improve the wine's complexity and texture."

With an annual output of around 18,000 cases, Grove Mill Marlborough Sauvignon Blanc is well known overseas – more is exported than sold in New Zealand (where it retails at around $17). Pearce recommends drinking the wine at between 18 months and two and a half years old, but "depending on the quality of the season, it can mature well for six years". The vertical tasting (below) suggests the wine varies in terms of its longevity, but top vintages can hold well for at least eight years.

The 1996 vintage was the first to win a gold medal in New Zealand, but previous vintages of Grove Mill Marlborough Sauvignon Blanc had won high awards overseas. Pearce is especially delighted by the gold medal awarded to the 1998 vintage at the 1999 Sydney International Wine Competition: "It's our third Sauvignon Blanc gold medal in a row at that show."

Concentrated, rich and lush, Grove Mill is a strikingly powerful Sauvignon Blanc, opulent and weighty, with huge drinkability. Since the 1996 vintage, it has emerged as one of Marlborough's – and New Zealand's – most outstanding Sauvignon Blancs.

tasting notes

These notes are from a vertical tasting of the 1990 to 1998 vintages, held at the winery in January 1999.

1998 ☆☆☆☆☆ Pale lemon/green. Fresh, limey nose. Very powerful and weighty (13.5 per cent alcohol), yet also has plenty of vigour. Magnificent now, with very intense melon/lime flavours, fresh, zesty and long. A top vintage, perhaps the best of all. **Drink 1999-2005.**

1997 ☆☆☆☆☆ Pale lemon/green. Lovely, very intense fruit characters. Classic, deep, freshly herbaceous flavours, beautifully balanced, lively and long. Drier and more understated than the 1996, but should be longer lived. **Drink 1999-2003.**

1996 ☆☆☆☆☆ Bright, light lemon/green. Bold, lush, rich palate, deliciously concentrated. A sliver of sweetness (5 grams per litre) adds to the overall impact, balanced by firm underlying acidity. Very punchy and powerful wine, but more advanced than the 1997. **Drink 1999-2001.**

1995 ☆☆☆☆ Light lemon/green. Lighter style (11 per cent alcohol) but still fresh, clean and crisp, with good persistence. Limey, flinty. From a bad year, surprisingly good. **Drink 1999-2000.**

1994 ☆☆☆☆☆ Light lemon/green. The most powerful and beautifully focused of the older wines, with a strong surge of tropical/capsicum flavours, appetising acidity and a rich, rounded finish. Highly scented, with excellent weight, intensity and softness. **Drink 1999-2000.**

1993 ☆☆☆☆ Medium yellow. Bouquet of honey and hay. Moderately ripe, with gooseberry and green capsicum characters, a touch of honey and high acidity. Slightly hollow, but still flavoursome and lively. **Drink 1999.**

1992 ☆☆☆☆ Bright, light yellow/green. Mature, canned peas aromas. Full, soft and strongly herbal. Good mouthfeel. Clearly a cooler year. Smooth, fractionally sweet finish. **Drink 1999.**

1991 ☆☆☆☆ ☆ ("Beatrice Estate") Bright, light yellow/green. Scented, ripe, slightly honied bouquet. Bigger, lusher than the 1990, with deep gooseberry/capsicum flavours, lively acidity and excellent mouthfeel. Lots of vigour and pleasure here. **Drink 1999-2000.**

1990 ☆☆☆☆ ☆ ("Oak Aged") Light-medium yellow/green. Attractive, well-rounded wine with melon and capsicum flavours and no "canned peas". Non-aggressive, with good but not great intensity. **Drink 1999.**

1998
SAUVIGNON BLANC

Marlborough

℮750ml.   PRODUCED AND BOTTLED BY HUNTER'S
WINES, RAPAURA ROAD, BLENHEIM.   13.0% alc/vol.
PRODUCE OF NEW ZEALAND.

Hunter's Marlborough Sauvignon Blanc

SUPER CLASSIC

In the crowded field of Marlborough Sauvignon Blancs, Hunter's stands alongside Cloudy Bay as one of the aristocrats, with a record of consistent excellence stretching back to the mid 1980s. With its "leap-out-of-the-glass" aromas and rich, vibrant flavours threaded with racy acidity, Hunter's Marlborough Sauvignon Blanc is an impeccable wine with great elegance and verve.

Hunter's owner, Jane Hunter, aims for a "classic Marlborough Sauvignon Blanc", but the wine's style has still changed over the years. "We've gone from a one-dimensional, grassy wine to a more complex style. In the early 1990s we went to a ripe, lush style, but we're now back to a complex style in which we keep the characters people expect in a classic Marlborough Sauvignon Blanc, but make it more multi-dimensional."

Dr Tony Jordan, an eminent Australian oenologist, has been a consultant to Hunter's since the 1986 vintage. "We want a strong expression of Marlborough fruit – a bell-clear wine with a mix of tropical and searing gooseberry characters." By sourcing fruit from a range of vineyards, picking at different levels of ripeness and keeping crop levels down to below four tonnes per acre, he also aims to achieve "mid-palate generosity".

Jane Hunter sees blending as a crucial ingredient in Hunter's Sauvignon Blanc recipe. The grapes are sourced from eight vineyards (seven in the Wairau Valley, one in the Awatere Valley), of which some are planted in stony sites, and others in non-irrigated, heavier soils. "This gives complexity," says Jane. "For example, in 1998, a hot year, we had two vineyards that didn't go beyond grassy herbaceous characters,

with highish acidity, whereas some of the others were super-ripe. The trick is the final percentage of each."

Top Sauvignon Blanc needs a lot of effort in the vineyard; the vines grow luxuriantly and must be tamed. Extensive shoot-thinning and leaf-plucking (55 per cent of the leaves are removed by hand) assists fruit ripening, by allowing better light penetration into the canopy and reducing the disease risk.

Deciding when to harvest is vital. "We're out most days during the vintage, Gary [winemaker Gary Duke] and I," says Jane. "We eat Sauvignon Blanc grapes, talk about their flavours – and walk miles."

Selection is another key part of the production process. Not all of the grapes harvested are kept - in lesser years a lot of the fruit is sold to other companies. The grapes from each vineyard are also fermented in separate batches, to give the winemakers the opportunity for a further selection at the blending stage.

To retain their fresh, vibrant characters, the grapes are processed quickly, with protective anaerobic techniques and minimal handling. The fruit is machine-harvested in the cool of the morning, then gently destemmed, crushed and pressed. After cold-settling and filtering, the juice is cool-fermented in stainless steel tanks for about four weeks, to maximise the retention of its aroma and flavour constituents. Tony Jordan reports "playing around with a bit of malolactic fermentation and lees-aging in tank, but it's nothing like Chardonnay."

With an annual production of around 10,000 cases, Hunter's Marlborough Sauvignon Blanc ($18) is widely available in New Zealand and overseas. Jane recommends consuming the wine within two years. "We can release it in New Zealand in September, but in the UK and Australia our agents prefer to hold it back until after Christmas, to soften it." Although at its most explosive and invigorating best in its first couple of years, like other top Sauvignon Blancs it can live for a decade, gradually softening and mellowing.

The gold medal awarded the 1998 vintage of Hunter's Marlborough Sauvignon Blanc at that year's Air New Zealand Wine Awards was the latest in a long list of top awards for the label. The 1989 vintage placed first in a *Decanter* magazine tasting of about 130 New World Sauvignon Blancs, and the 1991 won the Marquis de Goulaine Trophy for top Sauvignon Blanc at the International Wine and Spirit Competition in London.

Despite the challenges from the multitude of newer Marlborough labels, Hunter's remains at the top of the Sauvignon Blanc tree. It can be breathtakingly intense, yet also show great delicacy and finesse. With its consistently outstanding quality and lengthy pedigree, Hunter's Marlborough Sauvignon Blanc must be ranked among the country's greatest white wines.

tasting notes

These notes are from a vertical tasting of the 1985 to 1998 vintages, held at the winery in January 1999.

1998 ☆☆☆☆☆ Pale, green-tinged. Weighty yet gentle wine, with deliciously intense flavours of melon, passionfruit and capsicum and fresh, lively acidity. A ripe style with less "attack" than in a cooler vintage, but retains vigour. Still clearly Marlborough, and Hunter's. **Drink 1999-2005.**

1997 ☆☆☆☆☆ Pale, green-tinged. Fresh, lifted passionfruit/lime aromas. Classic Hunter's – sweet, ripe fruit flavours with a lime/capsicum edge. Deliciously fresh and crisp, and intensely varietal. **Drink 1999-2004.**

1996 ☆☆☆☆☆ Light lemon/green. Tight, poised wine with deep tropical/capsicum characters. Beautiful freshness, balance and vivacity. Aristocratic, slightly flinty wine with some complexity, still evolving. **Drink 1999-2003.**

1995 ☆☆☆☆ Light lemon/green. Tight. Less ripe and rich than the 1994. Flinty, distinctly green and slightly austere. Clean and fresh, but lacks ripe fruit characters. **Drink 1999-2000.**

1994 ☆☆☆☆☆ Light-medium lemon/green. Very clean, fresh nose. Lush, ripe and still very lively, with delicious depth of ripely herbaceous flavour, enlivened with fresh acidity. A classic vintage, still in full stride – complex, persistent, beautiful. **Drink 1999-2001.**

1993 ☆☆☆☆ Medium yellow. Scented bouquet, showing distinct *Botrytis* characters. Slightly honied palate, with good weight and flavour concentration. Still lively and enjoyable drinking. **Drink 1999.**

1992 ☆ Gold, with a hint of brown. Oxidised nose and palate. Gone. Looked excellent in its youth. Bad bottle?

1991 ☆☆☆☆ Light-medium yellow/green. Grassy, herbaceous bouquet, still fresh. Crisp and lively, in a high-acid, flinty style. Verdant, asparagus-like flavours, incisive and intensely varietal, although less ripe than in the more recent vintages. Could be very long-lived. **Drink 1999-2000.**

1990 ☆☆☆☆ (First two bottles corked.) Medium yellow, with green tints. Slightly austere, with canned peas flavours and a dry, flinty finish. Slightly hollow – lacks a bit of fruit sweetness – but still alive. **Drink 1999.**

1989 ☆☆☆☆☆ Medium yellow. Fairly subdued but clean bouquet. Mouthfilling, ripely flavoured style with good intensity and a long, tight finish. Much richer than the older vintages, and still vigorous, with a touch of mature "canned peas" character which doesn't dominate. **Drink 1999.**

1988 ☆☆☆☆ Medium-full yellow/green. Toasty, lively bouquet. Bigger wine than the 1986 or 1987, crisp and full-bodied, with strong lemon, lime and grass flavours. Zesty and holding its freshness. Excellent now. **Drink 1999.**

1987 ☆☆☆ Deep gold – more developed than 1985 or 1986. Dull nose. Oxidised. Slightly honied. Past it. **Drink ASAP.**

1986 ☆☆☆☆ Full yellow, slightly green. Citrus and lime flavours, with distinct overtones of Riesling, but also clearly herbaceous. Medium-full body, with quite good depth of crisp, lively flavour, but not intense. **Drink 1999.**

1985 ☆☆☆☆ Full yellow/light gold with a slight green tint. Clearly herbaceous nose – asparagus and peas. Still alive, but very rounded. Medium-full body, with a sliver of sweetness on the finish. Not hugely concentrated, but can still be drunk with pleasure. **Drink 1999.**

1997

SAUVIGNON BLANC
{OAK AGED}

Marlborough

℮750ml.   Produced and bottled by Hunter's   13.0% alc/vol.
           Wines, Rapaura Road, Blenheim
           Produce of New Zealand

Hunter's Sauvignon Blanc Oak Aged

SUPER CLASSIC

Equally distinguished, but rarer than its non-wooded stablemate, Hunter's Marlborough Sauvignon Blanc, this slightly higher-priced wine adds a subtle twist of oak to very ripe, less herbaceous fruit characters. The smoky vanillin characters add complexity to the wine, without overwhelming its pure, deep, incisive fruit flavours.

Length of flavour, rather than an "upfront hit of Sauvignon Blanc", is the style goal. "The barrel fermentation and oak-aging help achieve that," says Hunter's marketing manager, Peter MacDonald. "It's still a fairly upfront style, but the oak adds subtlety, rather than intensity."

The firm's ripest Sauvignon Blanc grapes, possessing tropical fruit rather than pungently herbaceous flavours, provide the basis of the wine.

Grown usually in the early-ripening estate vineyard in Rapaura Road, adjacent to the winery, the grapes must be "varietal but riper than usual", says Dr Tony Jordan, a leading Australian oenologist who acts as a consultant to Hunter's. "The advanced ripeness gives the wine weight, which works better with oak."

For the Hunter's style, the wood mustn't be overt. Part of the blend is handled entirely in stainless steel tanks; another portion is barrel-fermented; another is

The Hunter's team: winemaker Gary Duke, marketing manager Peter MacDonald and Jane Hunter.

tank-fermented but barrel-aged. "If anyone describes the wine as oaky, I think: 'We've made a mistake'," says Jordan.

The grapes are machine-harvested, crushed and gently pressed, and the juice is fermented with a neutral yeast. Forty per cent is fermented in new and one-year-old, medium-toast French oak barriques, and then matured on its yeast lees for nine months, with some lees-stirring. The majority of the tank-fermented component is matured for about eight months in one and two-year-old casks, while a portion is kept in stainless steel to give freshness to the final blend.

Jane Hunter believes that the style of the Sauvignon Blanc Oak Aged has changed more over the years than its unwooded stablemate. "It's softer and richer. We used to hold it back longer, for eight months after bottling, because the wood character tended to be overpowering, but now with really ripe fruit, we can release it within three months of bottling." The gradual refinement of picking dates and oak types, and the introduction of *bâtonnage*

(lees stirring) and a small proportion of malolactic fermentation, have all contributed to a softer, more complex style.

Only 1000 to 2500 cases of the Sauvignon Blanc Oak Aged are made each year, retailing at around $22. A wine that benefits from bottle age, it drinks at its best at between one and three years old, but top vintages can mature gracefully for many years.

Hunter's Sauvignon Blanc Oak Aged is a finely crafted wine, with rich, clearly varietal but not aggressive fruit flavours gently seasoned with oak. An attractive balance between the fruit and wood can be hard to achieve, given the natural assertiveness of Marlborough grapes but, from one vintage to the next, Hunter's get it right.

Over the years, the wine has won many accolades. The most memorable success came at the 1986 *Sunday Times* Wine Club Festival in London, when the public voted Hunter's 1985 Fumé Blanc (as the Sauvignon Blanc Oak Aged was originally called) the most popular wine of the show. 🍂

tasting notes

These notes are mainly from a vertical tasting of the 1986 to 1997 vintages, held at the winery in January 1999. The 1998 vintage was tasted in Auckland in April 1999.

1998 ☆☆☆☆¾ Pale lemon/green. Very ripe, fresh bouquet. Weighty and rounded, with soft tropical fruit flavours, a touch of toasty oak and a lively, long finish. Forward, fleshy, flavoursome wine, very non-herbaceous. **Drink 2000-2003.**

1997 ☆☆☆☆☆ Pale lemon/green. Powerful wine, with intense fruit and a stronger oak influence than in past vintages. Sweet, well-ripened tropical fruit/passionfruit characters, seasoned with spicy oak. Full, rounded and lovely now. **Drink 1999-2004.**

1996 ☆☆☆☆☆ Light lemon/green. Full body, sweet fruit flavours and subtle wood. Tropical/passionfruit characters, still very fresh, with richness right through the palate and a slightly creamy texture. **Drink 1999-2003.**

1995 Not made.

1994 ☆☆☆☆☆ Yellow/green, medium depth. A classic vintage, weighty, ripe and non-aggresssive, in a very elegant style. Deep tropical/capsicum flavours, still very lively, fleshed out with spicy oak. Very satisfying now – complex and harmonious. **Drink 1999-2002.**

1993 ☆☆☆ Deep yellow/light gold. Grassy, toasty bouquet and flavours, showing lots of bottle-age development. Lacks lush, ripe fruit. Very herbaceous style, with firm acidity. Lacks charm. **Drink 1999.**

1992 ☆☆☆☆¾ Medium-full yellow. Mature, strongly herbaceous, canned peas aromas. Rounded and high flavoured, with incisive melon/capsicum characters and restrained toasty oak. Enjoyable now, although less ripe than the 1991. **Drink 1999-2000.**

1991 ☆☆☆☆☆ Full, bright yellow. Generous, mouthfilling and ripe, with rich tropical fruit and spicy oak flavours, very integrated and smooth. Powerful, slightly creamy finish. Still in great condition. **Drink 1999-2000.**

1990 ☆☆☆☆ Bright, full yellow. Full and rounded, with good but not outstanding depth. Ripe flavours with subtle oak. Moderately herbaceous, elegant wine with a tight finish. **Drink 1999.**

1989 ☆☆☆☆☆ Full yellow, slightly green-tinged. Weighty, generous and concentrated. Tremendous wine for 10 years old, with deep, ripe tropical/capsicum flavours and harmonious oak. Still vigorous, with a rich, resounding finish. **Drink 1999.**

1986 ☆☆☆☆ (Fumé Blanc) Full yellow/slightly green. Fascinating museum piece, with grassy, strongly herbaceous flavours, overlaid with toasty bottle-aged characters. Drying out, but still moderately enjoyable. **Drink ASAP.**

Jackson Estate Sauvignon Blanc

CLASSIC

R ich, ripe and rounded – that's the distinctive style of this Marlborough beauty. It's typically a delicious wine, highly scented, with impressive depth of ripe, tropical fruit characters in a generous, wonderfully easy-drinking style with lots of class.

Proprietor John Stichbury say he aims for a "traditional Marlborough style of Sauvignon Blanc – meaning simple, direct, but clean and ripe fruit flavours, with not too many bells and whistles. We're not trying to reproduce a European style – there's no oak – but achieving advanced fruit ripeness makes us successful."

Stichbury is emphatic about where the wine's quality springs from. "You can't copy the climate. But the vineyard management is also critical." The vines are cultivated in heavy, moisture-retaining soils in the heart of the Wairau Valley, where Stichbury admits that vine vigour can be a challenge. The only surface stones are those Stichbury has carried in his pockets to throw to the dogs over the years. "So we don't irrigate the vines; we use Scott Henry trellising and leaf-plucking to open up the canopy, maximise the grapes' exposure to the sun and reduce disease; and we fruit-thin to ensure a light crop."

Jackson Estate is a vineyard; not a winery. The grapes are mechanically harvested in the cool of evening and processed at a local contract winemaking facility, Rapaura Vintners, by consultant winemaker, Martin Shaw, an Australian based in Adelaide, where he has his own company, Shaw and Smith. Three times each year – pre-harvest, during vintage and at blending – Shaw visits Marlborough to make the key winemaking decisions.

"I'm not a winemaker or a wine connoisseur," admits Stichbury, who has a background in mechanical engineering. "But with our vineyard manager, Geoff Woollcombe [who has worked for Jackson Estate since he planted the first vines in 1988] and Martin, we've got two highly experienced people in the key production roles."

Jackson Estate Marlborough Sauvignon Blanc ($17) is produced in large volumes (13,500 cases in 1998) and is well known in export markets. Stichbury recommends drinking the wine from one year old onwards: "It often gets a silver medal at the Air New Zealand Wine Awards in October/November, followed by a gold at the Liquorland Royal Easter Wine Show in March." Its most memorable show triumph came when the 1992 vintage won the trophy for best Sauvignon Blanc at the 1993 International Wine Challenge in London.

Jackson Estate Marlborough Sauvignon Blanc is a notably ripe-flavoured style, fragrant, vibrantly fruity and zingy, with lovely concentration and vigour. A distinctive wine, it's seductively rich, lush and soft – and of all the region's Sauvignon Blancs, one of the hardest to resist. 🍇

Jackson Estate owner John Stichbury and his partner, Joe Bailey.

tasting notes

These notes are from a vertical tasting of the 1991 to 1998 vintages, held at the winery in January 1999.

1998 ☆☆☆☆✧ Pale lemon/green. Fresh, very ripe fruit aromas. Very weighty and rounded, with strong flavours of passionfruit and limes and fresh acidity. Slightly less intense than the 1997, but still highly attractive, with very sweet fruit characters and good mouthfeel. **Drink 1999-2003.**

1997 ☆☆☆☆☆ Pale lemon/green. Big wine with an abundance of very ripe, passionfruit-like flavours and an undercurrent of fresh, herbaceous characters. Still youthful, with sweet-fruit delights in a weighty, rounded style. **Drink 1999-2002.**

1996 ☆☆☆☆☆ Light lemon/green. Absolutely classic – full, juicy and vibrant, with rich passionfruit/lime flavours and fresh acidity. Concentrated, beautifully focused wine, lovely now, with explosive fruit characters and a very powerful finish. **Drink 1999-2002.**

1995 ☆☆☆ Light lemon/green. A leaner and greener model than usual, lacking its customary lush fruit characters. Hint of honey. Very solid, with a high-acid finish. **Drink 1999-2000.**

1994 ☆☆☆☆✧ Medium yellow. Ripe, pineapple and passionfruit characters on nose and palate, with an overlay of toasty bottle-aged characters. Big, ripe style, with firm acidity. Characterful wine. No rush. **Drink 1999-2000.**

1993 ☆☆☆✧ Medium yellow. Mature, slightly honied bouquet. Less-ripe style, with good depth of flinty, honeyish flavour. Still reasonably lively, but starting to lose its fruit. **Drink 1999.**

1992 ☆☆☆☆ Light yellow/green. Grassy/capsicum aromas. Fresh, herbaceous and lemony. Distinctly green-edged but very lively, with cool vintage characters. Impressive flavour depth. **Drink 1999-2000.**

1991 ☆☆☆☆☆ Light-medium yellow. A special wine – great vigour, freshness and interest. Incisive gooseberry, capsicum and pineapple flavours. Rich, ripe, pungent wine, lush and penetrating. Maturing very gracefully. **Drink 1999.**

Kim Crawford Marlborough Sauvignon Blanc

POTENTIAL CLASSIC

Kim Crawford first carved out a high profile in his several roles as winemaker at Coopers Creek and consultant winemaker for Cairnbrae and Saint Clair in Marlborough. The first person to win the Liquorland Royal Easter Wine Show's trophy for winemaker of the year two years in a row, in 1996 he launched his own personalised label – Kim Crawford. The 1998 mislabelling scandal at Coopers Creek embroiled Crawford in controversy, but the initial vintages of his Marlborough Sauvignon Blanc show tremendous depth of character and the high impact style that is classic Crawford.

Crawford goes for a bold, punchy style of Marlborough Sauvignon Blanc – and hits the target with ease. "Most of the wine is sent overseas, especially to the UK, where they prefer a clearly herbal style. But we don't want the grassiness typical of the early 1990s. We get herbal notes, but not cut-grass."

Kim Crawford's use of his own name as his brand is a common practice in Australia, but a relatively new development in New Zealand. His move, says Crawford, reflects "growing recognition of the winemaker's commitment to excellence as a crucial factor in making quality wine."

Raised in Matamata, Crawford graduated from Massey University in 1983 with a degree in microbiology and botany. Armed with a graduate diploma in winemaking from Roseworthy Agricultural College in South Australia, he worked briefly as a cellarhand at Arrowfield Wines in the upper Hunter Valley of New South Wales, then spent six months as assistant winemaker at Stags' Leap Winery in California's Napa Valley. After a one-year stint at Backsberg Estate in Paarl, South Africa, in 1989 Crawford took over as winemaker at Coopers Creek, where he stayed until 1998.

Crawford aims for wines "with distinctive characters and a natural, uncluttered taste. In my view, New Zealand wines benefit from a natural fruitiness and really don't need vast quantities of additives to improve their taste. With every wine I make, I aim to let the natural flavour of the grape flow through into the final product."

The foundation of Kim Crawford Marlborough Sauvignon Blanc is the fruit grown by Neal Ibbotson, proprietor of Saint Clair, who owns a spread of vineyards in the Wairau and Awatere valleys. "That gives us a lot of blending options," says Crawford. "For example, the 1998s from the individual sites looked a bit simple separately, but when we put them together ..." The wine is processed to the juice or finished wine stage at various Marlborough wineries by Matt Thomson, an ex-Vintech (now Rapaura Vintners) winemaker who is now Crawford's partner in a consultancy

Kim Crawford makes a strikingly full-flavoured Sauvignon Blanc.

business, Kiwi Oeno.

The grapes are machine-harvested, mainly in the cool of night (sometimes at 2 am) and processed immediately. After cold settling, the juice is inoculated with a pure yeast culture selected for its production of aromatic compounds, and the ensuing fermentation is long and slow, to preserve maximum varietal character. Bottling is early, to retain the wine's youthful vitality.

With 10,000 cases produced in 1998, the wine is widely available in the UK, and retails in New Zealand at around $17. Crawford suggests drinking it "before Christmas [in the year of the vintage] or at five years old".

The 1997 vintage won major awards ("about three golds, I think," says Crawford) and the 1998 won a gold medal at that year's International Wine Challenge in London. In a blind tasting, Crawford's Marlborough Sauvignon Blanc stands out for its sheer explosiveness – a notably bold, super-ripe style with a delicious surge of fresh, crisp tropical/capsicum flavours and exceptional overall intensity. This is a classic new label on the rise. 🍷

tasting notes

These notes are from a vertical tasting of the 1996 to 1998 vintages, held in Auckland in November 1998.

1998 ☆☆☆☆☆ Light lemon/green. Fresh, ripe aromas. Big, juicy wine with very sweet fruit characters. Delicious, powerful wine with great mouthfeel. Strong tropical fruit flavours and soft acidity in a concentrated, rounded, hugely drinkable style. **Drink 1999-2003.**

1997 ☆☆☆☆☆ Light lemon/green. Broad, mouthfilling wine with tropical fruit and capsicum flavours and a very rich, powerful finish. Fleshy, with sweet fruit characters. More forward than the 1996, with more restrained fruit aromas (reflecting a small degree of malolactic fermentation). Rounded. **Drink 1999-2001.**

1996 ☆☆☆☆☆ Light lemon/green. Rich, ripely herbaceous bouquet. Still very fresh and lively, with deep melon/capsicum flavours and a flinty, fairly high-acid finish. Should be very long-lived. **Drink 1999-2001.**

Kumeu River Sauvignon Blanc

CLASSIC

Aworld apart from the briskly herbaceous Sauvignon Blancs of Marlborough, this Kumeu River label has proved Sauvignon Blanc's ability in Auckland to yield stylish, rather than strident, wine. A distinctive wine, weighty and subtle, with oak/lees-aging complexity and lush, tropical and stone-fruit flavours, rounded and long, it clearly reflects winemaker Michael Brajkovich's fondness for French wine styles.

"The original influence was white Graves," says marketing manager Paul Brajkovich. "That meant whole-bunch pressing and barrel fermentation, and malolactic fermentation to reduce what Michael sometimes calls the 'wickedly high' acidity in New Zealand Sauvignon Blanc."

The wine itself has remained highly consistent in style over the years, but its name has not. The debut 1986 vintage was labelled Sauvignon Fumé, which caused problems in Europe due to its similarity to Pouilly Fumé (a classic Sauvignon Blanc of the Upper Loire). The *Botrytis*-affected 1987 and 1988 vintages were labelled Sauvignon Noble Dry. From 1989 to 1992, the wine was simply called Sauvignon (as the French usually refer to Sauvignon Blanc); then Sauvignon/Sémillon from 1993 to 1996. In 1997, the Brajkoviches finally gave in to their US agent's urgings to put the word "Blanc" on the label.

The Sauvignon Blanc grapes are all grown on the top of the hill, across the road from the winery, in the company's HH3 (Hunter's Hill Block 3) vineyard. The wine also has a tiny amount of Sémillon, drawn from Kumeu River's company-owned vineyard in Waitakere Road.

The U-trellis system used by Kumeu River, which divides the vines' canopies horizontally (rather than vertically like Scott Henry), is a significant factor in the Sauvignon Blanc's quality, believes Paul Brajkovich. "We grow all the grapes ourselves, which is important in terms of control," says Brajkovich, "and especially in cooler years, the U-trellis gives us richer flavours. Because we don't have dense canopies, we can get the flavours beyond the green, grassy style and achieve full ripeness."

The vineyard work is very "hands-on", with a 20-strong team plucking the leaves by hand during summer. The vines' shoots are mechanically trimmed, and all the Sauvignon Blanc vines are covered with nets to ward off birds. Yields are kept low, at 3 to 3.5 tonnes per acre, and the grapes are all harvested by hand.

Winemaker Michael Brajkovich wants a "fuller" style of Sauvignon Blanc than most New Zealand examples, "with sufficient body and complexity to be able to mature in the bottle". Extracted gently by whole-bunch pressing, the juice is cold-settled for six hours and then racked to barrels, where it is fermented entirely with indigenous yeasts. Mainly older French oak barriques are used, with no more than five per cent new oak. The wine is given a full, softening malolactic fermentation and barrel-aged on its yeast lees, with regular stirring, for about 10 months.

Only about 1000 to 1200 cases of Kumeu River Sauvignon Blanc ($22) are made each year. It's a serious, understated wine, rather than the leap-out-of-the-glass style that is widely popular. Paul Brajkovich recommends drinking it after one or two years, "when it still retains its freshness, but has settled down in the bottle." It matures gracefully and does not develop the asparagus characters commonly associated with bottle-aged Marlborough Sauvignon Blancs.

Kumeu River is one of New Zealand's most absorbing Sauvignon Blancs. Recognising that Auckland's warm climate was not ideal for making the zesty, intensely herbaceous Sauvignon Blancs that flow from Marlborough, the Brajkoviches have succeeding in producing a richer, more multi-faceted and subtle wine. A rare beast, it's a sort of thinking person's Sauvignon Blanc. 🍇

Michael Brajkovich makes a complex, rounded style of Sauvignon Blanc.

tasting notes

These notes are from a vertical tasting of the 1989 to 1998 vintages, held at the winery in March 1999.

1998 ☆☆☆☆☆ Pale lemon/green. Fresh, very ripe, non-herbaceous fig, quince and citrus fruit flavours, with a subtle oak seasoning. A complex style, mouthfilling, rounded and rich. Already delicious. **Drink 2000-02.**

1997 ☆☆☆☆ Light-medium yellow. Slightly herbaceous bouquet. Mouthfilling, with good depth of tropical fruit (pineapple) and oak flavours, and a touch of cooler-vintage grassiness. Fresh, lively and still developing. **Drink 1999-2000.**

1996 ☆☆☆☆☆ (Sauvignon/Sémillon) Light yellow. Lovely drinking now – smooth and deep. Deliciously harmonious and complex wine with tropical fruit characters, a herbal undercurrent, gentle oak and a hint of butterscotch. Seamless, complete wine with a rich finish. **Drink 1999-2000.**

1995 Not made.

1994 ☆☆☆☆⯪ (Sauvignon/Sémillon) Full yellow. Maturing, toasty, bottle-aged characters on nose and palate. Rich flavours of pineapples, oak and butterscotch, with a faint herbal edge. Just starting to dry out a bit on the finish, but still full of character. **Drink 1999.**

1993 ☆☆☆☆ (Sauvignon/Sémillon) Light gold. A markedly more austere style than usual, reflecting the relatively high (30 per cent) Sémillon content. Not very fragrant, but offers lots of grapefruit-like, flinty flavour, with a very dry feel. Tight and persistent. Should be long-lived. **Drink 1999-2000.**

1992 ☆☆☆☆☆ (Sauvignon) Bright, medium yellow. From a low-yielding, ripe year, a rich, concentrated wine, maturing well. Tropical and citrus flavours with some toasty bottle-aged characters. Plump, complex wine, deliciously integrated. Tasted from a magnum (which may have contributed to its impressive freshness and vigour). **Drink 1999-2000.**

1991 ☆☆☆☆ (Sauvignon) Less-ripe style, with a firm-acid finish. Less fruity than the 1992, but tight and complex, with slightly biscuity, tropical/citrus flavours. Good body and concentration, with a very dry feel. Ready. **Drink 1999.**

1990 Not tasted.

1989 ☆☆☆☆☆ (Sauvignon) Medium-full yellow. Maturing superbly. Intense, steely and still vibrantly fruity. Penetrating, slightly toasty, grapefruit and lime flavours and firm acid backbone. **Drink 1999-2000.**

Matua Valley Reserve Sauvignon Blanc

CLASSIC

After 13 vintages, it's never won a gold medal in New Zealand, yet Matua Valley's wine is clearly one of New Zealand's finest oak-aged Sauvignon Blancs. The Aussies appreciate the style more – the 1992, 1993 and 1994 vintages were all placed in the Top 100 at the Sydney International Wine Competition.

Labelled Matheson Reserve Sauvignon Blanc since the 1998 vintage, in the past the wine was usually estate-grown at Waimauku in West Auckland. Since 1998, the grapes have been drawn from the Maraekakaho district of Hawke's Bay, where Matua Valley finds it can achieve earlier ripening and superior fruit flavours in the comparatively low fertility, "red metal" soils.

At its best, this is a beautifully harmonious and subtle wine in the white Bordeaux mould, with good body and excellent depth of fresh, ripe passionfruit and melon-like flavours, lightly seasoned with oak. Rather than the assertive style of Marlborough Sauvignon Blancs, the Matua Valley wine hangs its hat on depth, complexity and finesse.

For winemaker Mark Robertson, the Reserve Sauvignon Blanc is a labour of love. "It's the white wine I enjoy making the most – I've an affinity with the style. My wife, Jane, and I drink it as a standard wine at home – with food. Most Marlborough wines, by contrast, are better as an aperitif."

Robertson's approach to oak-aged Sauvignon Blanc was strongly influenced by his 1991 trip to Bordeaux, when he spent a week making dry white wine in Entre-Deux-Mers.

"It was all about producing ripe, weighty, serious, long-flavoured wine. They were picking obviously ripe fruit; giving the juice three days of skin contact; using no sulphur but purging the storage vessels with CO_2 to prevent oxidation; barrel-fermenting with reasonably high solids in the juice; using malolactic fermentation; barrel-aging. When I returned, I set out to emulate all that with our Reserve Sauvignon Blanc."

The key factor in producing top class, oak-matured Sauvignon Blanc, Robertson believes, is fruit quality: "You need ripe, figgy fruit, which means low cropping levels and lots of sun exposure." At Waimauku, the vines have been cropped lightly (at 2.5 to 3.5 tonnes per acre), with "extreme" leaf-plucking activity, to get the bunches fully ripe prior to the arrival of autumn rains.

The grapes are harvested by hand and machine, and the juice is given a lengthy period of skin contact. ("But that doesn't give hard flavours," says Robertson. "That's an issue related to rot and stalks.") The juice is fermented with high solids at fairly warm temperatures – up to 18°C. About 50 per cent of the final blend is barrel-fermented, and about 80 per cent is wood-aged (principally in French oak, but also in up to 30 per cent American oak, for "vanillin sweetness"). The wine is handled oxidatively, which Robertson finds makes it "more silky, with greater longevity".

For the consistently top-flight quality offered, Matua Valley Reserve Sauvignon Blanc is an irresistible buy at around $17. Up to 3000 cases are made each year, and it has an established niche in the US and UK fine wine markets.

When is the best time to broach it? "It must be pleasureable at the time of release," says Robertson. "Anything else thereafter is a bonus, but it does reward aging." Some vintages have matured well for five to eight years.

It's easy to overlook a wine like Matua Valley Reserve Sauvignon Blanc. It doesn't win gold medals in local competitions, isn't expensive and doesn't leap out of the glass at you like many Sauvignon Blancs. But if you enjoy weighty, richly flavoured and rounded dry white wine with character, complexity and enormous drinkability, this underrated Sauvignon Blanc is well worth discovering.

Matua Valley's founders, brothers Bill (left) and Ross Spence, with winemaker Mark Robertson.

tasting notes

These notes are mainly from a vertical tasting of the 1986 to 1997 vintages, held at the winery in November 1998. The 1998 vintage was tasted in Auckland in April 1999.

1998 ☆☆☆☆☆ (Labelled "Matheson") Hawke's Bay fruit (first since 1992). Pale lemon hue. Ripe aromas of pineapple and quince. Very mouthfilling, with lush tropical fruit flavours, toasty oak and balanced acidity. Still very fresh and youthful, in a very ripe, non-herbaceous style with a slightly creamy texture and rich finish. Hugely drinkable. Potentially quite complex. **Drink 2000-08.**

1997 ☆☆☆☆ ⚹ Light yellow-green. Fresh bouquet. Soft and mouthfilling, with strong citrus fruit and quince flavours, slightly buttery and complex. Quite forward. **Drink 1999-2003.**

1996 ☆☆☆☆☆ Pale yellow, green tint. Soft impression on the palate, with deep, well-ripened flavours of quince and fig, balanced oak and Chardonnay-like complexity, subtlety and mouthfeel. Slightly buttery, long finish. **Drink 1999-2006.**

1995 ☆☆☆☆☆ ⚹ Medium yellow. Very fleshy and mouthfilling (13 per cent alcohol). Tight, crisp and finely balanced, with strong flavours of tropical fruits, overlaid with mealy, buttery characters. Evolving well. Surprisingly good. **Drink 1999-2005.**

1994 ☆☆☆☆☆ Full yellow. Richly fragrant, creamy and full-bodied, with very satisfying mouthfeel. Rich, ripe, pineapple flavours, still tight. **Drink 1999-2004.**

1993 ☆☆☆☆☆ Medium-full yellow. Mouthfilling, with concentrated, ripe tropical fruit flavours and a creamy texture in a fairly Chardonnay-like style, maturing superbly. Should be long-lived (from a great Auckland vintage). **Drink 1999-2003.**

1992 ☆☆☆☆ (Hawke's Bay) Light gold. Bouquet of toast, honey and canned peas. From a cool year (too cool in Waimauku), a distinctly more herbaceous style, soft and very developed. Full-flavoured, with good weight. Ready. **Drink 1999.**

1991 ☆☆☆☆☆ Pale gold. Slightly grassy bouquet. Still fresh, with good weight and beautifully balanced flavours of melons, capsicums and oak. Complex, tight wine with a slightly buttery, very harmonious finish. Delightful now. **Drink 1999-2001.**

1990 ☆☆☆☆ ⚹ Light gold. Attractive bouquet of ripe fruit and toasty oak. Pineappley fruit characters, still lively, with balanced acidity and good length. Mellow. Very good now. **Drink 1999-2000.**

1989 ☆☆☆ ⚹ Medium gold. Very developed wine with tropical fruit and toast characters. Plenty of flavour, with a crisp, slightly hard finish. **Drink ASAP.**

1988 ☆☆☆ Deep gold. Still alive, but a bit dull and honied. Pineappley, with highish acidity and an obvious *Botrytis* influence. Near the end. **Drink ASAP.**

1987 Not tasted.

1986 ☆☆☆☆☆ Light gold. Honey and toast bouquet, with a limey edge. Slightly Riesling-like, minerally, full and still alive, with developed toasty characters. Rich and mellow. Has matured superbly. **Drink 1999.**

Nautilus Marlborough Sauvignon Blanc

CLASSIC

Wine judges often disagree, but the judges at the 1994 Australia National Wine Show in Canberra, 1994 Royal Hobart Wine Show, 1994 Air New Zealand Wine Awards, 1995 Sydney International Wine Competition, 1995 International Wine Challenge in London, and 1995 International Wine and Spirit Competition in London were unanimous on one point: Nautilus Marlborough Sauvignon Blanc 1994 deserved a gold medal. No other New Zealand Sauvignon Blanc has enjoyed such striking success on the international show circuit.

From one vintage to the next, this is a striking wine with a voluminous fragrance, lush, incisive flavours and zingy acidity – Marlborough Sauvignon Blanc at its inimitable best.

"We're in every part of the New Zealand wine industry – except retailing," says Clive Weston, Negociants' managing director. Apart from distribution of the company's exclusive range of New Zealand and imported wines and wine accessories throughout New Zealand, Negociants are also importers and exporters of wine, vineyard owners and winemakers under the Twin Islands and Nautilus brands.

The Nautilus brand was launched well over a decade ago. Weston recently stumbled across a surviving bottle of Nautilus Hawke's Bay Sauvignon Blanc 1985 – wine he hadn't realised existed. "It was probably only ever sold in Australia."

The first Nautilus Chardonnay and first Nautilus Hawke's Bay Sauvignon Blanc sold in New Zealand were produced in 1989, and the first Cabernet Sauvignon/Merlot in 1990. The first sparkling wine base was laid down in 1991, and 1992 brought the first Nautilus Marlborough Sauvignon Blanc.

One of New Zealand's best-known wine distributors, Negociants New Zealand is itself controlled by S. Smith & Son, owner of the Yalumba winery in the Barossa Valley. The wine is made at Rapaura Vintners in Marlborough, in which Negociants has a 25 per cent stake.

Winemaker Clive Jones aims for a Sauvignon Blanc that "is more than one-dimensional".

Two-dimensional? "Yes, but being Sauvignon Blanc, it probably won't be three-dimensional!" Only the best fruit is selected for the Nautilus label; the rest is used for the company's second-tier wine, Twin Islands Sauvignon Blanc.

The phenomenal show success of the 1994 vintage, which included a significant proportion of Awatere Valley fruit, led Nautilus to focus on the Awatere Valley as an ongoing source of grapes. Over the years, six vineyard sites have been selected, with a range of silty and shingly soils, in various parts of the Wairau Valley and the Awatere Valley. "That gives us a range of fruit characters," says Jones. "There aren't any wild extremes, but it does increase the wine's overall complexity."

In the pursuit of quality, a key element is controlling the size of the crop. "We do that by choosing lower-cropping sites and then manipulating the yields to below four tonnes per acre." The grapes are mechanically harvested in the cool of night, with the first load arriving at the winery at around 4 am.

The juice is cool-fermented in stainless steel tanks, at 10 to 14°C. Some skin contact is allowed: "If you crunch on the skin of a Sauvignon Blanc berry, you get a lot of flavour," says Jones, "but you don't want to extract too many phenolics." Oak plays no part in the wine, but after the ferment has subsided, the new wine is briefly matured on its yeast lees (for four to eight weeks).

With its large annual production of 15,000 cases, Nautilus Marlborough Sauvignon Blanc is widely available in New Zealand at around $18. About half the total volume is exported, principally to Australia, the UK and USA. Jones sees it as basically a drink-young wine. "It typically builds up to Christmas, then stays at its peak until about 18 months old." The vertical tasting showed that top vintages remain attractively fresh and lively for at least three years.

Nautilus Marlborough Sauvignon Blanc is a classy, richly fragrant wine with mouthfilling body and a strong surge of ripe, passionfruit and lime-like flavours, enlivened by fresh acidity. It's pure Marlborough – fresh, vibrant, mouthwateringly crisp and awash with flavour. 🍷

Clive Jones took over the winemaking reins at Nautilus in 1998.

tasting notes

These notes are from a vertical tasting of the 1992 to 1998 vintages, held in Auckland in February 1999.

1998 ☆☆☆☆✦ Pale lemon/green. Big, limey wine with real power. Not aggressive but clearly varietal, with deep tropical fruit flavours and good zest. Works well as a weighty style from an unusually hot year. **Drink 1999-2003.**

1997 ☆☆☆☆☆ Pale. Fresh, lifted aromas, very attractive. Rich and lively palate, mouthfilling, with intense, pure, delicate flavours of passionfruit and lime, cut with appetising acidity. Lovely concentration and vigour. Maturing well. **Drink 1999-2002.**

1996 ☆☆☆☆☆ Bright, light yellow/green. Richly, ripely scented. Generous palate, full and soft, with sweet fruit characters, lovely flavour depth and a rounded, lingering finish. Delightful now. **Drink 1999-2001.**

1995 ☆☆☆✦ Light yellow/green. Strongly herbaceous bouquet. Penetrating, green-edged flavour with a sliver of sweetness and firm acid spine. Medium-bodied. Just starting to soften. **Drink 1999.**

1994 ☆☆☆☆☆ Light-medium yellow/green. Strongly herbaceous bouquet, with developed, asparagus characters. Lush, rich palate of tropical fruits, again displaying mature asparagus and canned peas notes. Rich, rounded finish, with hints of tea and honey. Still highly enjoyable, with some complexity, but fully mature. **Drink 1999.**

1993 Not tasted.

1992 ☆☆☆✦ Medium gold. Very mature bouquet, starting to lose its varietal definition. Crisp, slightly honied wine with good vigour. Citrusy flavours, with only a touch of canned peas character. Leaner and crisper than most of the other vintages. **Drink 1999.**

Nga Waka
Sauvignon Blanc

CLASSIC

One of New Zealand's most powerful, robust and richly flavoured Sauvignon Blancs flows from the small Nga Waka winery in Martinborough. Nga Waka's deep-scented and vibrantly fruity Sauvignon Blanc 1995 stood in solitary splendour at the end of the 1995 Air New Zealand Wine Awards – the only wine out of several hundred from the exceptionally wet 1995 vintage to score a gold medal.

Roger Parkinson's wine stands out for its substantial body and highly concentrated, ripe flavour. How does it acquire such strength through the palate? "It's the vineyard, essentially – and the region," says Parkinson. "Martinborough's warm days and cool nights give the fruit freshness and zip. You get some of the tangy, grassy characters typical of Marlborough and some of the weight, richness and pineappley flavours of Hawke's Bay. And the vineyard expresses itself through the variety, regardless of the vintage, with clarity or purity of flavour and excellent concentration."

Nga Waka takes its name from the three nearby hills, Nga Waka a Kupe (the canoes of Kupe), which lie like upturned canoes not far from Martinborough. The stony, silty estate vineyard was established in 1988.

In a region famed for its Pinot Noirs, to date Nga Waka has been a white-wine specialist, although Roger Parkinson succumbed to the pressure and made his first Pinot Noir in 1998. He makes penetratingly flavoured, steely white wines, designed for long-term cellaring.

The vines are trellised on the twin-tier Scott Henry system (to reduce disease and shading of

the fruit), shoot-thinned, trimmed and vigorously leaf-plucked. Yields are kept low – around 3.5 tonnes per acre. Variation in soil types within the vineyard is another key factor in the wine's quality and style, Parkinson has found. "The more gravelly blocks give you fruit with fineness and structure, whereas the deeper, siltier blocks give you weightier, richer wine."

At the winery, the machine-harvested grapes are handled simply. The juice is cold-settled, inoculated with a neutral yeast, and fermented at cool temperatures, typically ranging from 10 to 18°C, for two to three weeks. Parkinson has no interest in oak: "With aromatic varieties like Sauvignon Blanc, wood simply interferes with what the wine is all about. The structure of the wine is exactly as I want it."

The ability to mature gracefully for several years is a hallmark of Nga Waka Sauvignon Blanc – the debut, gold medal 1993 vintage opened superbly in 1997. "When young, the wine always shows tropical fruit characters, especially passionfruit, but after a year gooseberry flavours come through, and at two years you get both. That's

126

Roger Parkinson makes a powerful, ripe, impressively concentrated Sauvignon Blanc.

when I think it's approaching its best."

Nga Waka Sauvignon Blanc ($22) is a rare wine. Past production has averaged only 750 cases, but as new plantings come on stream, this will double.

A cool-climate style of Sauvignon Blanc, Nga Waka is an immaculate wine, always highly aromatic, ripe and zingy. Power and concentration are its key attributes. An exciting mouthful, it stands out from the crowd with its great weight and depth of lush, ripe flavour. 🌿

tasting notes

These notes are from a vertical tasting of the 1993 to 1998 vintages, held at the winery in November 1998.

1998 ☆☆☆☆¼ Pale lemon/green. Ripely scented. Big, powerful, concentrated wine with tropical fruit flavours, balanced acidity and a rich finish. Crying out for time. Still very tight, but should mature well. **Drink 2000-03.**

1997 ☆☆☆☆¼ Pale lemon/green. Fleshy wine with concentrated, passionfruit-like flavours and limey characters too. Slightly less ripe than the 1996, with a slightly less rich finish, but fresh and tangy, with excellent weight and depth. **Drink 1999-2001.**

1996 ☆☆☆☆☆ Pale lemon/green – still youthful. From a warm season, very ripe passionfruit characters, with an undercurrent of limes. Richly fragrant and vibrantly fruity wine with intense flavour and excellent varietal definition. Just starting to round out and immensely drinkable now. A star of the lineup. **Drink 1999-2001.**

1995 ☆☆☆☆¼ Pale lemon/green. Immaculate, freshly herbaceous wine, with a hint of maturity but still fresh and lively. Good weight. Limey and appley, in a slightly less ripe style than the 1994 or 1996. **Drink 1999-2000.**

1994 ☆☆☆☆☆ Light lemon/green – very youthful. From a very low-cropping year, mouthfilling wine with lush tropical fruit flavours dominating and a touch of green capsicum. Crisp and vigorous, with slightly toasty characters emerging. Maturing superbly. **Drink 1999-2000.**

1993 ☆☆☆☆¼ Light-medium yellow/green. Very aromatic and still lively, with strong flavours and high acidity. Opened magnificently in 1997, but now showing canned peas characters and starting to dry out. A great wine in its day. **Drink 1999.**

Palliser Estate Sauvignon Blanc

This wholly seductive wine is one of the greatest Sauvignon Blancs in the country, with a distinguished track record in shows to prove it – every vintage has won a gold medal at a major wine competition.

Grown in Martinborough, it is typically an immaculate, classy wine, fresh, lively and simply overflowing with flavour. Ripe, sweet-fruit aromas lead into a deliciously full- bodied palate with fresh, pure, incisive flavours of tropical fruits and capsicums and a crisp, sustained finish.

Winemaker Allan Johnson's goal is "an intense style of Sauvignon Blanc, with flavours in the gooseberry/passionfruit spectrum. We want full-flavoured wine, but it must be an easy-drinking style. People say that Sauvignon Blancs are acidic, but they often confuse acidity with a phenolic edge, which I go out of my way to avoid." Great delicacy of flavour is one of the hallmarks of Johnson's wine.

For Johnson, the Sauvignon Blanc is produced not in the winery, but the vineyard. "It's a combination of climate and viticultural techniques. In Martinborough we get day-long warmth, without cooling sea breezes, so the wine is slightly riper and richer than most of Marlborough's. We make sure the vines have an open canopy, but don't want the bunches to be completely exposed to the sun – if you do too much leaf-plucking, the methoxypyrazines won't play their part and you won't get penetrating gooseberry characters." For Johnson, the timing of the harvest is crucial: "We go through the vineyards about every three days, tasting the fruit, watching the flavours develop. You can select your wine style prior to the picking."

Palliser Estate's Sauvignon Blanc vines are planted in some of the district's heavier soils, but Scott Henry (two-tier) trellising helps to spread the canopy and promote fruit ripening. Yields average four tonnes per acre.

At the winery, Johnson says he handles Sauvignon Blanc in a similar way to his equally outstanding Riesling. "It's very careful winemaking. We ferment the wine cool (at 11 to 15°C), with reasonably clear juice. There's no blending with Sémillon, no barrel fermentation, no oak-aging – the fruit gives us the breadth of flavour."

Palliser Estate Sauvignon Blanc is exported to Australia, Switzerland, the UK and the US, and sells in New Zealand at around $20. The annual production is currently 5000 cases, but Johnson reports the company could sell twice that much – and is in the process of doubling its output.

The best time to drink his superb Sauvignon Blanc is at nine to 18 months old, believes Johnson. "Let it settle until Christmas, and then drink it over the next year. The riper wines lose their vivacity faster than those from cooler years."

Palliser Estate Sauvignon Blanc once collected the trophy for champion Sauvignon Blanc at the Air New Zealand Wine Awards, but Johnson doesn't

Palliser Estate produces a very rich, pure and penetrating Sauvignon Blanc.

remember which vintage it was (1992): "I don't take individual show results too seriously." Along the way, the gold medals have been numerous. The 1997 vintage won the trophy for top Sauvignon Blanc at the International Wine Challenge in London.

A very classy wine of distinctly cool climate origin, Palliser Estate Sauvignon Blanc offers an exquisite harmony of crisp acidity, mouthfilling body and fresh, penetrating fruit flavours. Widely recognised as the Martinborough district's top Sauvignon Blanc, it's one of the most memorable Sauvignon Blancs in the country.

tasting notes
These notes are from a vertical tasting of the 1991 to 1998 vintages, held at the winery in November 1998.

1998 ☆☆☆☆☆ Pale lemon/green. Ripe, sweet-fruit aromas. Great depth – weighty wine with intense ripe flavours, which retain raciness. Very rich, pure and penetrating. A real standout. **Drink 1999-2002.**

1997 ☆☆☆☆☆ Fresh aromas of passionfruit, limes and melons. Superbly ripe fruit characters, while still very lively. Mouthfilling and concentrated, with a rounded, rich finish. Lovely now. **Drink 1999-2001.**

1996 ☆☆☆☆☆ Light lemon/green. Still youngish, with fresh, very ripe flavours of passionfruit and melon. Sweet fruit characters in abundance. Gentle, delicious wine with balanced acidity and impressive length. **Drink 1999-2000.**

1995 Not tasted (but one of the classiest wines of the vintage).

1994 ☆☆☆☆☆ Light lemon/green. Minerally, nettley bouquet. Very high-flavoured, with tropical fruit, capsicum and toasty bottle-aged characters threaded with firm acidity. Developed, but still very lively. **Drink 1999.**

1993 Not tasted.

1992 ☆☆☆☆ Bright lemon/green, still fairly light. Mature and mellow, with canned peas characters on the nose. Herbaceous style, citrusy too. Still alive and full-flavoured, with fairly high acidity. Clearly reflects the cool season. **Drink 1999.**

1991 ☆☆☆☆☆ Light lemon/green. Mature, toasty, bottle-aged characters dominate the nose. The palate is mouthfilling and still very alive, with good mouthfeel, sweet fruit characters and deep flavours of passionfruit and citrus fruits. **Drink 1999.**

CAPE CREST
SAUVIGNON BLANC
Te MATA
ESTATE
HAWKES BAY
1998

Te Mata Cape Crest Sauvignon Blanc

CLASSIC

Cape Crest is a sophisticated Hawke's Bay Sauvignon Blanc, with a touch of smoky oak, sweet-fruit characters and strong, ripe melon/lime flavours enlivened with fresh acidity. Full-bodied, firm and complex, it impresses not for the rapier-like herbaceousness that is the hallmark of Marlborough wines, but for its mouthfilling body and ripely herbal, subtle, sustained flavours.

One of New Zealand's most prestigious wineries, Te Mata's roots lie in the late nineteenth century. A hobby vineyard, planted in 1892 by Bernard Chambers of the Te Mata Station, thrived, encouraging him to convert a stable built in 1872 into a cellar and, in 1896, to embark on commercial wine production. By 1909, Chambers' vineyard covered 14 hectares and was the largest in the country. A long period of decline followed, but today this historic Havelock North winery is renowned for its distinguished claret-style reds, Coleraine and Awatea Cabernet/Merlots, high-flying Elston Chardonnay and two fine Sauvignon Blancs, Castle Hill and Cape Crest.

Proprietor John Buck isn't looking for a fresh, simple, drink-young Sauvignon Blanc. Te Mata strives for a style "that has the ability to develop in bottle; that has ripe flavours and some length and breadth to the palate. As a general rule-of-thumb, we consider these wines to be at their peak between 18 and 36 months of age." Since the 1991 vintage, oak-aging has added depth and clearly differentiated Cape Crest from its non-wooded stablemate, Castle Hill Sauvignon Blanc. Of the two, Cape Crest is typically slightly bigger, richer and more complex.

In Buck's opinion, the "spicy, fennel-like, figgy" characters of the fruit go well with spicy oak. "Herbaceous Sauvignon Blanc doesn't go with oak, but in Hawke's Bay we get lower-acid fruit, with more body."

The style has evolved over the years. Cape Crest was tank-fermented during the 1980s, but has gradually shifted towards a Graves (Bordeaux)-like style, with 100 per cent cask fermentation. The 1991 vintage was the first to be partly (30 per cent) oak-fermented, and since 1996 the wine has been fully barrel fermented.

The grapes were sourced from the Cape Crest vineyard at Te Awanga between 1983 and 1992. From 1993 onwards, Cape Crest Sauvignon Blanc became a marriage of Te Awanga and estate-grown, Havelock North fruit. A name change is in the wings, because it is now blended from grapes grown entirely in the company's own vineyards adjacent to the Havelock North winery and at Woodthorpe Terraces, on the south side of the Dartmoor Valley.

Some of the vines are vertically shoot-positioned, while others are trained on the two-tier Scott Henry trellising system. "Serious" leaf-plucking promotes ripeness, and bunch-thinning keeps the vines' yields down to 3.5 tonnes per acre.

Cape Crest "isn't a complicated wine" says winemaker Peter Cowley. The hand-picked grapes are destemmed, crushed and drained, and the juice is settled overnight before being fermented (with some indigenous yeasts in 1998) in French oak barriques (mainly second and third-use). The young wine is then matured for several more months on its light yeast lees, with "a bit" of stirring.

Te Mata Cape Crest Sauvignon Blanc ($21) is only made in small volumes (600 to 1000 cases per year). As Buck puts it: "It's not a mainstream style." The winery recommends drinking the wine at two to four years old, but top vintages (like the 1994) can hold their top form for at least five years.

New Zealand produces very few stylish, subtle Sauvignon Blancs that don't leap out of the glass, but draw you back for a second glass ... and a third. Substantial, ripely herbal and sustained, Cape Crest is not a dramatic Sauvignon Blanc, but a classic example of the satisfying, weighty, richly flavoured Hawke's Bay style.

Hand-picked grapes grown near Havelock North for Te Mata.

tasting notes

These notes are mainly from a vertical tasting of the 1991 to 1997 vintages, held at the winery in December 1998. The 1998 vintage was tasted in Auckland in March 1999.

1998 ☆☆☆☆☆ Weighty, crisp and tight-knit. Fresh, rich tropical fruit flavours, with oak and lees-aging characters and a long, structured finish. Noticeable wood at this stage, but already showing considerable complexity. **Drink 2000-02.**

1997 ☆☆☆☆☆ Pale lemon/green. Fresh, sweet-fruit characters. Very delicate, mouthfilling, deeply flavoured wine, slightly less wood-influenced than the 1996, with a hint of malolactic fermentation and crisp finish. Big wine with lovely concentration. **Drink 1999-2001.**

1996 ☆☆☆☆☆ Light lemon/green. Slightly oaky bouquet. Complex wine with ripe melon/lime fruit characters and oak/lees richness. A less fruit-driven, more wood-influenced style than previously, reflecting the heavier-cropping vintage. Maturing well. **Drink 1999-2000.**

1995 ☆☆☆☆ Light lemon/green. Full, fresh melon/lime flavours, with ripe fruit characters and restrained wood. Less rich than the 1994, but crisp and lively, with good depth. **Drink 1999.**

1994 ☆☆☆☆☆ Light lemon/green. Plump wine with fresh, rich, incisive melon/lime flavours and oak/lees complexity. Lovely vigour and balance. Clearly varietal yet unusually complex for Sauvignon Blanc. A star of the flight. Wonderful now. **Drink 1999.**

1993 ☆☆☆☆ Light-medium yellow. Rich bouquet of gooseberries, capsicums and toast. Crisp wine with good weight and strong, slightly herbaceous flavours. Holding well, with firm acidity. Toasty and mature. **Drink 1999.**

1992 ☆☆☆☆ Light-medium yellow. Herbaceous bouquet. Crisp, developed wine with gooseberryish, grassy flavours. Limey and penetrating. Good body and still very alive. Clearly a cool year. **Drink 1999.**

1991 ☆☆☆☆☆ Medium-full yellow. Pineappley fragrance and flavour. Toasty and lively. Full bodied wine, maturing gracefully, with very good depth of ripe fruit flavours and a crisp, firm finish. **Drink 1999.**

Vavasour Single Vineyard Sauvignon Blanc

CLASSIC

The debut 1989 vintage instantly established this label among Marlborough's most classy Sauvignon Blancs. Bursting with pure, intense fruit flavours, lightly seasoned with oak, it is a consistently immaculate wine, full-bodied and complex, with an intensity of flavour that can be quite breathtaking.

The Vavasour winery sits on terraces bordering the Awatere River, over the hills from the more extensively planted Wairau Valley. Mt Tupaenuku's 2900-metre peak rears to the south; to the north, four kilometres away, lies the sea. The wines are consistently impressive.

The name has changed over the years (from Fumé Blanc in 1989 and 1990, to Reserve Sauvignon Blanc between 1991 and 1993, and Single Vineyard Sauvignon Blanc since 1994), but winemaker Glenn Thomas' goal has stayed the same: "It's a concentrated, subtle wine, designed to stay fresh and age well over two or three years."

The key to its success lies in the vineyard. "That means site selection and crop load, above all," says Thomas. "We go for low crops [two to three tonnes per acre] and the vines are well balanced, with small canopies. We hand-pick the fruit, and whole-bunch press at least part of the blend. High quality, second or third-fill French oak barriques are also important."

In most vintages (except the 1996, grown in the Awatere River vineyard, now owned by Nautilus), the grapes have been cultivated in Vavasour's estate vineyard, in the lower Awatere Valley. "It's a sheltered, very free-draining site," says Thomas, "with some gravels, some loam, and enough substance to give the wine plenty of body."

The hand-picked fruit is at least 50 per cent, and sometimes fully, whole-bunch-pressed, which Thomas finds increases the juice's flavour delicacy and later minimises the development of asparagus characters. Retaining some solids in the juice for the ferment, rather than removing them by cold settling and racking, helps to boost the flavour and impart a slight "mealiness or toastiness". A proportion of indigenous yeasts have been used since 1997.

The degree of fermentation in French oak barriques ranges from 50 to 100 per cent. In ripe vintages, the wine is exposed to more oak, but in leaner, less-ripe years, the wood influence is cut back. The tank-fermented wine gives "freshness and varietal intensity", says Thomas, while oak fermentation improves the wine's "mouthfeel and texture, and imparts savoury, mealy characters". A small percentage of the final blend is also put through malolactic fermentation, to soften the palate.

Vavasour Single Vineyard Sauvignon Blanc is only made in small volumes – 500 to 1000 cases per year. At around $27, it's one of the country's priciest Sauvignon Blancs, but at 18 months old, it offers truly exciting drinking.

Strikingly powerful and intense, Vavasour Single

Glenn Thomas makes an exceptionally deep-scented, intense and zingy Sauvignon Blanc.

Vineyard Sauvignon Blanc is weighty and elegant, with flinty, concentrated, melon/herbal flavours. A delicate seasoning of oak enriches the wine without dominating, and the finish is rich and persistent. A classy, high impact wine, it's a very seductive and memorable mouthful.

tasting notes

These notes are from a vertical tasting of the 1989 to 1997 vintages, held at the winery in January 1999.

1998 Not made.

1997 ☆☆☆☆✓ Creamy oak on nose and palate. Big wine (13.5 per cent alcohol), still youthful. Elegant and persistent. Not pungent, but complex and restrained. Still opening out. **Drink 1999-2001.**

1996 ☆☆☆☆☆ Pale. Awatere Valley at its best, with tropical fruit characters, very pure and lush. Fruitier than the 1994; ripe and rounded. Mouthfilling, subtly oaked wine with lovely delicacy. Maturing superbly. **Drink 1999-2001.**

1995 Not made.

1994 ☆☆☆☆☆ Broader style, complex and leesy. Slightly spicy nose. Ripe, less herbaceous and overtly varietal style; more subtle and multi-faceted. Rounded, deep. Lovely now. **Drink 1999-2000.**

1993 ☆☆☆☆ (Reserve) Medium yellow. Very aromatic. Fresh and lively. High acidity. Citrus/lime flavours, tangy and slightly toasty. Still in very good shape. **Drink 1999.**

1992 ☆☆☆☆ (Reserve) Medium gold. Strong herbaceous aromas – canned peas and toast. Soft and generous. Full-bodied (13.5 per cent alcohol). Buttery, toasty and grassy, with lots of flavour. Ready. **Drink 1999.**

1991 ☆☆☆☆☆ (Reserve) Full yellow/light gold. Probably at full stretch, but still lively, with concentrated tropical, citrus fruit and oak flavours and a firm finish. Not grassy. Toasty and deep. **Drink 1999.**

1990 ☆☆ (Fumé Blanc) Developed gold, slightly brown. Dull, tired nose and palate. Past its best, by a few years.

1989 ☆☆☆☆☆ (Fumé Blanc) Youthful, light lemon/green. Developed, canned peas characters on the nose. Big wine (13.5 per cent alcohol). Rich, ripe fruit characters, with toasty oak adding richness. Classy wine. **Drink 1999.**

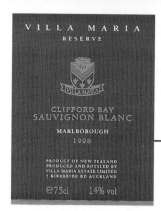

Villa Maria Reserve Clifford Bay Sauvignon Blanc

POTENTIAL CLASSIC

Grown in the Awatere Valley, east and over the hills from Marlborough's more heavily planted Wairau Valley, this is an exceptional wine. Unlike its stablemate, the Reserve Wairau Valley Sauvignon Blanc, it is virtually unwooded, but it's still of magnificent quality.

Sweet fruit delights are the key attraction. First produced in 1996, Villa Maria Reserve Clifford Bay Sauvignon Blanc is typically crisp, lively and zesty, with notable weight and loads of rich, ripe flavour, spreading across the palate to a resounding finish.

Villa Maria is New Zealand's third largest wine company. With its subsidiaries, Vidal and Esk Valley, it claims a nine per cent share of the domestic market for New Zealand wine, and an over 20 per cent share of the bottled white and red wine market. Its owner, George Fistonich, is a quiet man whose outward restraint gives little hint of his lifelong passion for Villa Maria.

Villa Maria boasts not only a range of good, sometimes excellent, "private bin" (in reality widely available) wines, but also "reserve" wines equal in quality to any other wines in the country. Its extraordinary avalanche of gold medals and trophies in the past decade tells its own story of wine quality.

Most of the fruit for the Reserve Clifford Bay Sauvignon Blanc comes from Seddon Vineyards, a large block of vines in the Awatere Valley owned by a group of small investors but managed by Villa Maria, which also purchases the grapes. Other sites in the Awatere Valley are also starting to come on stream. To maximise ripeness levels, the vines'

canopies are kept small, with the bunches well exposed to sunshine, and "deficit irrigation" is used to keep the berries small and flavour-intense.

After the grapes have been lightly crushed and pressed to extract the finest grade of juice, the "must" is cold-settled overnight and the clear juice is racked to tanks, where it is cool-fermented to ensure the preservation of its intense fruit characters. After the ferments have been blended, the wine is gently fined, filtered and bottled.

The 1996 and 1997 vintages were faintly influenced by oak (12 per cent of the 1997 was barrel-fermented), but in 1998 winemaker Michelle Richardson handled the wine entirely in stainless steel tanks. "The fruit from the Awatere is more herbaceous than from the Wairau," she notes. "It's less suited to oak; wood squashes the fruit and leaves the wine unbalanced. Oak makes the fruit lose its richness and taste vegetal."

With an annual output of around 3000 cases, Villa Maria Reserve Clifford Bay Sauvignon Blanc ($23) is readily available. Michelle Richardson finds the wine unleashes its charms earlier than its stablemate, the Reserve Wairau Valley Sauvignon Blanc. "The Wairau Valley holds back initially, when the Clifford Bay is out there. Then the Wairau Valley comes through."

Villa Maria manages and buys the grapes from Seddon Vineyards in the Awatere Valley.

The Reserve Clifford Bay Sauvignon Blanc has enjoyed huge success on the show circuit. The 1996 vintage won the trophy for champion Sauvignon Blanc at that year's Air New Zealand Wine Awards; a feat repeated the following year by the 1997 vintage.

Typically a stunning wine, Villa Maria Reserve Clifford Bay Sauvignon Blanc exhibits the leap-out-of-the-glass fragrance and zingy, explosive flavour of Marlborough Sauvignon Blanc at its inimitable best. 🍇

tasting notes
These notes are from a vertical tasting of the 1996 to 1998 vintages, held at the winery in April 1999.

1998 ☆☆☆☆☆ Pale lemon/green. Fresh, ripe tropical fruit aromas, less pungent than 1996 and 1997. Very big wine (14 per cent alcohol) with deep, pure flavours of passionfruit and melon. Strong yet delicate, with lovely weight and clarity of flavour. Slightly creamy mouthfeel. Less zingy than a cooler year, but still delicious. **Drink 1999-2001.**

1997 ☆☆☆☆☆ Very light yellow. More herbaceous than the 1998, on nose and palate. Big, punchy, zesty wine with loads of tropical fruit and capsicum flavour. Good "attack". Long finish, just starting to soften. **Drink 1999-2000.**

1996 ☆☆☆☆☆ Bright, medium-full yellow. Lush, weighty and rounded. Deep pineapple and capsicum flavours, crisp and clearly herbaceous. Very rich and concentrated, with slight honey and toast characters emerging with age. **Drink 1999.**

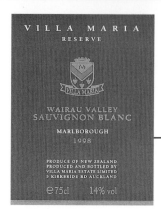

Villa Maria Reserve Wairau Valley Sauvignon Blanc

CLASSIC

With seven trophies and 10 gold medals, the 1996 and 1997 vintages of Villa Maria's Reserve Wairau Valley Sauvignon Blanc took the international show circuit by storm. When the 1996 captured the trophy for champion wine of the 1997 Sydney International Wine Competition (ahead of all the Australian reds), it was the first time in the show's history that a white wine had won the ultimate prize.

In the past labelled Reserve Marlborough Sauvignon Blanc, this is a brilliant wine. The bouquet is real leap-out-of-the-glass stuff, with deliciously ripe tropical fruit aromas. The palate is ripe and zingy, with marvellous weight and length of flavour – fresh, vibrant and concentrated. The 1996 and later releases have all ranked among the top Sauvignon Blancs of the vintage.

For winemaker Michelle Richardson, the *terroir* (natural environment) is the key to the wine's success. "It's primarily the climate and the soil. But there's a lot of work done in the vineyards. It's also the winemaking. Peter Jackson, the owner of the main vineyard, off Renwick Road, had some of his grapes processed by someone else. It was pressed aggressively and handled oxidatively. He was very disappointed. The differences in the wines were remarkable."

The vines are shoot-thinned, but to retain some herbaceousness in the fruit, often only one side of the vine row is leaf-plucked. To avoid problems in flavour development, it is vital to prevent the vines becoming water-stressed in early summer. Yields are a very important quality factor; the crop is kept to a maximum of 3.5 tonnes per acre.

Although the Jackson vineyard has been an important component in each vintage of the wine, vineyards established on slightly cooler, elevated sites in the Brancott Valley, warm riverbed gravels in the Rapaura area, and deep silt loams on the Wairau River floodplain, all contribute to the blend. The grapes from each site are machine-harvested and fermented individually and each parcel of wine is kept separate until blending.

The grapes are lightly crushed and pressed, and the clear juice is mostly tank-fermented at cool temperatures (12 to 14°C) with neutral yeasts that do not influence the flavours. About 15 per cent is fermented and/or matured in French oak barriques, with weekly lees-stirring. After about four months, the wine is blended, gently fined and filtered, and bottled.

Although the Reserve Wairau Valley Sauvignon Blanc is gently oaked, Richardson insists that the fruit must "express itself. The fruit can handle a bit of barrel fermentation, but we don't want it to be an obviously wooded style. The oak puts a bow around the other flavours."

Michelle Richardson was chosen as Winemaker of the Show at the 1998 Liquorland Royal Easter Wine

Artist Cynthia Taylor's impression of Villa Maria's new winery in Marlborough.

Show, winning the title for the second year in a row. Her success came at the end of a competition in which four of her Sauvignon Blancs won gold medals – Villa Maria Private Bin 1997, Cellar Selection 1997, Reserve Clifford Bay 1997 and Reserve Wairau Valley 1997.

High-priced at $23, but worth every cent, the Reserve Wairau Valley Sauvignon Blanc is readily available, with an annual production of 3000 cases.

Richardson suggests drinking it within three years of the vintage: "I don't like the fruit development beyond that – it gets flabby. I like it when it's firm and toned."

Villa Maria Reserve Wairau Valley Sauvignon Blanc is a mouthfilling, authoritative wine, with tremendous depth and drive. Overflowing with rich, piercing, ripely herbaceous flavour, fleshed out with subtle wood, it's a striking mouthful. 🍷

tasting notes

These notes are from a vertical tasting of the 1991 to 1998 vintages, held at the winery in April 1999.

1998 ☆☆☆☆☆ Pale lemon/green. Rich bouquet of fresh, zingy tropical fruits. Mouthfilling and ripe, with tropical/capsicum flavours and good vigour. Not punchy, but still a lovely mouthful, with layers of flavour, sweet fruit characters and a lush, lasting finish. **Drink 1999-2001.**

1997 ☆☆☆☆☆ Light lemon/green. Clearly herbaceous nose, with rich tropical fruit and herbal flavours, starting to round out, and a touch of complexity. Much more herbaceous than the 1998, with excellent body and plenty of zing. Flavour builds across the palate to a crisp, very rich finish. **Drink 1999-2000.**

1996 ☆☆☆☆☆ Light lemon/green. Still fresh and zingy. Powerful, with concentrated tropical fruit and capsicum flavours and good acidity. Herbaceous characters becoming a

bit more accentuated with age, but maturing well. Weighty, crisp wine, still delicious. **Drink 1999-2000.**

1995 Not made.

1994 ☆☆☆☆☆ (Reserve Marlborough Sauvignon Blanc) Medium yellow/green. Rich, mellowing but still fully alive, with vibrant, passionfruit-like, gently herbaceous flavours, slightly toasty and firm. Just a touch of drying out. Ready. **Drink 1999.**

1991 ☆☆☆☆☆ (Reserve Marlborough Sauvignon Blanc) Bright, full yellow/green. A less complex style than the 1996 to 1998 Reserve Wairau Valleys, but very harmonious and rounded. Melon and lime flavours, with balanced oak, now developing attractive minerally notes. **Drink 1999.**

Wairau River Marlborough Sauvignon Blanc

CLASSIC

The back label of Wairau River Sauvignon Blanc promises "elegance and power" – and delivers the goods. Mouthfilling and vibrant, with an exciting rush of fresh, pure flavour, this is one of Marlborough's most distinctive Sauvignon Blancs, coupling lush, rich fruit with piercing nettley characters.

Phil and Chris Rose own over 100 hectares of vines in the Wairau Valley. "We've got 60 hectares of Sauvignon Blanc to choose from," says Chris. "We do an awful lot of work in the vineyards; harvest from three sites in the Rapaura district; and ferment our Sauvignon Blanc in 10 to 15 different batches, all kept separate. We sell about 60 per cent of the wine to other companies; only the best gets kept for Wairau River."

Wairau River Sauvignon Blanc's notable weight and flavour richness reflects Phil Rose's desire for "a big, full-bodied wine with ripe fruit and reasonable legs [life-span]. After six months in the bottle, our wine is at its best, unlike the green, zingy style of Sauvignon Blanc encouraged by the UK market, which quickly develops cabbage and asparagus characters." The wine's mid-palate weight comes from a combination of low crops and ripe fruit. "In the past, when we were specialist grape-growers, the average yield for Sauvignon Blanc in Marlborough was said to be 5.5 tonnes per acre. The vines for Wairau River Sauvignon Blanc are cropped at an average of three tonnes per acre."

Of the Roses' three vineyards, the key site for the Sauvignon Blanc is the 60-hectare Giffords Road vineyard, planted in sandy, silty soils alongside the Wairau River, on the north side of the valley. "We

harvest late, when the fruit is extremely ripe, but still retains sufficient acidity," says Phil Rose.

The wine is made by John Belsham at Rapaura Vintners, in which the Roses own a 25 per cent stake. The grapes are crushed very gently, with minimal skin contact, and the juice is fermented at cool temperatures. The young wine is bottled early to maximise the retention of its fresh, incisive fruit aromas and flavour.

Wairau River Sauvignon Blanc ($19) is made in large volumes – about 8000 cases per year – of which the majority is sold overseas. The label instantly gained a high profile when the debut 1991 vintage won the champion Sauvignon Blanc trophy at that year's Air New Zealand Wine Awards, and later vintages have been awarded gold medals in Australia and the UK.

Chris Rose suggests the wine is typically at its peak from May of the year after vintage, until it is two years old. The vertical tasting shows that top vintages can mature well for at least five years.

Wairau River Sauvignon Blanc is an exceptionally robust and ripe style with a tantalising interplay of rich, tropical fruit flavours and more pungent, zingy, herbaceous characters. Of all Marlborough's Sauvignon Blancs, this is one of the most powerful and deeply satisfying.

Phil and Chris Rose with their weighty, superbly rich Sauvignon Blanc.

tasting notes
These notes are from a vertical tasting of the 1991 to 1998 vintages, held at the winery in January 1999.

1998 ☆☆☆☆ Pale. Still a baby – fresh, crisp and very youthful. Very ripely scented, with passionfruit and lime flavours, slightly less intense than the 1997, and a strong, zingy finish. Worth keeping. **Drink 2000-02.**

1997 ☆☆☆☆☆ Pale lemon/green. Sweet, ripe aromas. Tight, still youthful, with ripe passionfruit and lime flavours and lovely richness through the palate. Crisp, very long finish. Classic vintage. **Drink 1999-2001.**

1996 ☆☆☆☆½ Pale lemon/green. Rounded and persistent, with good weight and sweet fruit characters. Fractionally less intense than the 1994, but offers attractive tropical fruit flavours, with age becoming slightly honeyish. **Drink 1999-2000.**

1995 ☆☆☆ Light yellow/green. Solid, crisp, reasonably ripe-tasting but lacks its customary lushness. Gooseberryish flavours, not intense. **Drink 1999.**

1994 ☆☆☆☆☆ Big wine (13.5 per cent alcohol). Light-medium lemon/green. Powerful and still fresh, with lush, tropical fruit flavours, very ripe and very persistent. Delicious now. **Drink 1999.**

1993 ☆☆☆½ Bright, medium yellow/green. Herbaceous style with good depth of gooseberryish flavour and firm acidity beneath. Vigorous, slightly honied and more developed than the 1992. **Drink 1999.**

1992 ☆☆☆☆ Bright, light lemon/green. Restrained bouquet. Greener than the 1991, less ripe, but shows some flavour richness and good length. Still lively, with firm acid spine. **Drink 1999.**

1991 ☆☆☆☆☆ Bright, medium yellow/green. Mature, ripe-tasting wine, with a touch of canned peas on the nose. Soft, rich palate, with lovely weight and concentration. Intense tropical fruit flavours, with a gentle herbal undercurrent. Still a delicious mouthful. **Drink 1999.**

Wither Hills Marlborough Sauvignon Blanc

With a trophy and seven gold medals in New Zealand and Australian shows for his first three vintages, there's no doubting the quality of Brent Marris' wine. This is a striking Sauvignon Blanc, with a voluminous fragrance, mouthfilling body and very rich, sweet-tasting fruit flavours.

Marris, who built his reputation at Delegat's between 1986 and 1997, says he wants to let the region and variety "present themselves" in the wine. "I want full, unadulterated fruit flavours. I'm not looking for a high-acid, steely wine; I want a fleshy, ripe, weighty style with charm and elegance." While at Delegat's, Marris made the first eight vintages of Oyster Bay Sauvignon Blanc, typically chock-full of zingy, tropical fruit and fresh-cut grass flavour. The debut 1990 vintage carried off a gold medal and the top Sauvignon Blanc trophy at the 1991 International Wine and Spirit Competition in London.

The grapes are grown in Marris' own vineyard in the middle of the Wairau Valley, and another block planted for Wither Hills when Jim Delegat was involved in the company (Marris bought Delegat's share of Wither Hills in 1997). Marris has also purchased the 50-hectares Taylor River vineyard, previously owned by his parents, where the Wither Hills winery will eventually be erected.

The Wither Hills catch-phrase is "created in the vineyard" – and that's where Marris says his wine's quality stems from. "I identify the different blocks of land – the stonier areas and the siltier areas – and manage the vines' balance and health accordingly, to get clean, *Botrytis*-free grapes with very concentrated

flavours. By keeping each parcel of fruit separate, right through to the stage of completed wine, I get plenty of scope for blending." Rather than fermenting all his fruit together, Marris has 12 to 14 tanks of different Sauvignon Blanc for blending. Sub-standard grapes and sub-standard batches of wine are both sold off.

The grapes, harvested both by hand and machine, are dejuiced in Marlborough, then the juice is chilled and sent to the Pleasant Valley winery in Auckland, where Marris is currently based. There's a subliminal oak influence, but maturation on yeast lees (and regular lees-stirring) play a much more significant role in the wine's style, "adding to the layers of complexity, without interfering with the fruit." Typically, only five per cent of the final blend is barrel-fermented, but since the 1997 vintage, 50 per cent has been lees-aged and lees-stirred in stainless steel tanks.

Marris recommends drinking his superb Sauvignon Blanc "at the time of release and over the next two or three years". His key challenge in the future will be to retain the wine's outstanding quality while increasing its availability: production soared from 250 cases in 1994 to 5500 cases in 1998.

Wither Hills Sauvignon Blanc 1997 won the trophy for top Sauvignon Blanc in *Winestate* magazine's Wine of the Year Awards in 1997, beating 290 other Sauvignon Blancs from New Zealand and Australia. "The panel discussed whether a very young wine should win this honour and decided that the varietal definition was far too good. Yes! In the battle between more complex aged styles or young, fresh and lively styles, they decided that Sauvignon Blanc is better in youthful mode."

The *Winestate* Australian judges described the Wither Hills as "a powerful, herbaceous and tropical fruit style, yet crisp, fresh and clean. As one judge put it: 'Nicely intense – a dozen oysters please!' "

Always an astutely assembled wine, Wither Hills Sauvignon Blanc remains essentially a celebration of Marlborough's smashing fruit flavours, in a richly fragrant and weighty, hugely drinkable style. ₹

The Wither Hills line the south side of the Wairau Valley.

tasting notes

These notes are from a vertical tasting of the 1994 to 1998 vintages, held in Auckland in November 1998.

1998 ☆☆☆☆ Pale. Very fresh and juicy, but a more restrained style this vintage. Ripely aromatic, with mouthfilling body and plenty of mango and melon-like flavour. Fleshy, with sweet, ripe fruit characters, but lacks the sheer excitement of its predecessors. **Drink 1999-2002.**

1997 ☆☆☆☆☆ Light lemon/green. Strikingly scented bouquet, with a more herbaceous edge than the 1996. Weighty and penetrating, with rich, ripe tropical fruit flavours, a herbal undercurrent and a very rich finish. Still very fresh. Intensely varietal. My pick of the four vintages. **Drink 1999-2001.**

1996 ☆☆☆☆☆ Light yellow/green, with a hint of straw.

Scented bouquet, with a hint of bottle-aged toastiness adding complexity. Bigger than the 1994, with lovely depth of tropical fruit flavours, succulent and bursting with sweet-fruit appeal. Very non-herbaceous style, packed with fruit. Good acid backbone. Maturing superbly. **Drink 1999-2000.**

1995 Not made.

1994 ☆☆☆☆☆ Light yellow/green, very youthful for its age. Mature, ripely herbaceous bouquet, with a touch of canned peas. Weighty, rounded. Still lively, with passionfruit/melon flavours, showing good concentration. Hint of drying out on the finish, but holding well. **Drink 1999.**

The best of New Zealand's sweet white wines have been praised as "truly world class" by Robert Joseph, editor of the influential British magazine, *Wine*. Only a few classic labels have emerged, but they come from all over the country – the Waikato, Hawke's Bay, Martinborough, Marlborough and Canterbury.

Riesling is the paramount grape, yielding ravishingly perfumed wines with intense varietal flavours to which "noble rot", the desirable form of *Botrytis cinerea*, adds a honied, apricot-like richness. Other sweet whites have been made from Gewürztraminer, Pinot Gris, Chardonnay, Müller-Thurgau, Sauvignon Blanc, Sémillon, Chenin Blanc – even (by Rongopai) Pinot Noir.

New Zealand's most luscious sweet wines are made from late-harvested, *Botrytis*-infected fruit. Misty mornings, followed by clear, fine days with light winds and low humidity, are ideal conditions for the spread of "noble rot". One prerequisite is that the fruit is healthy and ripe. The fungus, which forms a fluffy coating over the berries, transforms their contents by thrusting tiny filaments through the grape skins and feeding on the interior. Through dehydration the grape sugars and extractives become highly concentrated – perfect for making sweet wine.

sweet white wines

Corbans Cottage Block Noble Riesling

"It's scary how good they are," enthuses Australian Michael Kluczko, Corbans' wine operations manager, about his company's stunning dessert wines. The Cottage Block label enjoys a distinguished heritage.

For many years before the Cottage Block label was launched, Private Bin was Corbans' top label. Corbans Private Bin Noble Riesling 1996 enjoyed a stunning career in competitions, twice scooping the trophy for overall champion wine at the Air New Zealand Wine Awards. The botrytised grapes were harvested in Marlborough in mid-June, when in Corbans' words "the vines were adorned with icicles and not a leaf remained". With its ravishing scent and thrillingly intense *Botrytis*, the 1986 vintage had a Rheingau-like balance and richness.

However, Corbans' production of sweet white table wines goes back much further than the Private Bin Noble Rhine Riesling. In the journey of the popular palate from sweet fortified wines to dry table wines, from the beginning Corbans played a crucial role. At the Easter Show wine competition in 1953, the top wine was Corbans Sauternes – described as "an unfortified white, sweet Sauternes-type".

Montel Sauternes, one of Corbans' oldest brands, reached the summit of its popularity 20 or 30 years ago, when sweetness, rather than quality, was most in demand by New Zealand wine drinkers. However, when wine arrived on supermarket shelves in 1990, its sales surged again. Today, known as Montel Sweet White and very low-priced, it is a light, essentially nondescript wine, juicy, lemony, mild, sweet and soft.

A rich, luscious 1980 Auslese set the scene for several outstanding sweet white wines from Corbans in the early-mid 1980s. The memorable Noble Reichensteiner 1985, a deep amber, treacly wine made from rampantly botrytised grapes grown at Tolaga Bay, near Gisborne, was followed in 1986 by the spectacularly successful Private Bin Noble Rhine Riesling.

To understand the sublime quality of the Cottage Block Riesling, Kluczko believes "you have to go back to the site. What drives a good noble Riesling? You need appropriate levels of *Botrytis*, and the Stoneleigh Vineyard in Marlborough delivers a noble Riesling fairly consistently."

The grapes are grown in a block where "we back off on our *Botrytis* management [with no sprays]. We keep the vines' canopies exposed and crops low, to get a good *Botrytis* strike, without sour rot."

The grapes are hand-picked – up to four times each season – by shaking individual berries from the vines. At the winery, the fruit is whole-bunch pressed. Some of the juice is fermented in stainless tanks, "to keep its pristine flavours"; another portion is barrel-fermented, "to give the wine weight and tannins".

Corbans Cottage Block Noble Riesling ($23 per half bottle) is made in very small volumes – between

From Corbans' Marlborough vineyards flow exceptional botrytised sweet Rieslings.

100 and 1000 cases, and on average every second year. Kluczko finds its longevity fascinating: "the 1991 vintage shows no sign of deteriorating, reflecting its sugars, balance and extract".

Having inherited the mantle of the 1986 Private Bin, the quality of Corbans Cottage Block Riesling is widely recognised. The 1991 vintage won a gold medal at the 1993 Air New Zealand Wine Awards, and the 1997 was awarded five stars in the May/June 1999 issue of *Winestate*. Ravishingly perfumed, oily and honey-sweet, with an apricot-like intensity, at its best (as in 1991 and 1997) this is a glorious dessert wine – the equal of any in the country.

tasting notes

These notes are from a vertical tasting of the 1991 to 1997 vintages, held at the winery in April 1999.

1997 ☆☆☆☆☆ Amber-hued. Harvested at a soaring 40 brix. Very rich and soft, with great concentration of apricot and honey flavours and enormous body (despite its modest 11 per cent alcohol level). Very strong *Botrytis* influence. Firm acidity. The most powerful of the trio, very sweet and very luscious. Liquid honey. **Drink 2000-06.**

1996 ☆☆☆☆¾ Medium gold. Harvested less ripe (32 brix) than the 1997 or 1991. Minerally nose. Lush palate with intense grapefruit and honey flavours, still fairly youthful. Tight and rich, with steely acidity. Packed with Riesling character. Should develop for ages. **Drink 2001-05.**

1995 Not tasted. My most recent note indicates the wine is "stunning – deep amber with rich, apricot-like aromas and a mouthfilling, oily, well-spined palate awash with nectareous, rampantly botrytised flavour." Not tasted since 1997.

1994 Not made.

1993 Not made.

1992 Not made.

1991 ☆☆☆☆☆ Deep gold/amber. Harvested at 41 brix. Authoritative wine, with rich, complex apricot and honey aromas. Gorgeously concentrated. Sweet, mature and slightly toasty, in an intense, strongly botrytised style with great acid spine. Apricot-like, minerally flavours and a very lasting finish. Great wine. **Drink 1999-2001.**

RIESLING
1997

DRY RIVER
Craighall
BOTRYTIS SELECTION

No 1638
BOTTLED BY DRY RIVER WINES LTD, PURUATANGA RD, MARTINBOROUGH
PRODUCE OF NEW ZEALAND
e 375ml   CONTAINS PRESERVATIVE (220)   9.5% VOL

Dry River Sweet and Medium-Sweet Whites

SUPER CLASSIC

No other winery in the country can match Dry River for the diversity of its superb sweet white wines. Riesling and Gewürztraminer are the pillars of Neil McCallum's dessert wine production, but he has also made ravishing sweet whites in Martinborough from Sauvignon Blanc, Chardonnay, Pinot Gris and Müller-Thurgau.

McCallum's sweet wines are designed for cellaring, rather than drink-young appeal. "The hallmark of classy dessert wines is their restraint while young," he says. "They don't show strong colour or overt *Botrytis* characters. Our wines aren't spectacular when they're young. I'm interested in preserving the varietal flavours, and the *Botrytis* characters will follow in time."

Martinborough's weather is ideal in some vintages for the spread of "noble rot". "We always do a *triage* – three or four pickings spread over about a month. Other than at Château d'Yquem and a few other properties, that's not done very commonly."

In McCallum's view, the queen of dessert wines is Riesling. He admires the late-harvest wines of the Mosel, "notable for their purity of expression unobscured by overt *Botrytis* notes or other add-ons such as barrel flavour. This is not to say that *Botrytis* cannot subtly modify the flavours found in the wine, but it would be my expectation that such changes would arise from *Botrytis* metabolism of flavours, such as the peaches of unaffected wine being seen as apricot in the dessert version. These are changes

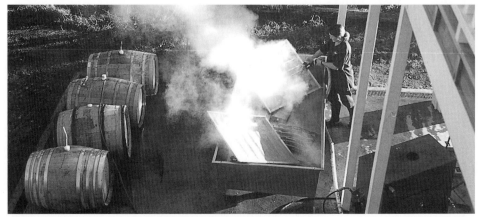

Assistant winemaker Merie Cannon steam-cleans pressing equipment at Dry River.

which do not obscure the essential varietal flavours and nature of [Riesling]."

Gewürztraminer is more of a challenge. "High sugar levels are hard to achieve and *Botrytis* is more difficult to contract. The *Botrytis* modifies or destroys the natural varietal flavours so that a balance must be struck with the extent of infection – the wine gaining its benefits but preserving sufficient intensity of varietal flavour."

In the winery, everything is aimed at enabling the wines to realise their full potential over time. "Leaving the juice on the skins for prolonged periods prior to fermentation may well extract more varietal and modified varietal flavours, leaving the wine more golden in colour, more powerful in character and more obviously appealing as a young wine," says McCallum. "However, this also raises the question of skin phenolics, so that the wine will appear more coarse as it gets older, and it will probably oxidise and age faster."

Botrytis-affected juices contain high levels of laccases (natural enzymes) which render them highly vulnerable to oxidation. "Extra exposure to air early in the life of the wine will make it more golden, and will provide obvious and interesting *Botrytis* characters in a young wine. The downside of this is that oxidation can damage varietal and still-to-be developed varietal flavours [and] the wine's long-term potential (as far as varietal characters) is compromised."

Dry River sweet wines are rare. The total output from the 1996 vintage, which yielded more than any other, was 133 cases. Prices are moderate, given the quality – the 1997 Craighall Botrytis Selection Riesling was released at $22 per half bottle, $40 per full bottle.

The wines mature superbly. "They should be good for at least 10 years, unless there is something amiss with the cork," says McCallum. He points out that for long-term cellaring, 750 ml bottles are best.

Dry River produces breathtakingly beautiful botrytised sweet wines, sometimes light and fragile, sometimes high in alcohol and very powerful. Don't look for them in your corner store – these memorable wines are very quickly snaffled by McCallum's mail-order customers.

tasting notes

These notes are from a vertical tasting of Dry River's sweet and medium-sweet white wines from the 1989 to 1997 vintages, held at the winery in November 1998.

1997 ☆☆☆☆☆ (Chardonnay Botrytis Bunch Selection) Golden. An opulent style with searching apricot, peach and honey flavours, enlivened with fresh acidity. Oily mouthfeel and texture. Very forward. Sweet style – 165 grams/litre residual sugar. (375 ml.) **Drink 1999-2000+.**

1996 ☆☆☆☆☆ (Riesling Craighall Botrytis Bunch Selection) Medium gold. Very lush and concentrated, with deep citrus, pear and honey flavours, good acid spine and a super-rich finish. Oily, with thrilling intensity. Sweet style – 170 grams/litre residual sugar. (375 ml.) **Drink 1999-2005.**

1995 ☆☆☆☆☆ (Riesling Craighall Botrytis Bunch Selection) Light gold. Highly perfumed bouquet, with slight minerally notes. Grapefruit and honey flavours with lovely freshness and poise. Firm acid backbone. Sweet style – 140 grams/litre residual sugar. (375 ml.) **Drink 1999-2003.**

1995 ☆☆☆☆☆ (Gewürztraminer Botrytis Bunch Selection) Heady (14 per cent alcohol), powerful wine with lovely, intense, peppery, gingery varietal flavours, unobtrusive sweetness and balanced acidity. Notably weighty and concentrated. Sweet style – 100 grams/litre residual sugar. (750 ml.) **Drink 1999-2002.**

1994 ☆☆☆☆ ☆ (Gewürztraminer Selection) Medium-full yellow. Mouthfilling (13.5 per cent alcohol) and soft, with intense lemony, peppery varietal characters, nuances of peaches and apricots and unobtrusive sweetness. 60 grams/litre residual sugar. (375 ml.) **Drink 1999-2002.**

1993 ☆☆☆☆☆ (Sauvignon Botrytis Selection) Golden. Very ripe, honied bouquet. Very non-herbaceous on the palate, with tropical fruit (passionfruit) flavours and a honied richness. Maturing well. (375 ml.) **Drink 1999-2000.**

1991 ☆☆☆☆☆ (Gewürztraminer Botrytis Bunch Selection) A star. Medium-full yellow. Superb bouquet of honey and spice. Marvellously rich, powerful and concentrated, with bottomless depth of musky, lemony, slightly honied flavours and great vigour. A great classic. Sweet but not super-sweet at 50 grams/litre residual sugar. (750 ml.) **Drink 1999-2001+.**

1989 ☆☆☆☆☆ (Riesling Botrytis Bunch Selection Framingham Marlborough) Medium gold. Attractive although not intense bouquet of honey and apricots. Still fresh, with citrus/honey flavours and classic Riesling poise. Lovely balance of fruit, sweetness and acidity. (750 ml.) **Drink 1999-2000.**

Giesen Botrytised Riesling

CLASSIC

Stunningly perfumed, with exceptional depth of succulent, honey-sweet flavour threaded with steely acidity, Giesen Botrytised Riesling is one of New Zealand's most brilliant sweet whites. "We were inspired by Germany's *trockenbeerenauslesen*, which are very prestigious in New Zealand," says winemaker Marcel Giesen, born in the Rheinpfalz. "We thought that if we could make a similar wine here, it would be great for the company's reputation."

The 1990 vintage was the champion wine of the Liquorland Royal Easter Wine Show in 1991, the 1991 "won a gold in London", and the glorious 1995 won "six or seven golds, all up".

Marcel Giesen has strong views on New Zealand Rieslings, which in recent years have finally started to find popularity with wine lovers. "Most of it is an upmarket version of Müller-Thurgau: fruity, mild wine which tones down Riesling's natural racy acidity." Why? "Because many winemakers sell their Rieslings too young, and the public don't like sharp acidity. And if the wine is light in body, a high level of acidity can be unbalanced."

Giesen delights in Riesling's mouth-wateringly crisp acidity: "You need steely acidity for structure, elegance and longevity. With the low yields we get in Canterbury, our grapes have high extract [stuffing] and the wines can carry more acidity. Riesling like this ages longer than Chardonnay or Sauvignon Blanc."

With the Botrytised Riesling, Giesen says he is after a wine with "*real* concentration of flavour, with lots of dried fruit characters." *Botrytis* plays a crucial role. The company's first sweet wine, produced in 1985, was freeze-concentrated in the winery rather

than naturally late-harvested; the 1987 was artificially inoculated with *Botrytis* in the Giesens' sauna (and thereafter known unofficially as "the sauna wine"). The breakthrough came in 1989, when rampantly botrytised fruit at soaring sugar levels was hand-harvested in the estate vineyard at Burnham, south-west of Christchurch.

The grapes are grown in a block alongside the main highway, especially designated for *Botrytis* wines. "Over the years, it's built up a lot of *Botrytis* spores," says Giesen. "Late in the season, when the fruit is ripe, we get cool nights and morning dews, which helps to get it going. But the weather must be right. If autumn isn't warm enough, the *Botrytis* spreads but we don't get the concentrating effect."

The grapes are normally hand-harvested. If the *Botrytis* infection is uneven, the fruit may be picked on two separate occasions. In 1995, so even was the *Botrytis* spread, the mechanical harvester was used.

At the winery, the grapes are pressed gently and the juice is inoculated with a yeast selected for its tolerance to high sugar levels. When the desired alcohol level of nine to 11 per cent has been achieved, the fermentation is stopped. The wine is

The Giesen brothers. (Left to right): Marcel, Theo and Alex.

handled entirely in stainless steel tanks, and bottled with 100 to 150 grams per litre of residual sugar.

Giesen Botrytised Riesling ($20 per half bottle) is made intermittently: none was produced in the 1992-94 and 1996-98 vintages. "We could have made it in 1997 and 1998," says Marcel Giesen, "but we produced a lot in 1995 [1000 cases]. Now we realise just how important the wine is for us, in future we'll make it as often as possible."

Giesen suggests drinking the wine at five to 10 years old. "I'm extremely cautious about recommending longer periods. Who is cellaring wine properly these days?" The vertical tasting indicates the wine holds well, but doesn't show any huge improvement, past the five-year mark.

Deep gold, with a thrilling depth of luscious honey and apricot flavours, Giesen Botrytised Riesling is a rampantly botrytised sweet wine with firm acid spine and a rich, oily texture. Not only is it the first classic wine to emerge from central Canterbury – it is right in the vanguard of New Zealand's sweet whites. ▼

tasting notes
These notes are from a vertical tasting of the 1989 to 1995 vintages, held in Auckland in February 1999.

1995 ☆☆☆☆☆ Deep gold/amber. Fresh, lush and beautifully perfumed, with sweet, apricot-rich flavours threaded with steely acid. Classic sweet Riesling. Oily, with tremendous concentration. Exciting wine. **Drink 1999-2002.**

1994 Not made.

1993 Not made.

1992 Not made.

1991 Not tasted.

1990 ☆☆☆☆☆ Deep amber/green, with a hint of brown. Sweet and luscious, with a treacly bouquet and flavour. Fresher than the 1989, but mellow and ready. Very rich apricot/honey flavours, now softening.

1989 ☆☆☆☆☆ Dark amber/green, slightly brown. Less scented than the 1990, but shows great weight and flavour density. Liquid honey, with a powerful *Botrytis* influence and ultra-rich apricot-like characters. Soft, mellow, and fully mature. **Drink 1999-2000.**

Glazebrook Noble Harvest Riesling

CLASSIC

Winemaker Alwyn Corban's devotion to Riesling is rare in Hawke's Bay, and his Glazebrook Noble Harvest is the region's only classic sweet white wine. Named after Garry Glazebrook, Corban's partner in the Ngatarawa winery, this gloriously perfumed and nectareous beauty is one of New Zealand's most exceptional "stickies".

Corban (a great-grandson of Assid Abraham Corban, the founder of Corbans Wines), goes for "a full-on *Botrytis* character. We get 70 to 80 per cent of the berries raisined, which gives us only 20 per cent of the normal juice yields. They're high alcohol wines, at 12 to 13 per cent, which enhances their vinosity."

The grapes are all estate-grown at Ngatarawa, in a block in front of the winery specifically dedicated to the production of nobly rotten grapes. "We encourage *Botrytis*," says Corban. "By not leaf-plucking the vines, we get more humid conditions in the canopy, which encourages *Botrytis* infection, and we don't use anti-*Botrytis* sprays. We run the risk of getting sour rot, but that usually only happens where the berries have been damaged by bird pecks." However, the miracle of noble rot can't be taken for granted. The 1989 vintage was too dry; 1995 was too wet.

To produce a high quality sweet wine, it is important that the grapes are ripe before the onset of *Botrytis*, so that the mould is concentrating fully ripe flavours. Any berries with sour rot are rejected. To get the shrivelled, nobly rotten Riesling fruit, the pickers make several separate sweeps through the vineyard. "In 1996, our pickers went through the

vineyard *eleven* times selecting fruit," recalls Corban.

To extract maximum sweetness from the grapes, the juice is held in contact with the skins overnight, then slowly pressed. The fermentation, conducted at 12 to 15°C, is long and slow. "You have to watch that it doesn't get too sluggish," says Corban. If it does, he stimulates the yeasts by warming the juice. When the wine has about 120 grams per litre of sugar remaining, the fermentation is arrested.

Production of Glazebrook Noble Harvest Riesling ($30 per half bottle) is low – about 100 cases per year. Corban recommends drinking it at between two and five years old, but it lives much longer.

The 1994 vintage was awarded five stars in *Winestate*, followed by five stars for the 1996 vintage in *Wine Star*. The wine has also excited overseas critics. Oz Clarke, in *New Classic Wine*, called Glazebrook Noble Harvest "a wonderful, golden orange wine, so thick and syrupy it plops out of the bottle like oil and swims lazily from side to side as you swirl your glass."

Amber-hued, with a heady, intensely honeyish fragrance, this is typically a highly refined, richly botrytised, honey-sweet wine, strikingly concentrated and treacly. Corban delights in serving it gently

Ngatarawa has pioneered botrytised sweet wines in Hawke's Bay.

chilled with a soft blue cheese.

If you enjoy Glazebrook Noble Harvest Riesling, look out for Alwyn Noble Harvest. In 1994, Alwyn Corban set aside a tiny amount of ultra-ripe (42 brix) Riesling with 100 per cent noble rot infection. Searching for "an extra dimension and complexity", he barrel-fermented the wine and matured it in wood

for 18 months. Light gold, with a ravishing, honied perfume, it is powerful and succulent, with great weight through the palate. Yet it is not a Sauternes style – the wood adds richness, but the fruit flavours show the finesse and acid spine of Riesling. At $60 per 375ml bottle, this is one of New Zealand's most expensive wines. 🍷

tasting notes
These notes are from a vertical tasting of the 1987 to 1996 vintages, held at the winery in December 1998.

1996 ☆☆☆☆☆ (Glazebrook Noble Harvest Riesling) Deep gold – darker than the 1994. Soaring, treacly bouquet. Gorgeously concentrated honey-sweet flavours, oily and rich. Very intense, with a very long and powerful finish. The best yet? **Drink 1999-2010.**

1995 Not made.

1994 ☆☆☆☆☆ (Ngatarawa Glazebrook Reserve Noble Harvest) Medium gold. Lovely poise. Intense flavours of honey, pears and citrus fruits. Mouthfilling (13 per cent alcohol.) *Botrytis* enriches but doesn't dominate the rich Riesling characters. Good acid spine, giving a lovely sweet/sour interplay. **Drink 1999-2006.**

1993 Not made.

1992 ☆☆☆☆☆ (Ngatarawa Penny Noble Harvest Riesling Selection) Deep gold. Lovely, pure, searching citrus, pear and honey flavours. Very classy Riesling. Gentle wine, finely balanced. Looks capable of very long life. **Drink 1999-2005.**

1991 ☆☆☆☆☆ (Ngatarawa Penny Riesling Noble Selection) Deep gold. Rich *Botrytis* influence, although less rampant than in the 1987. Concentrated, honied flavours, clearly Riesling in character, with good acidity. Maturing well. **Drink 1999-2005.**

1990 Not made.

1989 Not made.

1988 ☆☆☆☆½ (Ngatarawa Penny Riesling Noble Selection) Amber-green. Very sweet, with rich apricot characters and firm acidity. Less concentrated than the 1987, and slightly sharper. **Drink 1999-2000.**

1987 ☆☆☆☆☆ (Ngatarawa Botrytised Berry Selection) Amber-green. Deep, honey/apricot fragrance. Very full-bodied, with rampant *Botrytis*. Majestic wine – treacly, oily and very intense. Maturing splendidly. Ready; no rush. **Drink 1999-2002.**

Rongopai Winemaker's Selection Botrytised Riesling

CLASSIC

Rongopai burst onto the wine scene in the mid 1980s with botrytised wines at a standard – and at prices – that compelled widespread interest. This small Waikato winery is still best known for its spectacular sweet whites, notably the Winemaker's Selection Botrytised Riesling, an alluring beauty with a gorgeous perfume and great depth of honey-sweet flavour, threaded with steely acidity.

Winemaker Tom van Dam aims for a low alcohol style of sweet Riesling – around 10 per cent. "That way, you keep more of the fruit characters. And you have to remember it's a dessert wine, and that people often feel they've had enough alcohol by that stage of a meal. So by stopping the ferment at 10 per cent alcohol, we end up with at least 100 grams per litre of residual sugar."

The key factors in the wine's quality, says van Dam, are "getting the grapes really ripe, to a minimum of 30 brix, and getting the right sort of rot." The 1987 vintage was grown in Ross Goodin's local vineyard; the subsequent vintages have all come from Rongopai's own vineyard in Waerenga Road, Te Kauwhata, an exposed site at the top of a small, north-facing hill.

Botrytis is a common occurrence, in its noble and ignoble (sour rot) forms. "Te Kauwhata is an island, surrounded by water," says van Dam. "We're close to Lake Waikare, the Waikato River and the Whangamarino wetlands. For dry wine styles, we have to work hard to avoid sour rot. But the Riesling vines are closely planted, which promotes high humidity in the canopies. If we get lots of foggy mornings followed by fine days, that's ideal for the spread of noble rot."

The pickers comb the vineyards two or three times, harvesting the ripest, nobly rotten bunches and trying to avoid any fruit with sour rot. Before being put into the press, the grapes are soaked for 24 hours to soften their skins: "Otherwise it's too hard to get the juice out of the raisins," says van Dam.

Riesling's fresh, racy acid attracts van Dam: "You need that acidity to balance the sugar." To get the firm acid structure he wants, in some years he supplements the juice's natural acidity by adding tartaric acid. To retain sweetness in the wine, the ferment is arrested by spinning the yeasts out in a centrifuge and adding sulphur. The wines from the individual pickings are fermented separately and blended prior to bottling.

Rongopai Winemaker's Selection Botrytised Riesling ($40 per half bottle) is a rare wine, produced in about one year in three. The 1987 vintage yielded just 136 cases.

Van Dam recommends drinking the wine at five to 10 years old, and the vertical tasting showed the 1987 is still in magnificent form. "We tell our mail-order customers that if they don't enjoy it at 10 years old, they can bring it back and we'll refund the money," says van Dam.

Tom van Dam makes full-bodied dry and dazzling sweet white wines.

Golden, oily and treacly, Rongopai Winemaker's Selection Botrytised Riesling is a real conversation piece – a rampantly botrytised wine with the inimitable beauty of classic sweet Riesling.

Rongopai's other sweet wines are usually based on early-ripening German varieties such as Müller-Thurgau, Scheurebe and Wurzer, late-harvested with soaring sugar levels and a degree of shrivelling and *Botrytis*. Promoted as "the ultimate aphrodisiac", the striking Winemaker's Selection Botrytised Chardonnay is liquid nectar, with great weight and rich, treacly, everlasting flavour. 🍇

tasting notes
These notes are from a vertical tasting of the 1987 to 1997 vintages, held in Auckland in March 1999.

1997 ☆☆☆☆☆ Amber-hued. Treacly, apricot-like aromas. Strong *Botrytis* influence. Fresh and crisp, with concentrated grapefruit and honey flavours threaded with firm acidity and a rich finish. Quite forward and already delicious, but has strong aging potential. **Drink 2000-06.**

1993 ☆☆☆☆☆ (Reserve Botrytised Riesling) Medium-full gold. Very elegant wine, still quite tense, with lovely lemon, pear and honey characters and good acid spine. Less powerful *Botrytis* influence than in the 1997. Slightly minerally, bottle-aged characters developing. Ready. **Drink 1999-2001.**

1991 ☆☆☆☆ ☆ (Reserve Botrytised Riesling.) Deep gold, light amber. Shy nose. Finely balanced, with rich flavours of grapefruit, pear, apricot and honey, and lovely sweet/sour harmony. Intense, with firm acidity and a lasting finish. **Drink 1999-2001.**

1987 ☆☆☆☆☆ (Riesling Auslese) Deep amber. Rich, mellow, complex bouquet. Soft, lush and lovely, with superbly rich and harmonious flavours of apricots, tea and honey, deliciously smooth and long. Great now. **Drink 1999-2000.**

Villa Maria Reserve Noble Riesling

SUPER CLASSIC

This is the country's most successful sweet white wine on the show circuit – every vintage has won at least one gold medal and most have won trophies. The 1991 vintage was the runner-up champion wine of the 1994 Air New Zealand Wine Awards. The 1994 went one better – champion wine of the 1995 Liquorland Royal Easter Wine Show. The 1998 vintage recently scooped the trophy for champion sweet white at the 1999 Liquorland Royal Easter Show. If you taste the wine ($40 for a half bottle) you'll see what all the fuss is about.

Ensconced in a soaring, see-through bottle, it is typically light gold, with a stunningly rich, honied perfume. It's a superbly weighty, oily wine with intense, very sweet honey/citrus flavours and a finely balanced, lush, long finish. In short, one of the most ravishingly beautiful wines in the country.

Winemaker Michelle Richardson is after a "Wow!" factor. "It mustn't be too heavy, too sweet or too soft – the balance is very important." Past vintages have been grown in Hawke's Bay or Marlborough; sometimes both. However, the winery has lost access to the fruit grown in Ian and Digger Gunn's vineyard near Fernhill, so future vintages will probably rely heavily on Marlborough – especially the Fletcher vineyard in the Wairau Valley, where sprinklers along the vines' fruit zone create ideal conditions for the spread of noble rot.

Careful, highly selective picking of the grapes is crucial. "It's a difficult job," says Richardson, "and the fruit looks disgusting. Some New Zealand dessert wines show sour rot characters, and fall over straight away. The pickers have to make sure they get the nobly rotten berries, not those with volatile, sour rot.

It's an expensive wine to make and you must have pickers who care."

Richardson, who grew up in Putaruru and Matamata, has a Bachelor of Science degree from Massey University, majoring in microbiology. At a loss what to do after graduating, she spent three years overseas, "dossing about without a care in the world", then did a one-year post-graduate diploma in wine science in Adelaide. After working for two years at the Cassegrain winery in New South Wales, she worked as a "flying winemaker" in France, then joined Villa Maria for the 1992 vintage – and has been there ever since, climbing swiftly through the ranks.

"My intention was to fly back from Europe to do a vintage in New Zealand for three months and then continue my working around the vineyards of the world," recalls Richardson. "What happened? When [company owner] George Fistonich offered me a job as assistant winemaker, it didn't take me long to decide. After dealing with fruit from Australia and France, I could not get over the fruit intensity of the whites in New Zealand."

The heavily botrytised grapes are loaded into the

Noble rot dehydrates Riesling grapes, concentrating their sugars and flavours – perfect for making sweet wine.

press for up to 24 hours of skin contact, to extract the skins' flavours, and the juice is then pressed off and left to settle for several days. The pressings are added back to the free-run juice, "because you have squeezed the yummy apricot characters out of the skins, so need to put it back in," says Richardson. After a slow fermentation lasting several weeks, when the flavours, sugar, acid and alcohol are in balance the ferment is arrested by chilling, and the wine is racked off its

yeast lees, fined, filtered and bottled.

With a production level of around 500 cases, Villa Maria Reserve Noble Riesling is in reasonable supply. Richardson thinks it drinks well "from the day it's bottled until it's at least 10 years old." The wines from the early 1990s are still in outstanding form.

Succulent, honey-sweet, gloriously perfumed – this exquisite wine is one of the country's most memorable taste experiences.

tasting notes
These notes are from a vertical tasting of the 1991 to 1998 vintages, held at the winery in April 1999.

1998 ☆☆☆☆☆ Bright yellow/light gold. Beautiful, enticing scents of honey and pears. Pure, delicate, superbly concentrated Riesling fruit flavours, overlaid with honey. Crisp, very harmonious, lingering finish. **Drink 2000-05.**

1997 Not made.

1996 ☆☆☆☆☆ Light-medium gold, slightly green-tinged. A real stunner. Gloriously perfumed. Richly honied, with highly concentrated grapefruit and pear flavours. Beautifully poised. Starting to acquire slight toasty characters and soften, but still developing. **Drink 1999-2003.**

1995 Not made.

1994 Not tasted.

1993 ☆☆☆☆☆ Deep gold, slightly green-tinged. Nose lacks any

great perfume, but offers a hint of honey and apricots. Less ripe than the 1996 or 1998, with crisp acid and strong lemon/lime flavours. *Botrytis* adds apricot/honey characters. **Drink 1999-2000.**

1992 ☆☆☆☆☆ Full yellow/light gold. Toast, honey and minerally characters on the nose and palate. Rich, honied wine, aging very gracefully. Poised and very vigorous, with a powerful finish. **Drink 1999-2000.**

1991 ☆☆☆☆☆ Deep gold. Treacly, highly botrytised nose and palate. Soft, lush and intense. Apricot, lemon and honey flavours, toasty, deep and complex. Lovely bottle development. **Drink 1999-2000.**

New Zealand's top sparkling wines are made exclusively by the classic technique known until recently as *méthode champenoise*, but now widely called *méthode traditionnelle*, in which the secondary, bubble-creating fermentation takes place not in a tank, as with cheaper wines, but in the bottle, as in Champagne itself.

During the wine's lengthy maturation in the bottle (anything between nine months and three years, but most commonly 18 months to two years) the yeast cells gradually decompose, conferring distinctive, bready, yeasty characters on the wine that greatly add to its richness and complexity. The quality of a fine sparkling wine reflects not only its lengthy maturation in the bottle in contact with its yeast lees, but also the standard of its base wine. Pinot Noir and Chardonnay, both varieties of key importance in Champagne, are also the foundation of New Zealand's top sparkling wines (although Meunier, the least prestigious but most extensively planted grape in Champagne, is still rare here).

Marlborough has emerged as the country's premier region for bottle-fermented sparkling wines (although Corbans has achieved glowing success with Verde and – until recently – Amadeus in Hawke's Bay). The piercing flavours and tense acidity of Marlborough fruit have attracted not only local producers, but such illustrious Champagne houses as Deutz and Moët & Chandon.

New Zealand bubblies are carving out a strong international reputation. "The range of Champagne-method wines was one of the most exciting I have seen anywhere," enthused Robert Joseph, editor of the UK magazine, *Wine*, after judging at the 1997 Air New Zealand Wine Awards. "And anywhere includes that certain self-satisfied region in the north-east of France. The range of styles and flavours was simply stunning."

Most bubblies are ready to drink when released, but a short spell in the cellar can benefit the top bottle-fermented sparklings. Montana has found that Deutz Marlborough Cuvée improves markedly "on cork", during its first six months after disgorging.

sparkling wines

Amadeus Classic Reserve

CLASSIC

For many years, Corbans' Hawke's Bay sparkling was a "steal" – the finest sub-$20 bubbly in the country. The grape supply has recently switched to Marlborough and the price has climbed to $25, but Amadeus remains one of New Zealand's most distinguished sparklings, with a glowing record in show judgings.

Amadeus is typically a stylish wine with an enticingly rich and yeasty bouquet, persistent bead, impressive delicacy, complexity and liveliness, and a long, slightly creamy finish. Pinot Noir dominates the blend – 80 per cent in 1992, 90 per cent in 1995 (with 10 per cent Chardonnay). "It's a rich style of sparkling, intended to have greater flavour and complexity than our crisp, elegant Verde," says Michael Kluczko, Corbans' wine operations manager, who was formerly the head of sparkling wine production at Southcorp, the Australian wine giant.

Under Kluczko's direction, the style of Amadeus is evolving. "We're switching the grape supply to the South Island, using a higher percentage of good Chardonnay and introducing the third Champagne variety, Meunier."

Three years ago, when I chose the 1992 vintage of Amadeus as Best Buy of the Year in my annual *Buyer's Guide to New Zealand Wines*, Corbans showed no interest in making Amadeus a Marlborough wine. "I don't see why Marlborough should make better sparklings than Hawke's Bay," said Kirsty Walton, Corbans' Hawke's Bay winemaker. "Our base wine is wonderful, with an ideal balance of acid, sugar and pH."

Why has Amadeus, long admired as a great

example of Hawke's Bay's potential to make fine quality sparkling, become principally a South Island wine since the 1995 vintage? "We don't get the tightness of fruit characters in the Bay that we do in Marlborough," says Kluczko. "The Hawke's Bay grapes give flavour richness, so they'll always be there, but they don't have the same structure as cooler climate fruit." In the future, Kluczko expects Amadeus to include about 10 per cent Hawke's Bay fruit, but Corbans may also draw grapes from further south than Marlborough.

The keys to the wine's quality, Kluczko believes, are fruit selection and blending. "You must treat sparkling wine grapes the same as table wine fruit. The days are gone when you could use less-ripe fruit for bubbly. You need grapes that are physiologically ripe at lower sugar levels [around 19 brix]. That means choosing a good site and appropriate vineyard practices to promote ripeness – crop management, shoot-thinning, leaf removal."

Tropical fruit flavours (noticeable in many low-priced Australian bubblies) are to be avoided. "We want lemon/lime flavours. By going south, we can retain those lemon/lime characters at higher brix levels and with greater flavour length, without getting tropical flavours."

In the winery, the emphasis is on processing the

The grapes for Amadeus are now sourced primarily from Corbans' Marlborough vineyards.

fruit very gently. The hand-picked grapes are whole-bunch pressed, with only the free-run juice retained for Amadeus; the pressings are blended away. Oak historically played no part in the wine, but a portion of the juice is now fermented in seasoned oak barrels, in a bid to achieve greater complexity. The Marlborough fruit is also put through malolactic fermentation: "You can do that with cool-climate fruit without making it blowsy and buttery," says Kluczko. Following its secondary fermentation, the wine is matured in the bottle and finally disgorged from its yeast lees after about three years.

Amadeus is a readily available wine, with an annual production of between 5000 and 12,000 cases. Kluczko suggests drinking it within a year or two of the release date, although the outstanding 1992 vintage is still in top form.

The 1990 to 1993 vintages of Amadeus all won gold medals at the Air New Zealand Wine Awards. Amadeus' finest moment came at the Air New Zealand Wine Awards in 1997, when the 1992 vintage won a gold medal, the trophy for champion sparkling, and the ultimate trophy for champion wine of the show. 🍇

tasting notes

These notes are from a vertical tasting of the 1991 to 1995 vintages, held at the winery in April 1999.

1995 ☆☆☆☆☆ Pale straw. Fresh, attractive nose. Very lively palate, crisp and fresh. Highly refined, with lemony, slightly appley flavours and subtle biscuity yeast characters. Tight and flinty. **Drink 1999-2001.**

1994 Not made.

1993 ☆☆☆☆ ⚹ Straw hue. Inviting nutty aromas and a steady bead. Grapefruit and nut flavours, with strong yeast autolysis complexity. Quite high acid on the finish, which is long and rich. Taut, searching flavour. **Drink 1999-2000.**

1992 ☆☆☆☆☆ Full yellow/light gold. Stylish bouquet, fresher and less toasty than the 1991. Elegant and tight-knit, with crisp, lemony, yeasty flavour and rich, bready yeast autolysis characters. Good vigour and a rich finish. Still lovely. The star of the lineup. **Drink 1999-2000.**

1991 ☆☆☆☆☆ Straw/gold. Rich, toasty bouquet, yeasty and complex. Still lively on the palate, with a steady bead. Big, high-flavoured style, peachy, lemony and yeasty, with a lingering finish. Weighty, intense and complex. Quite developed. **Drink 1999.**

Daniel Le Brun
Vintage Brut

CLASSIC

Daniel Le Brun severed his ties with the Marlborough winery that bears his name in 1996, but of his highly acclaimed range of sparkling wines, the vintage was always his favourite. A powerful, yeasty, flavour-packed wine, enticingly fragrant, in several vintages it has risen to great heights.

Allan McWilliams, the current winemaker, sees the Le Brun vintage sparklings of the past as "a full-bodied, oxidative style based on rich Pinot Noir characters and developed yeast autolysis characters, with a backbone of Chardonnay acidity. That's still our style objective – rich, full, well-matured."

Daniel Le Brun was born in the Champagne region, and McWilliams believes his personal experience of Champagne production was invaluable in the early days. "The wines Daniel made in the mid 1980s were the first in New Zealand to show similar characters to true Champagne. He had centuries of first-hand knowledge behind him, so used all the right varieties and techniques."

The grapes are grown in the company's vineyards adjacent to the winery at Renwick, in free-draining soils of moderate vigour. The vines were originally densely planted in rows only 1.4 metres apart (with 1.2 metres between the vines), but a lack of air movement caused problems with powdery mildew. Now the rows are 2.8 metres apart.

The Vintage Brut is a 50/50 blend of Pinot Noir and Chardonnay, with no Meunier (which would make the wine age faster). Yields are kept to a maximum of 4.5 tonnes per acre. The grapes are all harvested by hand in the cool of morning, to reduce

the need for sulphur dioxide additions. "Hand picking is very important," says McWilliams. "That way, we can leave any diseased or unripe berries and ensure we get elegant fruit characters."

In the winery, McWilliams pursues a "minimal intervention" approach. He tastes the juice out of the press, keeping only the most delicate grades. A quick, warm ferment (five to seven days at 20 to 25°C) is designed to remove some varietal characters, especially the tropical fruit flavours typical of Mendoza clone Chardonnay.

A full malolactic fermentation helps to give the wine its full, rich style, and the base wine is also matured on its gross lees before it is bottled, to add further creaminess. After a three to five-year period *en tirage* (maturing on its yeast lees) in cool underground cellars at a steady temperature of 12 to 14°C, the wine is disgorged over a year, typically on three separate occasions, the varying length of development introducing a degree of batch variation.

McWilliams has slightly changed the wine's production methods since Daniel Le Brun's departure, in a bid to "retain the traditional style but improve the quality control". New clones of Pinot Noir and Chardonnay are being planted (the Bachtobel clone of Pinot Noir and Mendoza Chardonnay dominated in the past); the row spacings have widened; the company has gone back to the initial practice of complete hand-harvesting; and "a bit more lab work" is being done.

Only about 1000 cases of Daniel Le Brun Vintage Brut ($35) are made in an average year. McWilliams says to drink it within two years of disgorging. "That's a personal preference, but it's also how the French read it. People in the UK appreciate the bottle-aged characters you get after two years, but you can lose the freshness."

A few years ago, I asked Daniel Le Brun how, in his eyes, the style of his vintage wine compared to Champagne. He quoted Tom Stevenson, author of the prize-winning book, *Champagne*. "When I first tasted this [Daniel Le Brun Vintage Brut 1989] in a blind tasting of 21 different New Zealand sparkling wines, my immediate reaction was that they had slipped in a Champagne. A typical Champagne straw colour, it seemed like Champagne on the nose and tasted like Champagne on the palate..."

The 1989, 1990 and 1991 vintages of Daniel Le Brun Vintage Brut all won gold medals in New Zealand; the exceptional 1990 also won New Zealand's first gold medal at the International Wine Challenge in London. Rich and smooth, with deep, strawberryish, yeasty flavours and tremendous power, complexity and liveliness, at its best this is one of the country's greatest bubblies.

Allan McWilliams is preserving and refining the Le Brun style.

tasting notes

These notes are from a vertical tasting of the 1986 to 1995 vintages, held at the winery in January 1999.

1995 ☆☆☆☆✫ (Very recently disgorged, so a tentative rating.) Light lemon/green. Lighter than the 1990 and 1991, but very fresh and refined. Appley, lemony, yeasty flavours of impressive delicacy. **Drink 1999-2001.**

1994 Not made.

1993 Not made.

1992 ☆☆☆☆✫ Full yellow, slightly pink. Broad, harmonious Pinot Noir style, complex and smooth. Strawberryish, yeasty flavours of excellent depth, although slightly less rich than the 1991 and 1990. Fully developed. **Drink 1999.**

1991 ☆☆☆☆☆ Light yellow/slightly pink. Rich, yeasty bouquet. Finer fragrance and fruitiness than the 1992. Slightly lighter than the 1990, but shows impressive complexity, flavour length and vigour. Ready. **Drink 1999-2000.**

1990 ☆☆☆☆☆ Light straw. Rich, refined, yeasty bouquet, deep and enticing. Tremendous vigour and richness in a punchy, complex style that retains its freshness and vivacity. No sign of decline. Always a great wine. **Drink 1999-2001.**

1989 Not tasted.

1986 ☆☆☆ Developed, medium-full gold. Very toasty, nutty bouquet. Slightly oxidised, with toasty, orangey flavours and a slightly hard finish. Has lost its fruitiness and freshness. **Drink ASAP.**

Deutz Marlborough Cuvée

CLASSIC

Montana's flagship sparkling wine is clearly its outstanding Deutz Marlborough Cuvée, produced since 1988 under a joint agreement between Montana and the Champagne house of Deutz and Gelderman. The partners' ambition, says Peter Hubscher, managing director of Montana, is "to produce the best sparkling wine outside Champagne itself".

The initial result was a rich style, bolder and riper-tasting than the true Champagnes with which it is inevitably compared. Of late, however, Deutz Marlborough Cuvée has become less overtly fruity, more refined and flinty, with an intense, yeasty fragrance and subtle, tight, lingering flavours.

Deutz (as Deutz and Gelderman is commonly known) is described by expatriate New Zealander Don Hewitson in his book, *The Glory of Champagne*, as "a house with great integrity, excellent wines and a low profile. I am offered regular glasses of Deutz when in London, New Zealand, Australia, the United States, or travelling around France – but usually by fellow restaurateurs. It seems to be the caterer's Champagne, which is a genuine compliment to its qualities." The house has been owned since 1995 by Louis Roederer, a leading Champagne company which also owns Delas Freres, an old Rhône firm, and Château De Pez, an outstanding *cru bourgeois* of St-Estephe.

Jeff Clarke, Montana's chief winemaker, sees Deutz Marlborough Cuvée as "an apéritif style, rather than a food wine. Deutz Champagne is popular as an aperitif in Parisian restaurants, and our wine is fashioned in that style – fine, delicate, elegant."

Clarke quickly puts his finger on the key aspects of the wine's quality. "There's the Deutz [French] influence, of course. The grapes are all grown in our own vineyards, so we have absolute control. That's a very large resource, so we can choose only the most suitable fruit. We hand-pick, have specialised equipment to obtain only the most delicate juice, and we select only the finest *cuvées* [base wines] for the final blend."

The grapes are drawn from Montana's vineyards throughout the Wairau Valley. The key Pinot Noir clone is Bachtobel, and Mendoza is the main Chardonnay clone, but for both varieties, other clones are being introduced. The company aims to harvest the fruit at a sugar level of around 19.5 brix: "That gives us good weight and mouthfeel in the wine," says Clarke, "but not too much varietal flavour."

The hand-picked grapes are pressed in a computer-controlled French Coquard Champagne press, which yields juice of great delicacy. The juice is warm-fermented at around 20°C, "to drive off its varietal fruit characters". Before being bottled, the base wine is lees-aged for up to three months and given a full malolactic fermentation, "to reduce the acidity and give extra nuttiness". After each

Deutz Marlborough Cuvée is a marriage of Montana's Marlborough grapes and French expertise.

vintage, the wine is blended in Blenheim, then shipped to Auckland to be matured on its yeast lees for two to three years in a specially built, climate-controlled cellar.

The next step for Deutz Marlborough Cuvée, says Clarke, is to incorporate older reserve wines. Already, 10 to 20 per cent of each batch is reserve wine, a year or two older than the rest. Clarke wants to see the age of the reserve stocks increase, to impart greater complexity to the final blend.

Deutz Marlborough Cuvée ($27) is produced in huge volumes by New Zealand standards (50,000 cases per year), and distributed widely in Australia and the UK. If it is released with insufficient time "on cork" after disgorging, it appears fresh and attractive, but simple. Six months after disgorging, however, it reveals its full character, is ready to drink and needs no further cellaring.

Deutz Marlborough Cuvée is not entered in local wine competitions, but has enjoyed wide international acclaim, including a Sparkling Wine of the Year trophy (awarded for quality, availability and price) at the 1998 International Wine Challenge. Refined, tight and searching, it floats across the palate with a Champagne-like delicacy, lightness and smoothness.

tasting notes

Deutz Marlborough Cuvée is not vintage-dated, and therefore not suited to a vertical tasting of past vintages. Montana, however, holds back small stocks of past releases, to assess the impact a longer period en tirage (maturing on its yeast lees) has on the wine. These wines were tasted in Auckland in April 1999.

NV ☆☆☆☆☆ (The current release, based principally on wine from the 1996 vintage.) Pale. Poised and very lively, with lovely freshness and vigour. Stylish wine with crisp, yeasty flavour, slightly nutty and very persistent. **Drink 1999-2000.**

Recently Disgorged 1992 ☆☆☆☆☆ Pale straw. Yeastier, much more aldehydic bouquet than the 1996. Retains its delicate, lemony, appley characters, but is a more complex, more deeply-flavoured style, with a richer finish.

Recently Disgorged 1991 ☆☆☆☆☆ Pale straw. The best of the trio – even richer than the 1992. Very weighty and complex, with great balance and smoothness. Powerful, nutty, long finish. Outstanding.

Domaine Chandon Marlborough Brut

CLASSIC

In 1993, the year Moët & Chandon, the great Champagne house, celebrated its 250th anniversary, it also launched the first 1990 vintage of its Domaine Chandon Marlborough Brut. The 1992 and subsequent vintages rank among the most scintillating sparkling wines ever made in New Zealand, with highly refined, intricate flavours, piercing, tight-knit and smooth.

Domaine Chandon (NZ) is a wholly owned subsidiary of Moët & Chandon and a sister company of the Yarra Valley winery, Domaine Chandon (Australia). Moët's stated objective with its Marlborough wine is "to produce a wine that reflects Marlborough *terroir* in its aroma and flavour but at the same time, by careful blending of the base wines, produce a flavoursome, rich, long palate structure with a dry, yet soft finish, which is in the Moët house style".

Best known for its non-vintage Brut Imperial and the liquid status symbol, Dom Perignon, Moët & Chandon is the world's single most important Champagne brand, selling more than twice as much as its closest competitors and commanding over 25 per cent of all Champagne exports. Founded in the 18th century by Claude Moët, it is now part of the giant LVMH (Moët Hennessy-Louis Vuitton) luxury goods conglomerate.

Moët & Chandon has a long history of investment in the New World. It founded Bodegas Chandon in Argentina in 1960, Domaine Chandon, a major sparkling wine producer in California's Napa Valley, in 1973, and Provifin in Brazil in 1974.

In Australia, wine writer James Halliday says Domaine Chandon's sparklings are "thought by many to be the best produced by Moët & Chandon in any of its overseas subsidiary operations, a complex blend of French and Australian style." The Yarra Valley facility, housing a winery, cellar and stunning tasting area, was opened in 1990. For a small fee, visitors can sit in the vaulted tasting area with its sweeping view over vineyards and mountains and enjoy a crystal flute of any of the Domaine Chandon range, including Domaine Chandon Brut, Blanc de Blancs, Blanc de Noir and Rosé.

The New Zealand wine is a blend of Pinot Noir, Chardonnay and Meunier, made at the Hunter's winery in Marlborough by Wayne Donaldson of Domaine Chandon (Australia), and Richard Geoffery, a Champagne-based senior winemaker for Moët & Chandon, working closely with Hunter's winemaker, Gary Duke. Jane Hunter uses her local knowledge and viticultural expertise to source premium quality grapes.

The French influence has been felt primarily in determining the wine's style, rather than dictating production details, reports Dr Tony Jordan, the former managing director of Domaine Chandon (Australia), who is now a consultant to Moët-Hennessy. "The French oenologists don't say: 'This is the recipe.' They do say the wine must have creaminess in the mid-palate and the finish should be dry and soft, not dry and acid."

The first vintage shuttled backwards and forwards across the Tasman during processing, but since 1992 the wine has been made entirely at Hunter's. The grapes are fed directly into the press, with no sulphur dioxide additions. Of the three juice fractions separated, none of the coarser pressings are retained for the Marlborough Brut. The juice is settled in tank for 24 hours, then fermented to produce the base wines.

At this stage, all the vineyards and grape varieties are kept separate, to maximise the final blending options in June. The wine is bottled for its secondary fermentation between August and October, and then matured for two and a half to three years on its yeast lees before disgorging, cork-aging and release.

The style of Domaine Chandon Marlborough Brut has evolved since the first 1990 release, reflecting the growing proportion of Pinot Noir (the 1994 vintage is 50 per cent Pinot Noir, 41 per cent Chardonnay and nine per cent Meunier) and increased (now 100 per cent) use of malolactic fermentation.

Production is small, climbing from 700 cases in 1990 to 3400 cases in 1996, but the wine is sold only in New Zealand, at around $32. "Like Champagne, it will age well in the bottle," says Jordan. "If you like big, complex bubblies, give it up to five years after release."

Domaine Chandon Marlborough Brut is a

Wayne Donaldson, winemaker at Domaine Chandon.

powerful yet refined wine with rich Pinot Noir flavours to the fore in an intense, yeasty, nutty, complex style, very harmonious and persistent. A New World style with French flair, it's one of New Zealand's greatest sparklings. 🍇

tasting notes

These notes are from a vertical tasting of the 1991 to 1994 vintages, held in Auckland in March 1999.

1994 ☆☆☆☆☆ Pale straw. Richly fragrant. Fresh and creamy, with rich citrusy, nutty flavours. Yeasty, ripe-tasting, fruity wine with impressive balance and complexity. Very harmonious and smooth-flowing. **Drink 1999-2002.**

1993 ☆☆☆☆☆ Light straw. Mouthfilling, rich wine, broader than the 1991 and 1992 (reflecting a higher Pinot Noir content) and more forward. Smooth, toasty and very yeasty indeed. Fat, creamy wine, flavour-packed, complex and powerful. **Drink 1999-2000.**

1992 ☆☆☆☆☆ Light lemon/green. Rich, citrusy, slightly buttery bouquet. Strong flavours of grapefruit and nuts in a clearly Chardonnay-predominant style. Crisp, lively and yeasty, with good acid spine and a long, rich, slightly creamy finish. More buttery than the 1991. **Drink 1999-2000.**

1991 ☆☆☆☆☆ Pale straw. Lemony, biscuity, slightly minerally bouquet. Still very vigorous. Crisp, elegant, complex flavours of citrus fruits, with good yeast autolysis and a firm finish. Tight-knit, high-flavoured wine, maturing gracefully. **Drink 1999-2000.**

Hunter's Brut

POTENTIAL CLASSIC

T his is Hunter's best-kept secret – a very stylish Marlborough bubbly with strong, yeasty, complex flavours, crisp, lively and long. Why is it not better known?

"We only make about 750 cases each year," says Jane Hunter. "If you have big stocks of sparkling wine, the demand on capital is huge. It's expensive to make – but fun to drink." She believes Marlborough fizz has a strong future, but has yet to decide whether Hunter's will expand its production to meet the growing international demand.

Deeply scented, elegant, richly flavoured white wines are Hunter's strength, so it's no surprise the Brut is so good. "New Zealand wines are going places. Australians can only dream of the intensity of fruit and natural acidity in Marlborough," says winemaker Gary Duke, a tall, quiet Australian who worked at the Tisdall and Hanging Rock wineries in Victoria before joining Hunter's in 1991.

Hunter's Brut is a classy, complex wine with more assertive fruit characters than are found in Champagne. "Richard Geoffory [a senior Moët & Chandon oenologist] told us: 'You can't get the Marlborough fruit characters out of the wine, so you might as well make it fruity,' " says Hunter. Dr Tony Jordan of Australia, a long-term winemaking consultant to Hunter's (and former head of Domaine Chandon in Australia) has the same view: "I'm helping to make New Zealand wine, not Champagne. In Marlborough, you get a very strong fruit expression, so we keep that as a character of Marlborough bubbly."

The typical blend in recent years has been 55 per cent Pinot Noir, 35 per cent Chardonnay and 10 per cent Meunier. However, Meunier, a key ingredient in Champagne, is currently being phased out of Hunter's Brut: "It's too hard to get uniform ripening," says Jane Hunter.

The style of the wine has evolved over the past decade, based on its increasing Pinot Noir content and the incorporation of new clones of Pinot Noir and Chardonnay. "Back in 1990, there was a lot of Bachtobel in Marlborough, which performs reasonably in bubbly, but little else in the way of Pinot Noir clones," recalls Jordan. "The wine was principally Chardonnay in the beginning, but we've changed it to a Pinot Noir-dominant style. That evolution will continue, with better clones coming through; we'll probably end up with a 70 per cent Pinot Noir content. Sparkling wines with a high Chardonnay level tend to be relatively restrained in their youth, whereas Pinot Noir gives a strongly aromatic, yeasty, bready character."

The grapes are grown in the Wairau Valley, on sites with heavier soils and slower ripening patterns than the estate vineyard. The fruit is hand-picked and whole-bunch pressed, and the wine is matured *en tirage* (on its yeast lees) for an average of three and a half years.

"To get yeast characters, you need at least 18 months," says Jordan. "For the Hunter's style, you

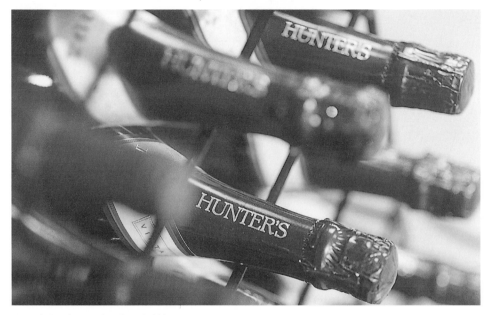

Hunter's Brut is a rare but classy bubbly.

need 30 months-plus. It depends on the blend; riper fruit components need less less-aging. A fine *blanc de blancs* (based entirely on Chardonnay) can still look very acidic after three years and may need four to five years on its lees." Full malolactic fermentation is used to soften the wine, and the riddling process (shaking the yeast deposits into the neck of the bottle) is done entirely by hand.

Hunter's Brut ($30) clearly benefits from the sparkling wine expertise of Dr Tony Jordan, who was formerly deeply involved with Domaine Chandon Marlborough Brut and remains a consultant to the Moët-Hennessy group. Full and vigorous, broad and generous, with loads of citrusy, yeasty, nutty flavour and a creamy, lingering finish, this is one of Marlborough's finest sparklings.

tasting notes

These notes are from a vertical tasting of the 1987 to 1995 vintages, held at the winery in January 1999.

1995 ☆☆☆☆ Pale straw. Strong, appley, yeasty, nutty flavours. Less concentrated than the 1994, but refined, with a crisp, long finish. **Drink 1999-2002.**

1994 ☆☆☆☆☆ Pale straw. Punchy, richly flavoured wine, very crisp and yeasty, seamless and long. Marlborough fruitiness with a Champagne-like power and complexity. Lovely wine. **Drink 1999-2002.**

1993 ☆☆☆☆ Pale straw. Very crisp and bready. Rich, nutty, buttery flavours, long and lively, but lacks the power of the 1992. **Drink 1999-2001.**

1992 ☆☆☆☆☆ Light/medium yellow. Very rich and complex nose. Punchy, deep flavours, lemony, with intense yeast autolysis characters. Long, bready finish. **Drink 1999-2001.**

1991 ☆☆☆☆✦ Light lemon/green. Fresh and full, with strong lemon, apple and yeast flavours. Slightly creamy, with lovely vigour and a crisp, dry, long, bready finish. **Drink 1999-2000.**

1990 ☆☆☆☆ Straw/slightly pink hue. Feathery-light, with well-subdued fruit characters. Dry and yeasty, with a creamy mouthfeel. Ready. **Drink 1999.**

1989 ☆☆☆☆ Light straw. Slightly cava-like, with toasty, moderately complex lemon/lime flavours, still fruity and lively, and a subtle yeastiness. Ready. **Drink 1999.**

1987 ☆☆☆✦ Light straw. Delicate, bready, appley aromas. Light (10.5 per cent alcohol) and lacks real richness, but shows some delicacy of flavour and good yeast development. Mellow, gentle wine. Ready. **Drink 1999.**

Mills Reef
Traditional Method

POTENTIAL CLASSIC

At the opulent Mills Reef winery near Tauranga, Paddy Preston makes one of New Zealand's most classy and characterful sparkling wines. The 1990 and 1992 vintages of Mills Reef Traditional Method both won a gold medal and collected the trophy for champion sparkling wine at the Liquorland Royal Easter Wine Show.

Past vintages of this barrel and then bottle-fermented Hawke's Bay bubbly were a strikingly rich and creamy celebration of Chardonnay fruit flavours, overlaid with nutty oak and yeast-derived complexity. The latest releases show greater delicacy and finesse, with searching, complex, tight-knit flavours in a more Champagne-like style.

In Paddy Preston's opinion, barrel-fermenting the base wine is a major factor in the wine's quality. "Most sparkling wines are tank-fermented, but ours is whole-bunch pressed and then fermented and matured in oak, before it goes into the bottle for its secondary fermentation. By fermenting and lees-aging the base wine in barrels, we get greater complexity – it makes a big difference." The early vintages were entirely Chardonnay-based, but the 1994 vintage is a blend of Chardonnay (70 per cent) and Pinot Noir (30 per cent).

The Chardonnay is grown in the company's free-draining vineyard in Mere Road, on the banks of the Ngaruroro River, and the Pinot Noir is bought from a vineyard in Morley Road, off Pakowhai Road. Both vineyards are near Hastings.

In the vineyard, the size of the crop is crucial, says Preston. Planted on their own roots, the Mendoza clone Chardonnay vines in the Mere Road vineyard are vulnerable to *Phylloxera*, and are being replaced

with Chardonnay and Pinot Noir vines, grafted onto *Phylloxera*-resistant rootstock. The yields to date have been low, varying from 1.5 to 3.5 tonnes per acre.

The grapes are hand-harvested and whole-bunch pressed. "We settle the juice in a tank, take the clear juice to barrels, add a cultured yeast and conduct the primary ferment in barrels," says Preston. Obvious oak flavours are not desired, so three to five-year-old barrels are used. The base wine goes through a full, softening malolactic fermentation in the barrel, and the yeast lees are stirred every two or three weeks.

After eight to 10 months in oak, the base wine is blended and bottled for its secondary, bubble-inducing fermentation. The wine is then stored *en tirage* in a very cool cellar (around 14°C) for three years or more, until it is disgorged.

Mills Reef Traditional Method ($28) is produced in quite large volumes of 2000 to 3000 cases per year, and exported to the UK. Preston believes the wine tastes best "if you leave it a bit" after disgorging. It drinks well soon after release, but the 1992 is still in superb form.

Mills Reef Traditional Method is a classy, delicious sparkling wine. Richly fragrant, with subtle, searching, intensely yeasty flavours, it's a mouthwateringly crisp, complex style with a lot of finesse.

Paddy Preston makes distinguished white, red and sparkling wines, all grown in Hawke's Bay.

tasting notes

These notes are from a vertical tasting of the 1990 to 1994 vintages, held in Auckland in March 1999.

1994 ☆☆☆☆☆ (70 per cent Chardonnay, 30 per cent Pinot Noir.) Straw hue. Very richly scented. Refined, crisp and intense, with lemony, appley, nutty flavours and pronounced yeast autolysis characters. Floats across the palate to a very long, creamy-rich finish. Lovely lightness and delicacy. **Drink 1999-2002.**

1993 Not made.

1992 ☆☆☆☆☆ (100 per cent Chardonnay.) Bright, medium-full yellow. Citrusy, slightly nutty aromas. Strong lemony, biscuity flavours, crisp and lively. More yeast-influenced than the 1990, and markedly more complex. Loads of flavour, rich and lingering. **Drink 1999-2000.**

1991 Not tasted.

1990 ☆☆☆☆ (100 per cent Chardonnay.) Light gold. Rich, citrusy bouquet with toasty, bottle-aged characters. Steady bead. Rich, very fruity, lemony flavours, moderately yeasty. A toasty, fruity New World style, mellow and ready. **Drink 1999.**

Pelorus

CLASSIC

B ubbly is hardly the first wine that springs to most drinkers' minds in connection with Cloudy Bay. Yet the illustrious Sauvignon Blanc producer also makes a notably rich, flavour-crammed bubbly, Pelorus, which for over a decade has ranked among New Zealand's few exceptional sparklings.

Grown in Marlborough, Pelorus is arrestingly bold, fruity and creamy. In style terms, it's a far cry from leaner, flintier wines like Deutz Marlborough Cuvée. Powerful, lush and opulent, Pelorus is an expression of Marlborough's rich, vibrant fruit flavours, overlaid with nutty, toasty, yeasty characters. It's an exciting mouthful – and as explosively flavoured a glass of fizz as you could hope to find.

David Hohnen, the quiet, entrepreneurial Australian who founded Cloudy Bay in 1985, at first concentrated on still wines – Sauvignon Blanc, with instant runaway success, then Chardonnay and Cabernet/Merlot. However, in the mid 1980s Australian winemakers were also starting to discover their country's potential for producing quality sparkling wine. In 1986, Hohnen invited American Harold Osborne, his former classmate at Fresno State University, to assess the scope for premium sparkling wine production in Marlborough.

After graduating from Fresno, in 1973 Osborne joined Schramsberg, one of California's first producers of quality sparkling wine. "[Schramsberg's] big, rich, complex sparklers are, even competitors admit, California's answer to Krug," wrote Jane MacQuitty in her *Guide To Champagne and Sparkling Wines*. After leaving Schramsberg in 1981, Osborne took a two-

year break for travel ("after eight years working in a cave [cellar], I needed to work on my tan," he quips), and refreshed his relationship with Hohnen by working a vintage at his Cape Mentelle winery in Western Australia.

When Osborne got Hohnen's call in 1986 to come to Marlborough, he was working for Champagne Deutz's California offshoot, Maison Deutz. From the beginning, Hohnen had suspected Marlborough had the capacity to produce exceptional sparkling wines. "All that was needed," he recalls, "was an open mind and broad experience in the traditional techniques of sparkling wine production, and Harold Osborne had both." Osborne visited the region, liked what he saw, and in 1987 returned to Marlborough to supervise Cloudy Bay's first crush of Pinot Noir, Chardonnay and Pinot Blanc for a sparkling base wine. Pelorus was born.

Named after Pelorus Jack, the dolphin which for many years guided seafarers through the Marlborough Sounds, Pelorus is a less steely, much softer and fruitier style of bubbly than the traditional Champagnes of France. "Marlborough has cool ripening conditions, so we retain the crisp acidity in the grapes that is ideal for sparkling wine, but we also get riper fruit characters," says Kevin Judd, Cloudy

Bay's manager. "We aim for a full-bodied, savoury wine, but with its riper fruit characters, Pelorus is a very different style to Champagne." Osborne deliberately set out to drive much of the fresh, vibrant fruitiness of Marlborough grapes out of the wine, to create a savoury, yeasty style with richness and complexity of flavour.

Pelorus is a blend of the great Champagne grapes, Pinot Noir and Chardonnay (the first vintage also included 15 per cent Pinot Blanc), with always a slightly greater Pinot Noir content than Chardonnay. The vines, planted in soils ranging from fine silt loams to free-draining gravels, are cultivated in the Wairau Valley by contract growers and in the company's own vineyards. The 1994 vintage, when the vines yielded 9 tonnes of grapes per hectare, was made from four clones of Pinot Noir (AM 10/5, UCD5, UCD6 and Bachtobel) and two clones of Chardonnay (Mendoza and UCD6).

Once at the winery, the machine-harvested fruit is "not handled with high-tech kid gloves," reports Cloudy Bay. "Rather, the wine is allowed to do its own thing." Juice handling is oxidative, with minimal use of sulphur dioxide, and the grapes are pressed without crushing. The alcoholic fermentation (in a mix of stainless steel tanks, large oak vats and French oak barrels) is warm (at 20 to 25°C) and quite short, to drive off some of the primary fruit characters.

A spontaneous, complete malolactic fermentation follows, "to transform the green apple characters into big, buttery flavours, much more delicious." The separate batches of wine are then matured for about nine months prior to *assemblage* (final blending of the base wines). The 1994 vintage was *tiraged* (prepared for its secondary, bubble-creating fermentation by the addition of sugar and yeast to the base wine) in January 1995. After three years' maturation on its yeast lees, the 1994 was finally disgorged in the winter of 1998.

In 1990 the great Champagne house, Veuve Clicquot, acquired a majority stake in Cloudy Bay, but does not have a big role in production. A senior Veuve Clicquot winemaker stands in on the blending tasting, but today the key figures steering Pelorus are still Hohnen, Osborne, Judd and the project co-ordinator, Cloudy Bay oenologist, James Healy.

You can expect to pay around $40 for the vintage Pelorus. That makes it one of New Zealand's most expensive sparklings, but it's still cheaper than most Champagnes. One of the country's most distinguished bubblies, it also matures well – top vintages like 1991, 1990 and 1989 are still in magnificent condition.

tasting notes

These tasting notes are from a vertical tasting of the 1987 to 1994 vintages of Pelorus hosted by Kevin Judd in Auckland in October 1998.

1994 ☆☆☆☆☆ From a vintage Judd describes as "cool, low-cropping and dry – ideal". Pink/straw hue. Toasty fragrance of nuts and oranges. Fresh, strong strawberry/yeast flavours with toasty, buttery characters. Soft, complex style with a creamy texture. An exciting, delicious mouthful. **Drink 1999-2006.**

1993 ☆☆☆☆ From an unusually cold year. Light gold. Slightly honied. Quite developed for its age, with some *Botrytis* influence and a rounded finish. Weighty and flavoursome, but not exciting. **Drink 1999-2000.**

1992 ☆☆☆☆ A lighter, less powerful vintage. Light yellow. Slightly leaner in body than usual, but with rich, citrusy flavours, still fresh and crisp. Delicate, with a creamy finish. **Drink 1999-2001.**

1991 ☆☆☆☆☆ From a "great vintage – average to cool temperatures and dry". Deep straw colour. Very yeasty and complex nose and palate. Structured, lively and lingering – clearly the most Champagne-like wine of the tasting. Powerful and harmonious. Top stuff. **Drink 1999-2003.**

1990 ☆☆☆☆☆ From a "warm, early-ripening year". Golden colour. Richly scented and robust, with loads of flavour – rich, biscuity, citrusy. Complex wine, vigorous and long, aging splendidly. **Drink 1999-2002.**

1989 ☆☆☆☆☆ From a "very warm, cruisy vintage". Light gold. Still very vigorous. Complex and smooth, with rich, strongly yeasty, citrusy flavours, good firm acid and a long, rich, creamy finish. **Drink 1999-2001.**

1988 ☆☆☆☆ From a wet, *Botrytis*-affected vintage. Light gold. Surprisingly good, with no sign of decline. Richly scented and full-bodied, with lovely depth of citrusy, yeasty, slightly honied flavour and a crisp, powerful finish. **Drink now.**

1987 ☆☆☆☆ From a "cool, moderately wet year". Light yellow colour. Citrusy, toasty bouquet. Leaner than the 1988, but still lively, with good acid spine and plenty of lemony, yeasty flavour, now showing toasty bottle-aged characters. **Drink now.**

Cabernet Sauvignon dominated New Zealand's red-wine output for decades. Viewed in the 1970s as the saviour of the country's red-wine quality, by the early 1980s the great grape of the Médoc was the second most widely planted variety in the country. Today, it still accounts for almost seven per cent of the national vineyard, but its ascendancy has been heavily eroded by the earlier-ripening Merlot and Pinot Noir.

In cool-climate regions, Cabernet Sauvignon is a late ripener. In Marlborough, the grape has typically struggled to achieve full ripeness, producing leafy-green wines that lack richness and warmth.

Cabernet Sauvignon performs better in the warmer temperatures of the North Island. In Hawke's Bay, where almost 60 per cent of the vines are clustered, in favourable (warm and dry) years it yields fragrant, sturdy wine of a richness only consistently rivalled by the Cabernet-based reds of Waiheke Island. The top wines can be of arresting quality, with a fragrance, flavour depth and delicacy that can be distinctly reminiscent of a fine Bordeaux. All of New Zealand's finest Cabernet Sauvignon-based reds flow from those two, relatively warm regions.

Many top reds are Cabernet/Merlot blends, in which the Merlot adds its lush fruit flavours and velvety mouthfeel to the more angular Cabernet Sauvignon. Other traditional grapes of Bordeaux (Cabernet Franc, and to a lesser extent, Malbec and Petit Verdot) are also blended with Cabernet Sauvignon, contributing colour, perfume, fruitiness, softness and complexity to the country's finest claret-style wines.

How good are New Zealand's best Cabernets, in international terms? A good vintage of Stonyridge Larose Cabernets, Goldwater Estate Cabernet Sauvignon & Merlot, or Te Mata Estate Coleraine Cabernet/Merlot can hold its own in all except the most illustrious company. In a blind tasting, these distinguished reds sit comfortably alongside *cru classé* (classed growth) Bordeaux. But New Zealand makes far fewer outstanding claret-style reds than, say, Chardonnays or Sauvignon Blancs, and most (especially those from Waiheke Island) are produced in tiny volumes.

cabernet sauvignon-predominant reds

Babich The Patriarch Cabernet Sauvignon

POTENTIAL CLASSIC

This is Babich's flagship red. Launched in 1996 as part of the company's 80th anniversary celebrations, it is named in honour of Josip Babich, who made the first Babich wine in 1916 and until his death in 1983 was the Babich family patriarch.

The Patriarch label is reserved by the Babich winemaking team, headed by Neill Culley, for the outstanding red and white wine of each vintage, regardless of variety or vineyard. Future Patriarch reds could therefore be based on Merlot, Syrah or Pinot Noir. All the early vintages, however, have been unblended Cabernet Sauvignons, grown in the company's shingly, free-draining vineyards in Gimblett Road, Hawke's Bay.

Dark and lush, with the aromas of blackcurrants and sweet, perfumed oak, The Patriarch Cabernet Sauvignon is a seductively warm, ripe and complex red with deliciously rich flavour. The 1994, 1995 and 1996 vintages have all won gold medals, and the 1994 won the trophy for champion Cabernet Sauvignon-predominant red at the 1997 Liquorland Royal Easter Wine Show.

Babich's instant success with The Patriarch Cabernet Sauvignon was based on the learning curve it went through with its former top (now second-tier) red, Irongate Cabernet/Merlot. "With the Irongate red [launched from the 1987 vintage], we initially followed the Australian model," recalls Joe Babich. "For example, we didn't do long macerations on the skins. We controlled the pH, but the wines sometimes lacked warmth and softness. Now the wine has

extended post-fermentation maceration, to soften the tannins and stabilise the colour. We hand-plunge, we've made equipment changes – there's been a whole raft of changes. We didn't settle on the right winery handling as quickly as for the Irongate Chardonnay."

Babich's early Cabernet Sauvignons, bearing distinctive black labels, between 1976 and 1984 were made solely from estate-grown Henderson fruit. The style was medium-bodied, with moderate colour depth and a pleasantly oaky palate. By far the pick of the bunch was the unusually ripe and scented, gold medal 1978 vintage. However, from the 1985 vintage onwards, the decision to draw fruit for red wine from Hawke's Bay paid a big quality dividend.

The Patriarch Cabernet Sauvignon is based on the very best grapes in the vineyard, where Babich has overcome its initial problems with irrigation management and adjusted to the braided soil pattern, in which silty areas of the vineyard have been linked to herbaceous fruit characters. The fruit is hand-picked and the juice is fermented at warm temperatures in small vats. During its long spell in oak, the wine is racked several times and lightly fined, but not filtered, before it is bottled.

The Patriarch Cabernet Sauvignon is a "'Hey,

174

Neill Culley has taken over the winemaking reins from Joe Babich.

look at me!' red," says Joe Babich. Its strong American oak influence (typically 80 per cent) gives it a "more lush, upfront style" than Irongate Cabernet/Merlot. The Patriarch is based entirely on Cabernet Sauvignon, rather than blended with Merlot, because "that's what stands out in the blending trials". And whereas the Irongate red spends a year to 18 months in oak, The Patriarch is barrel-aged for two years.

The Patriarch Cabernet Sauvignon ($30) is made in small volumes – the 1998 vintage yielded 700 cases. "The wine was designed to enhance the Babich image in New Zealand, but it's had a great reception overseas," reports Neill Culley. Small shipments have gone to the UK, Japan and Australia.

Babich The Patriarch Cabernet Sauvignon is a very complete red with an enticing perfume, full, vibrant colour, lovely, sweet-tasting fruit and highly concentrated, persistent flavour. A notably classy red, it has strong drink-young charm coupled with the power and structure to mature well over the long haul. ▼

tasting notes

These notes are from a vertical tasting of the 1994 to 1998 vintages, held at the winery in November 1998.

1998 (Not rated. Tasted as a representative barrel sample.) Dense colour. Huge wine, with a tidal wave of cassis/plum flavour. Enormous power.

1997 Not made.

1996 ☆☆☆☆✫ Full, purple-flushed colour. Powerful wine, especially for a 1996. Fresh and vibrant, with deep cassis, plum and spice flavours, ripe and chewy. Well-balanced acid and tannin structure. **Drink 2000-2005.**

1995 ☆☆☆☆☆ Bold, youthful hue. Highly concentrated and supple, with vibrant cassis/plum flavours, ripe and deep, nutty oak and mouthfilling body. Riper than the 1994, with chewy tannins. Impressive now, but still maturing. **Drink 2000-05.**

1994 ☆☆☆☆☆ Deep, still slightly purplish colour. Fragrant, brambly bouquet. Robust, very generous wine, nutty and chewy, with a sweet oak influence. A hint of herbaceousness, but very persuasive power and complexity. **Drink 2000-03.**

Brookfields Cabernet/Merlot

Brookfields' "gold label" Cabernet/Merlot ranks among Hawke's Bay's most powerful and delicious reds. The virtues of splendidly ripe fruit are reflected, as winemaker Peter Robertson puts it, in its "lovely ripe jammy flavours". A notably dark, fragrant and substantial red, it unfolds well over a decade.

Robertson, a Bordeaux-lover, stresses that his wine is for cellaring, rather than drinking in its youth. "In making this wine, I place a lot of value on what it will develop into. It goes through a trough at four to five years old, when it's ruby coloured and tannic, but at five to six years old, the colour changes and its special qualities start to emerge."

Up to and including the 1995 vintage, the grapes were grown on a warm, north-facing slope across the Tukituki River from the Akarangi winery. Now, the fruit is drawn from what Robertson believes will be a "more consistent" vineyard, planted in a shingly old riverbed in Ohiti Road, behind Roys Hill. The vines' yields are typically three to 3.5 tonnes per acre.

New oak is a crucial ingredient in the Cabernet/Merlot recipe. "You have to recognise good fruit, understand the fruit you're working with, and mature the wine in new wood," says Robertson. By leaving the young wine on its skins for about three weeks after the fermentation, it "gains in structure and the tannins soften". The Cabernet/Merlot is then matured for 18 months in French oak barriques, 95 per cent new.

About 500 cases of Brookfields Cabernet/Merlot are produced each year, retailing at $45. In

the belief that "the wines can talk for themselves", Peter Robertson withdrew from wine competitions many years ago, but occasionally gets talked into re-entering. The 1995 Cabernet/Merlot won a gold medal at the 1998 Liquorland Top 100 International Wine Competition.

Although Robertson is a fan of Pinot Noir, he's not interested in making it: "You can't do everything well." However, Brookfields does produce an outstanding Reserve Cabernet Sauvignon. Brookfields 1983 Cabernet Sauvignon announced the winery's arrival as a serious red wine producer, and that enticingly ripe and fragrant red has been followed by a string of equally successful Reserve Cabernet Sauvignons. Working with "punchy, ripe Hawke's Bay fruit", matured in American oak casks, Robertson fashions dark, weighty, flavour-packed wines that prove Cabernet Sauvignon's ability to produce superb unblended reds.

At its best, Brookfields Cabernet/Merlot is a thrilling red – perfumed, densely coloured and overflowing with very rich cassis, plum and mint flavours. Robust and tannin-laden in its youth, it is a chewy, exceptionally intense wine that handsomely rewards (and in top vintages demands) long-term cellaring.

Peter Robertson produces excellent white wines and a dark, sturdy red that flourishes for a decade.

tasting notes

These notes are from a vertical tasting of the 1987 to 1997 vintages, held at the winery in December 1998.

1997 ☆☆☆☆⚬ (Bottled for only three weeks.) Full colour. Minty bouquet. Rich, concentrated flavours of blackcurrant, spice and mint. More accessible in its youth than many past vintages, with softer tannins than the 1995. A different beast, reflecting the new site (first vintage Ohiti Road). **Drink 2002+.**

1996 Not made.

1995 ☆☆☆☆☆ Huge colour. Still a baby. Strapping, taut wine, crammed with highly concentrated cassis, spice and plum flavours. Complex, with powerful, ripe tannins. The biggest yet? Built for the long haul. **Drink 2002-10.**

1994 ☆☆☆☆ Full, maturing colour. Soft, savoury, plummy, leathery and forward, reflecting its unusually high (30 per cent) Merlot content. A relatively light vintage, but flavoursome and supple. **Drink 1999-2002.**

1993 Not made.

1992 Not made.

1991 ☆☆☆☆☆ Rich, still slightly purple-flushed colour. Big, rich wine. Lovely intensity of cassis, plum and spice flavour. Bold tannins. Nutty, complex and now reaching its high plateau. Slightly finer than the 1989. A star. **Drink 2000-05.**

1990 ☆☆☆☆⚬ Rich, fairly mature colour. Brambly, spicy and savoury. Less lush than the 1991, but lovely now. Firm but softening. Complex. Very Bordeaux-like. **Drink 1999-2001.**

1989 ☆☆☆☆☆ Dense colour, with a hint of approaching maturity. Robust, chewy, leathery, brambly, nutty and complex. Excitingly rich and bold. Big tannins, starting to soften. Slightly rustic, compared to the 1991. **Drink 1999-2002.**

1988 ☆☆☆⚬ Fullish, mature colour. Good effort for cyclone Bola. Still alive. Full bodied, mellow and leathery. Still some pleasure to be had. **Drink 1999.**

1987 ☆☆☆☆☆ Fullish, mature colour. At full stretch now. Very full-flavoured, mellow and leathery. Soft, complex and long. Has matured very well. Ready. **Drink 1999.**

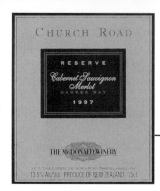

Church Road Reserve Cabernet Sauvignon/Merlot

CLASSIC

When Montana set out to produce outstanding reds at The McDonald Winery in Hawke's Bay, it enlisted the help of the Bordeaux house of Cordier, which owns or manages several properties, including the illustrious Châteaux Gruaud-Larose and Talbot in St Julien. Church Road Reserve Cabernet Sauvignon/Merlot is an eye-catching result – a distinctly Bordeaux-like wine, sturdy and supple, with superb depth of brambly, spicy, cedary flavour and very fine-grained tannins.

Cordier gave Montana clear guidelines, recalls winemaker Tony Prichard. "Prior to their involvement, we were trying lots of techniques, but didn't have a clear direction. Cordier have focused us on a narrower range of concerns: the quality and amount of tannins, barrel handling [no American oak], blending and – the key thing – eliminating herbaceousness."

What style of red is Montana after? "A wine that's more complex than most Hawke's Bay reds and designed for long-term aging," says assistant winemaker Peter Hurlstone. "We want a very soft wine which still has firm, ripe tannins. The fruit characters are not the be-all and end-all of the wine; we want some barn-yardy, earthy complexity."

Australian techniques, including what Hurlstone calls "a fixation with pH and adding acid to fruit that doesn't need it", were abandoned. Low acids became a priority. By leaving the young wine on its skins for an extended period after the fermentation, it builds up a solid foundation of tannins, which by acting as a preservative make pH (effective acidity) a less critical concern. "Huge work" has been done on amounts and types of tannins, including learning how to handle separate parcels of fruit in different ways.

From the start, the Hoy vineyard in the Esk Valley was an important source of grapes, but recently Montana's own vineyards have come to the fore, especially Phoenix Estate, near Clive, and The McDonald Estate, a warm, shingly site at Moteo.

Church Road Reserve Cabernet Sauvignon/Merlot has typically been only about 15 per cent Merlot, but that proportion is expected to rise as new Merlot plantings come on stream. The vines' crops are small, ranging from 2.5 tonnes per acre to an "absolute maximum" of 3.5 tonnes per acre.

The machine-harvested grapes are fermented in large (18,000-litre) cuves imported from France. Hurlstone admits it is "hard" to say exactly what advantage the cuves give, "but you can taste the difference, compared to fermenting the wine in stainless steel or concrete." The cuves taper at the top, which helps to keep the cap of skins under during the fermentation, and when the ferment subsides, the skins sink more easily, helping with extraction.

Church Road Reserve Cabernet Sauvignon/Merlot is matured for 18 months in French oak barriques, between 65 per cent and 80 per cent

Tony Prichard (right), winemaker at the McDonald Winery, with assistant winemaker Peter Hurlstone.

new. During its long spell in wood, the wine is racked regularly to stabilise its colour and soften the tannins. The final composition of the wine is decided when it is about 15 months old, at the time its stablemate, the non-reserve Church Road Cabernet Sauvignon/Merlot, is blended.

Church Road Reserve Cabernet Sauvignon/ Merlot ($35) is only made in favourable years, but then in substantial volumes – about 4000 cases. Hurlstone suggests drinking it at about six to seven

years old. It drinks superbly at three years old, but the releases to date have proved their ability to mature well for at least five years; the 1995 should be very long-lived.

Church Road Reserve Cabernet Sauvignon/ Merlot is a very bold and generous red with great depth of blackcurrant and plum flavours wrapped in quality oak. Fragrant and complex, with huge drinkability, it is clearly one of New Zealand's most distinguished claret-style reds. 🍷

tasting notes
These notes are from a vertical tasting of the 1994 to 1996 vintages, held at the winery in December 1998.

1997 Not made.

1996 ☆☆☆☆☆ Promisingly deep colour. Rich, delicate and smooth. Spicy, plummy, slightly minty and peppery flavours, still quite fresh. Slightly lighter and softer than the 1995, and in its youth more approachable, but shows surprising depth for the vintage, with a sustained finish. Very elegant wine that still needs time. **Drink 2000-04.**

1995 ☆☆☆☆☆ Dense colour. Mouthfilling and highly concentrated, with densely packed cassis, plum and spice flavours and firm but supple tannins. Big, rich wine, set for the

long haul. Warm, nutty. Classic Cabernet-based red of very high quality. Highly complex. Outstanding concentration and structure. **Drink 2000-07.**

1994 ☆☆☆☆☆ Deep colour, moderately aged. Maturing well, with strong, still vibrant cassis/plum flavours, sweet and ripe, wrapped in cedary oak. Chewy tannins. Developing subtle leathery characters. A top wine for the vintage, non-herbaceous, nutty and complex, with Bordeaux-like finesse. **Drink 1999-02.**

Fenton Cabernet Sauvignon/ Merlot/Franc

POTENTIAL CLASSIC

Fenton is a little-known Waiheke Island producer, but in the 1993 and 1994 vintages it made highly distinguished wines. Owner Barry Fenton admits the latest releases haven't been in the same league, but is determined Fenton (as most people refer to Fenton Cabernet Sauvignon/Merlot/Franc) will recapture its brilliant early form.

Inspired by his love of red Bordeaux (each month he drinks two or three bottles of first growth claret), Fenton, an Auckland businessman, bought land at Oneroa in 1988. His Twin Bays vineyard lies on a point, about 400 metres as the crow flies from Peninsula Estate. "The island is a good spot for reds," says vineyard manager Richard Barker Harland. "It's warm enough for long enough to get real flavour complexity."

A bit of a mystery man in Auckland wine circles, Barry Fenton is the owner of Passport United Holidays. He and his wife, Meg, have a holiday home at Twin Bays, but the vineyard is run strictly as a business venture. "It's great to be able to make a bloody good red," he says, "but I also enjoy the stimulation of making a business profitable. The only way to make money is to have an uncompromising attitude toward wine quality. If you make truly great wine the market will eventually recognise that quality and pay well for it."

Stephen White, of Stonyridge Vineyard, was employed as a consultant to establish the vineyard, and initially the future of Fenton looked to be closely tied to Stonyridge. In 1994, White publicised his intention to enter a winemaking joint venture with

Fenton. "Future plans... involve planting a high proportion of Merlot which performs beautifully on the site. Eventually I see Twin Bays as my Pomerol and [Stonyridge] Larose as my Pauillac/Margaux." However, Fenton and White later decided to pursue separate paths.

Sheltered by pines, the vineyard runs down a gentle north-facing slope to a sheer drop, 40 metres above the sea. Cabernet Sauvignon is the key variety in the 1.5-hectare vineyard, with the remaining 20 per cent devoted to Merlot and Cabernet Franc. The vines are heavily shoot-thinned and leaf-plucked, and the vineyard is managed organically; spraying is minimal. In the low-fertility clay soils, the plants yield light crops of only two to 2.5 tonnes of grapes per acre.

The 1993 and 1994 vintages of Fenton were made by Stephen White at the Stonyridge winery. "Stephen asked me: 'What sort of wine do you want?'" recalls Barry Fenton, "and I said: 'A wine like yours.'" Matured in French oak, those wines have matured splendidly, developing a notably Bordeaux-like richness and complexity.

From the exceptionally wet 1995 vintage, Fenton released only a lower-tier wine, labelled simply as The

Red. The 1996 to 1998 vintages were made by Kim Crawford of Coopers Creek. "I asked Kim to make an early-drinking claret-style red," says Barry Fenton. Crawford introduced perfumed, sweet-tasting new American oak, which gave the wine upfront appeal but left it more Australian than French in style.

In a bid to recapture the finesse and subtlety of the 1993 and 1994 vintages, in 1999 Barry Fenton arranged for the wine to be made by John Hancock at the Trinity Hill winery in Hawke's Bay. The grapes are picked into bins, trucked overnight to Hawke's Bay and crushed immediately.

Fenton ($50) is a small volume wine, with an annual output varying between 300 and 500 cases. It matures well – the 1993 and 1994 vintages are magnificent now and should continue to provide top drinking over the next two or three years. The lighter 1996 and 1997 vintages will probably peak at four to five years old.

The 1994 Fenton is the same wine that won a gold medal and trophy in 1995 at the Air New Zealand Wine Awards under the Stonyridge Airfield label. Labelled as Fenton, it was awarded five stars in *Cuisine* magazine, as was the 1996 vintage. If it recaptures its dazzling early form, Fenton will be a label to watch. 🍷

Fenton's initial 1993 and 1994 vintages are currently in brilliant form.

tasting notes

These notes are from a vertical tasting of the 1993 to 1997 vintages, held in Auckland in April 1999.

1997 ☆☆☆⯪ Fullish colour, not dense. Supple wine with cassis and red berry flavours. Good flavour depth but not highly concentrated. Ripe. A drink-young style, lacking the power of the 1993 and 1994. **Drink 2000-02.**

1996 ☆☆☆☆⯪ Full colour, with some development. Fragrant and sturdy, with rich flavours. Sweet, ripe fruit characters wrapped in sweet American oak. Mouthfilling, supple wine with good length. Delicious now. **Drink 1999-2002.**

1995 Not made.

1994 ☆☆☆☆☆ Dense, dark colour with a hint of maturity. Very concentrated and nutty. Softening, but has good tannin structure. Complex, powerful wine, developing mature, leathery characters. Outstanding wine, highly Bordeaux-like. **Drink 1999-2002.**

1993 ☆☆☆☆☆ Full colour, with a hint of maturity. Lovely, supple wine – a pleasure to drink. Very ripe fruit. All of the elegance and complexity of the 1994, in a slightly lighter mould. Again, highly reminiscent of Bordeaux. Outstanding wine, all spice and tobacco. **Drink 1999-2001.**

Goldwater Cabernet Sauvignon & Merlot

SUPER CLASSIC

Kim and Jeanette Goldwater were the first to unearth Waiheke Island's red-wine potential, and after 18 vintages their powerful Cabernet Sauvignon & Merlot is firmly established as one of the country's most prestigious reds. An aristocratic wine with masses of blackcurrant, spice and oak flavour and a strong tannin grip, it has the proven ability to flourish in the bottle for many years.

"To begin with, we were preoccupied with enormity," recalls Kim Goldwater. "Now we aim for elegance. The wine must have balance, finesse and concentration, in that order. Too many winemakers aim at concentration first, and the wine becomes an assault on the senses. Our key criteria are balance and harmony."

Goldwater is no fan of "fruit-driven" reds. "I don't like the modern emphasis on fruit-juice wines, made by reductive techniques [keeping the juice and wine away from air]. I prefer the more oxidative, French-style methods, whereby you transform the fruit into something vinous." The Goldwater red has a distinctly Bordeaux-like character – fragrant, rich and firm, with notable finesse.

The vines are cultivated in sandy clay soils on the hillside overlooking Putiki Bay. "Vines grown in stones can be quite simple," believes Goldwater. "Our clay isn't sticky – it drains well – and the clay fraction gives the vines abundant minerals, from which the grapes get extra flavour." He also views the island's maritime climate ("not too hot in the day and not too cold at night") as a critical quality factor.

Goldwater has found marked difference in the performance of various Cabernet Sauvignon clones:

"The old Corbans/Babich clone and clone 337 from Bordeaux have been vastly superior to others." The original vines, planted 20 years ago, are now extremely low-cropping (averaging only half a tonne of grapes per acre) and may soon be uprooted.

The vinification, says Goldwater, is based on "classic Bordeaux techniques used by the top châteaux." The fermenting juice is pumped over its skins, rather than hand-plunged: "I was told in Bordeaux that if you break the cap [the layer of skins on the surface of the fermenting wine] you break the wine." The young wine is held on its skins for 15 to 25 days after the ferment has subsided to soften its tannins, and then matured for 12 to 21 months in 225-litre French Nevers oak barriques (typically half new). Goldwater used 450 to 500-litre puncheons in the past, but reports "they're too heavy once you're past 50!"

Recently, as the older vines' crops have plummeted, the output of Goldwater Cabernet Sauvignon & Merlot ($50) has declined accordingly. Prior to 1992, the average annual output was 1000 cases, but the 1997 vintage yielded only 580 cases, and 1998 just 500 cases.

Goldwater recommends drinking his red at

between eight and 15 years old, depending on the vintage. The vertical tasting showed the lighter wines drink well at six or seven years old, and that top vintages reward cellaring for at least a decade.

Goldwater doesn't enter his wine in local shows, but it has been highly praised overseas, especially in the US. The 1989 vintage won a gold medal at the Intervin International Wine Competition in New York, and in 1997 a six-litre imperial of the 1990 vintage sold for $US3800 at a New York auction.

Dark and concentrated, Goldwater Cabernet Sauvignon & Merlot is a very classy red. In its youth powerful, brambly and strongly oak-influenced, it overflows with rich, ripe, blackcurrant and spice flavours framed by taut tannins. The early wines were among the finest reds of their era, but the 1990 and subsequent vintages, which offer remarkably consistent quality, have taken the label to new heights. 🍷

tasting notes

These notes are from a vertical tasting of the 1982 to 1997 vintages, held at the winery in April 1999.

1997 ☆☆☆☆☆ Full colour. Rich and strongly spiced, with very intense fruit wrapped in nutty oak. Ripe, balanced tannins and a supple, very long finish. **Drink 2001-10.**

1996 ☆☆☆☆☆ Full colour, although slightly lighter than some vintages. Supple and elegant, with deep cassis, plum and cedary oak flavours. Not a blockbuster, but deliciously balanced and very classy. A forward year, ideal for drinking now or cellaring. **Drink 2001-05.**

1995 ☆☆☆☆☆ Full colour. Elegant, supple and concentrated, with deep cassis/plum flavours and quality oak. Firm but balanced tannins. Nutty and complex. Still developing, but fairly forward. **Drink 2001-05.**

1994 ☆☆☆☆☆ Deep, still purplish hue. Slightly more forward than the 1993, but still youthful, with strong blackcurrant and nutty oak flavours, ripe, complex and chewy. **Drink 2001-04.**

1993 ☆☆☆☆☆ Deep, inky, youthful colour. Very bold and intense, ripe-tasting and taut, with buckets of blackcurrant fruit and spicy oak. A star year with big tannins, crying out for cellaring. **Drink 2002-08.**

1992 ☆☆☆☆ Fullish colour, with moderate age. Fairly reserved nose, but full-flavoured. Leathery and slightly herbaceous. Good but not great concentration. Fairly developed. A good drink-now candidate. **Drink 1999-2000.**

1991 ☆☆☆☆☆ Full colour, showing moderate age. Powerful, firm, concentrated and leathery. More developed than the 1990, with ripe cassis/spice flavours in a complex style with a rich, chewy finish. Offering a lot now. **Drink 1999-2001.**

1990 ☆☆☆☆☆ Full colour, still fairly youthful. A star vintage. Classy oak on the nose. Rich, structured wine with layers of cassis and cedary oak flavours, firm yet supple, with great power and finesse. Still fresh and vibrant. The greatest of the 1982 to 1990 vintages. **Drink 2001-05.**

1989 ☆☆☆☆☆ Fullish, mature colour. Savoury, elegant wine, developed and supple. Not quite as intense as the top vintages, but still very good. **Drink 1999.**

1988 ☆☆☆ ☆ Fullish, mature colour. No delights on the nose, and a herbal influence running through. Plenty of flavour, but slightly rustic, with a lack of fruit sweetness and drying tannins. **Drink ASAP.**

1987 ☆☆☆☆☆ Full colour, fairly mature. Good concentration. Rich cassis, spice and oak flavours, with a leathery complexity. Firm, subtle style with chewy tannins. The best of the older wines. **Drink 1999.**

1986 Not tasted.

1985 ☆☆☆☆☆ (Cabernet/Merlot/Franc) Fullish, mature colour. Quite rich and very savoury. Faintly herbal, but still fruity, with complex, leathery characters. Rounded finish. **Drink 1999.**

1985 ☆☆☆☆☆ (Cabernet Sauvignon) Fullish, mature hue. Leathery, spicy nose. Mellow, developed palate, complex and rounded. Still attractive but very ready, with a hint of drying out. **Drink 1999.**

1984 ☆☆☆ ☆ (Cabernet Sauvignon) Full, mature colour. Lacks real fragrance. Herbal influence. Full-flavoured, but slightly rustic, with highish acidity. **Drink ASAP.**

1983 ☆☆☆☆☆ (Cabernet Sauvignon) Full, mature colour. Slightly plumper than the 1982, with deep flavours of blackcurrant and liquorice. Sweet, ripe fruit characters, holding well. Savoury, complex, mellow and ready. **Drink 1999.**

1982 ☆☆☆☆ (Cabernet Sauvignon) Full, mature hue. Mellow, nutty, slightly herbaceous bouquet. Plenty of pruney, liquorice-like, mature, complex flavour, with a leafy streak. Starting to dry out, but still enjoyable. **Drink 1999.**

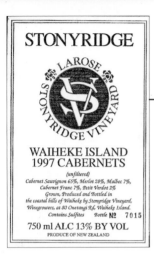

STONYRIDGE

LAROSE

WAIHEKE ISLAND
1997 CABERNETS
(unfiltered)
Cabernet Sauvignon 65%, Merlot 20%, Malbec 7%,
Cabernet Franc 7%, Petit Verdot 2%
Grown, Produced and Bottled in
the coastal hills of Waiheke by Stonyridge Vineyard,
Winegrowers, at 80 Onetangi Rd, Waiheke Island.
Contains Sulfites   Bottle № 7015
750 ml ALC 13% BY VOL
PRODUCE OF NEW ZEALAND

Stonyridge Larose Cabernets

SUPER CLASSIC

After tasting almost every vintage of Stephen White's famous Waiheke Island red in 1999, one conclusion was inescapable – over the past decade, no other red in the country has matched it for sheer vintage-to-vintage brilliance.

Dark and seductively perfumed, with smashing fruit flavours, Larose (as it is commonly known) is a magnificently concentrated red. It matures superbly for a decade and longer, acquiring savoury leather and tobacco characters and great overall complexity and harmony.

The accolades, local and international, have been many. Before White pulled Larose out of competitions, the 1987 and 1988 vintages won gold medals in New Zealand. Roger Voss, in *Cabernet Sauvignon Wines* (Mitchell Beazley, 1991) rated the 1987 vintage among his "20 Greatest Cabernets in the World". Stonyridge also has a maximum four-star rating ("grand, prestigious, expensive") in the huge-selling *Hugh Johnson's Pocket Wine Book.*

"Ripeness, smoothness and complexity" are the key qualities White seeks in Larose. "My original goal was to make a New Zealand red that expresses ripe fruit; so many were so green [herbaceous] when I started. In terms of Bordeaux, I wanted a wine that had some of the strength of Mouton [Château Mouton-Rothschild] and the elegance of [Château] Margaux."

A crucial factor in his success was the warm, relatively dry climate of Waiheke Island. "This valley [Onetangi], this site has an especially good climate. It's north-facing, we have rocks in the ground, and

our viticulture is meticulous. We have five staff working five hectares of vines – that's an unheard-of ratio. We crop the vines lightly, and are absolutely dedicated to the idea that wine is made in the vineyard. And we use all five Bordeaux varieties [Cabernet Sauvignon, Merlot, Cabernet Franc, Malbec and Petit Verdot]; five is better than four."

The vines grow in poor clay soils threaded with rotten rock, which aids good drainage. A kilometre away lies the sea, "which means the nights are not too cold; the Bordelaise like that." The vines are managed organically, with no use of herbicides, insecticides or systemic fungicides. So low are the yields (averaging 11 tonnes off 3.8 hectares of mature vines in 1998 and 1999), White has recently made two Hawke's Bay wines and been forced to "rely on the winery restaurant to keep the company going".

The vinification, says White, is "pretty low-tech and traditional". Extracted gently with a basket press, the juice is fermented with cultured yeasts: "Peter Sichel said that with indigenous yeasts, you run the risk of introducing strange flavours." Following the ferment, the wine is held on its skins for up to three weeks to stabilise its colour and soften the tannins. It is then matured for a year in oak barriques, predominantly French, but about 25 per cent of the casks are American oak, which White believes adds "more obvious characters, but also complexity; more winemakers use it than admit it". In a "big" year, the barrels are almost entirely new or freshly shaved, but in a lighter year half of the barrels are one year old.

Larose is a rare red, with an annual production ranging from 450 to 1200 cases. To buy it, get on the 3600-strong mail-order list. Sometimes the entire mail-order stock is sold to a "loyalty group" of 500, whose members have each bought Larose for the past four years in a row. The 1998 vintage was sold on an *en primeur* (reduced payment in advance of delivery) basis at $70. If you find Larose in a retail store, expect to pay around $95. A cheaper way to taste it is in the winery restaurant, where a "big" glass costs $19.

When should you open it? White suggests from about eight years old onwards: "It should do 12 years before weakening." The vertical tasting showed that the 1987 and 1989 vintages are now at their peak, and that the 1990 and subsequent releases are still developing.

In April 1999, I blind-tasted 12 top claret-style reds from 1995 and 1996, including all the most prestigious New Zealand labels, Château Lynch-Bages 1995 and Henschke Cyril Henschke Cabernet Sauvignon 1995, with wine writers Michael Brett, Bob Campbell and Vic Williams. The two top-scoring wines, both averaging 19 points out of 20, were the Henschke ($95), grown in the Eden Valley of South Australia – and Stonyridge Larose Cabernets 1996.

tasting notes

These notes are from a vertical tasting of the 1985 to 1997 vintages, held at the winery in April 1999.

1997 ☆☆☆☆☆ Rich, youthful colour. Lovely, fresh, vibrantly fruity wine with intense flavours of cassis and plums and a rich spiciness. Very concentrated, mouthfilling and long. **Drink 2003-09.**

1996 ☆☆☆☆☆ Dense, purplish hue. Scented bouquet of cassis and mint. Still very youthful and fresh, with concentrated blackcurrant, red berry and mint flavours framed by firm, chewy tannins. Should be very long-lived. **Drink 2003-08.**

1995 ☆☆☆☆☆ Full, youthful colour. From a wet vintage, not a huge wine, but still offers excellent depth. Very elegant wine with ripe berryish flavours and a slightly more obvious oak influence than usual. Slightly lower alcohol than usual (12.5 per cent) but still very stylish. **Drink 2001-05.**

1994 ☆☆☆☆☆ Dense, purple-flushed colour. Beautifully fragrant, minty nose. Wonderful depth of berry fruits and classy oak. Huge in the mouth. Creamy-rich, with great concentration and big tannins (from a hot, dry, low-cropping year). Still youthful. A star wine that will probably last 20 years. **Drink 2002-10.**

1993 ☆☆☆☆☆ Deep, still purplish colour. Rich, scented, minty bouquet. Vibrant cassis fruit. Still very youthful. A "pretty", supple wine with very sweet fruit characters and a long, lush finish. Highly approachable now, but still ascending. **Drink 2000-05.**

1992 Not made.

1991 ☆☆☆☆☆ Rich colour, with some development. Sweet, strong berry fruits, slightly minty and lush. Splendidly powerful wine with mouth-encircling flavour and balanced tannins, now developing real complexity. Still maturing. **Drink 1999-03.**

1990 ☆☆☆☆☆ Deep colour, still fairly youthful. Tight and elegant, with blackcurrant and spice flavours, still fresh and taut. Slightly leaner than the 1989, but very classy. Still developing. **Drink 2000-03.**

1989 ☆☆☆☆☆ Deep colour, with a hint of maturity. Very distinguished and concentrated. Intense, sweet fruit. Classic cassis, spice and nutty oak flavours, developing mature tobacco characters. Mouthfilling wine, now revealing real complexity. At peak. **Drink 1999-02.**

1988 ☆☆☆☆☆ Medium-full hue, with a hint of brown. Spicy, mellow but not rich bouquet. Not highly concentrated, but attractive – supple, leathery and smooth. Like a mellow, middle-tier Bordeaux.

1987 ☆☆☆☆☆ Rich colour with mature edges. Fragrant, with nuances of blackcurrants, liquorice and leather. Sweet, ripe fruit and firm tannins. Deliciously powerful and intense, with lots of savoury, complex characters from lengthy bottle-age. A legendary vintage, now fully mature. **Drink 1999-2000.**

1986 Not tasted.

1985 ☆☆☆☆☆ Medium-full, mature colour. Old, leathery, savoury nose. Mellow and rounded. Good flavour depth – prunes, plums, blackcurrant. Very ready. Like a very old claret. **Drink ASAP.**

AWATEA
CABERNET/MERLOT
Te MATA
ESTATE
HAWKES BAY
1997

Te Mata Awatea Cabernet/Merlot

CLASSIC

Positioned below Coleraine Cabernet/Merlot in the Te Mata hierarchy of red-wine labels, Awatea Cabernet/Merlot is nevertheless a fine wine in its own right. It is designed to be drunk earlier than Coleraine, and with its perfumed, silky charms, it often heads off its slower developing, more tannic big brother in blind tastings.

Awatea is typically a deeply coloured, richly fragrant wine with a lovely surge of ripe, blackcurrant and spice flavours and a well-rounded finish. It can mature gracefully for many years but is delicious at two years old, overflowing with sweet fruit flavours. "It's our top red-wine label for the restaurant market," says John Buck, co-owner and managing director of Te Mata.

From the 1982 to 1988 vintages, Awatea was a distinguished single-vineyard Hawke's Bay red, grown in the old Awatea vineyard near the winery at Havelock North, once owned by Vidal. Since the 1989 vintage, however, Awatea has evolved into a blend of wines· from Te Mata's vineyard sites, including the recently replanted Awatea vineyard and the Aitken vineyard, across the road from the winery. "We like the sites near here," says winemaker Peter Cowley. "In hot, dry years, their relatively heavy soils give us greater flavour richness." Fruit is also drawn from the Bullnose vineyard, planted in lighter soils at Maraekakaho, inland from Hastings.

Awatea is typically a blend of about 55 per cent Cabernet Sauvignon, 35 per cent Merlot and 10 per cent Cabernet Franc. The grapes are hand-picked about 10 days later than a decade ago, with "less emphasis on analytical data and more on

flavour," says Cowley. "The French call it *sur maturité* – above maturity." This greater ripeness has given Awatea a higher alcohol content and softer acidity than in the past.

The juice is fermented at warm temperatures, and after the ferment the young wine is held on its skins for a couple of weeks to "fill out the palate and increase its suppleness". Maturation is in French oak barriques, typically one-half new. At the time of the second racking, when the wine is due to be transferred from Te Mata's first-year cellar to the second-year cellar, tastings are held to determine the final blends for Coleraine and Awatea.

With an annual production of 2000 to 3000 cases, Awatea Cabernet/Merlot ($32) is fairly widely available. Buck recommends drinking the wine at five to eight years old, "but that's on the conservative side. Beyond eight years, it changes, but it doesn't necessarily get better." Top vintages, like the 1990 and 1991, can mature well for at least a decade.

Awatea lives in the shadow of its more illustrious stablemate, Coleraine, but in its youth is more open and expressive. If you want a truly classy, claret-style red, but don't want to cellar it for five or more years, this richly flavoured, complex and supple wine is hard to beat. ▼

Jonathan Buck with a pneumatic plunger used to immerse the skins in the wine during fermentation.

tasting notes

These notes are mainly from a vertical tasting of the 1985 to 1996 vintages, held at the winery in December 1998. The 1997 vintage was tasted in Auckland in March 1999.

1997 ☆☆☆☆ Full, youthful colour. Cedary bouquet. Mouthfilling, with warm cassis and plum flavours and spicy oak. Stylish wine with good depth but slightly less rich than usual. Already highly approachable. **Drink 2000-05.**

1996 ☆☆☆☆ Full, youthful, purple-flushed colour. Slightly minty nose. Smooth and vibrantly fruity, with very good depth of plummy, fractionally green-edged flavour. A cooler vintage. **Drink 2000-03.**

1995 ☆☆☆☆☆ Bright, deep colour. Tight-knit and very spicy, with excellent concentration. Built for the long haul. Very elegant wine, warm and satisfying, with positive tannins. A classic vintage. **Drink 2000-05.**

1994 ☆☆☆ Full, slightly purplish colour. Leafy nose. Fresh, plummy, green-edged flavour. Distinctly herbaceous. Spicy, with chewy tannins. Won't reach the same heights as 1990 or 1991. **Drink 1999-2000.**

1993 Not tasted.

1992 Not tasted.

1991 ☆☆☆☆☆ Bold colour, showing little development. Generous, very high-flavoured, densely packed wine, still developing. Powerful, spicy and chewy. Currently less seductive than the 1990, but needs more time. **Drink 2000-04.**

1990 ☆☆☆☆☆ Fullish colour. Beautifully perfumed, concentrated and harmonious, with deep cassis and spice flavours. A tight-knit, finely balanced wine, aging very gracefully. A real classic. **Drink 1999-2003.**

1989 ☆☆☆☆☆ Full, faintly purplish hue. Slightly herbaceous nose. Still fresh and buoyant – surprisingly youthful. There's a fractional lack of warmth here, but also loads of cassis, plum and spice flavour. Still developing. **Drink 1999-2002.**

1988 ☆☆☆ ☆ Fullish, browning colour. Smooth, slightly herbal palate, leathery and mellow, with good depth. Still quite enjoyable, but definitely drink-up time. Good effort for the year (cyclone Bola). **Drink 1999.**

1987 ☆☆☆☆☆ Deep, mature colour. Very stylish wine with concentrated flavours of cassis, plum and leather. Excellent depth and complexity. Has matured superbly. **Drink 1999.**

1986 ☆☆☆☆ Full, browning colour. Slightly herbaceous bouquet. Mellow red, still very intact, with good concentration and harmony. Leathery, smooth. **Drink 1999.**

1985 ☆☆☆☆☆ Full, brick-red colour. Holding magnificently. Generous wine, distinctly Bordeaux-like, with excellent depth of brambly, leathery, spicy, nutty flavour and slightly grippy tannins. A revelation. **Drink 1999-2000.**

COLERAINE
CABERNET/MERLOT
Te MATA
ESTATE
HAWKES BAY
1997

Te Mata Coleraine Cabernet/Merlot

SUPER CLASSIC

Named after the Irish town that was the home of John Buck's forebears, Coleraine is one of New Zealand's most prestigious reds, with a pedigree stretching back to the early 1980s. A good vintage Coleraine is a magical wine, with an intensity, complexity and subtlety on the level of a top class Bordeaux.

Te Mata's highest-profile wine, Coleraine Cabernet/Merlot is a deeply flavoured and tautly structured Hawke's Bay red, fragrant and multi-dimensional. More new oak-influenced than its stablemate, Awatea, it is more restrained in its youth. Breed and delicacy are the hallmarks of Coleraine – the sublime 1991 and 1995 vintages can hold their own in any company.

In 1997, Te Mata submitted the 1991 and 1995 Coleraines to a "European Grand Jury" review of Cabernet Sauvignon-based reds from two highly rated vintages in Bordeaux, 1990 and 1995. The 30 wines selected were from Bordeaux (including all of the first growths and a number of "super seconds"), Italy (the "super Tuscans"), California, Australia (Penfolds Bin 707) and New Zealand.

For both vintages, Coleraine finished in the middle of the field, demonstrating, as Buck, Te Mata's managing director, put it, that "we can compete regularly at the top international level, against Europe's best, in vintages of their choosing, in their forums, with their judges." The only two non-French wines that ranked in the top 20 in both tastings were Robert Mondavi Reserve Cabernet Sauvignon and Coleraine.

In assembling Coleraine, Buck (and winemaker

Peter Cowley) make "no concessions to accessibility when the wine is young. It's made to be the best it possibly can be. We go for a highly concentrated palate; the nose comes later. Coleraine is based on our most concentrated fruit, off our oldest, lowest-cropping vines, grown in the warmest sites."

The key quality factor, Buck believes, is "the vineyard site. It's site, site and site – as it is around the world. New Zealand is more site-specific than Europe. In a cool or relatively cool viticultural country, you need a favourable site to give you the ability to make quality wine in the poorer years."

The 1982 to 1988 vintages were grown in John and Wendy Buck's own two-hectare vineyard called Coleraine, but since 1989 Coleraine has been blended from Te Mata's spectrum of vineyards. The core sites today are the Coleraine vineyard ("Our hottest site," says Buck); the east side of the BDM block, first planted in 1892 by Bernard Chambers, the founder of Te Mata Vineyard; the nearby Awatea vineyard; and the Bullnose vineyard at Maraekakaho, inland from Hastings. The vines' yields are restricted to a maximum of three tonnes per acre.

Although based mainly on Cabernet Sauvignon (which forms about 55 per cent of the blend), Coleraine is a blend of three classic Bordeaux varieties. "A straight Cabernet Sauvignon is not as good as one that's blended with Merlot to fill out the middle palate," says Cowley, "and we use Cabernet Franc to add charm and red-berry fragrance."

At the winery, the fruit is destemmed and lightly crushed, and during the ferment the skins are pneumatically plunged into the wine three times per day. Cowley aims for a "more mouthfilling style with softer tannins" by macerating the skins in the wine for two weeks after the fermentation has subsided. The young wine is then matured for 18 to 20 months in French oak barriques, typically 70 per cent new.

With an annual output of 2500 to 3000 cases, Coleraine ($45) is available in reasonable commercial volumes. Buck and Cowley recommend drinking the lighter vintages within 10 years, and top years at 10 to 25 years old.

Breeding, rather than brute power, is the hallmark of Coleraine. Concentrated, complex and slowly evolving, at its best it is an outstanding wine, with exceptional harmony and finesse. No serious New Zealand cellar could be without it. 🍷

Te Mata's grapes are all harvested by hand.

tasting notes

These notes are mainly from a vertical tasting of the 1982 to 1996 vintages, held at the winery in December 1998. The 1997 vintage was tasted in Auckland in March 1999.

1997 ☆☆☆☆✦ Rich, youthful colour. Fresh, strong but not especially intense cassis, plum and spicy oak flavours. Firm yet supple, with a persistent finish. Not a top vintage, but forward and already very drinkable. **Drink 2001-05.**

1996 ☆☆☆☆☆ Full, bright colour. Fresh, strong, concentrated cassis, plum and spice flavours. Slightly less warm than the 1995, but shows classic Coleraine poise and structure. Not a blockbuster, but elegant and tight. **Drink 2001-05.**

1995 ☆☆☆☆☆ Dark. Nose still closed. Big, warm, concentrated and brambly. Densely packed and chewy, with noble tannins. One for the long haul. Beautifully proportioned and very complex. Best since 1991, and potentially the finest Coleraine yet. **Drink 2002-10.**

1994 ☆☆☆☆✦ Full, youthful colour. Slightly herbaceous nose. Deep cassis, plum and spice flavours, with a minty edge. Typical Coleraine harmony. Still developing. A good but not great year. **Drink 2000-05.**

1993 Not made.

1992 Not made.

1991 ☆☆☆☆☆ Rich, slightly youthful hue. Wonderful, sturdy wine, bigger than the 1990, with brambly, spicy flavours of great intensity and ripe, firm tannins. Mouthfilling and strikingly concentrated. A great vintage, arguably the best yet. **Drink 2001-06.**

1990 ☆☆☆☆☆ Full colour, with moderate maturity. Lovely delicacy. Not a blockbuster but sheer class. Deep flavours of cassis, spice and cedary oak, very complex and supple. Bliss for Bordeaux lovers. A widely (but wrongly) overlooked vintage. **Drink 1999-2002.**

1989 ☆☆☆☆☆ Full, slightly purplish hue. Still fresh and youthful, with rich cassis/plum flavours. Lovely concentration and harmony. Stylish, beautifully proportioned wine with a long finish. Developing great complexity, but worth holding longer. **Drink 2000-2004.**

1988 Not tasted.

1987 ☆☆☆☆ Full, moderately mature hue. Soft, mature and slightly herbaceous. Generous cassis, spice and cedary oak flavours. Lacks the ripeness of 1985, 1983 and 1982, but full of character. **Drink 1999.**

1986 Not tasted.

1985 ☆☆☆☆☆ Full, moderately mature colour. Maturing with great style. Generous, spicy, leathery flavours. Big, deep, supple and chewy. Still in full stride. **Drink 1999-2000.**

1984 Not tasted.

1983 ☆☆☆☆☆ Fresher colour and flavour than the 1982. Maturing superbly, with deep cassis and spice flavours, very concentrated. Sweet fruit characters. Chewy tannins. Currently outshines the 1982, and will be longer-lived. **Drink 1999-2003.**

1982 ☆☆☆☆☆ Deep, mature colour. Notably rich palate, now fully developed. Generous wine with firm tannins. Very brambly, nutty, leathery and ready. **Drink 1999-2000.**

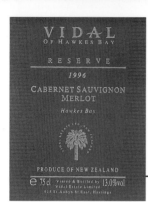

Vidal Reserve Cabernet Sauvignon and Reserve Cabernet Sauvignon/Merlot

CLASSIC

When Vidal Reserve Cabernet Sauvignon/Merlot 1987 won the trophy for champion wine of the 1990 Sydney International Wine Competition, Australian judges were forced to sit up and take notice of a New Zealand red. The gloriously perfumed, flavour-packed and complex 1990 vintage later won the trophies for champion wine of the 1992 Air New Zealand Wine Awards and 1993 Liquorland Royal Easter Wine Show.

Vidal's top Cabernet-based reds are among the greatest in Hawke's Bay. Alongside the Reserve Cabernet Sauvignon/Merlot there is a superb Reserve Cabernet Sauvignon, which serves as a reminder that New Zealand's top claret-style reds don't always have to be blended with Merlot to achieve distinction. Power-packed, with great richness and length, the wines are not made every vintage – neither the Reserve Cabernet Sauvignon nor the Reserve Cabernet Sauvignon/Merlot was produced in 1993, and the last time both appeared is 1991.

"Ripe fruit" is what the style is all about, says

winemaker Rod McDonald. "We specialise in Cabernet-based wines [unlike Esk Valley, Vidal's sister company, where the focus is on Merlot], and with Cabernet Sauvignon there's always a greater susceptibility to greenness."

The early wines were sourced from growers' vineyards around the Bay. Since 1995, the key source of fruit has been the dry, gravelly Ngakirikiri vineyard on State Highway 50, near Gimblett Road, owned by Vidal's parent company, Villa Maria. "Having your own vineyard gives you the chance to run trials," says McDonald, "and it's the best place in

The gravelly Ngakirikiri vineyard supplies some of Vidal's finest red-wine fruit.

Hawke's Bay to grow red-wine grapes."

At Ngakirikiri, warm temperatures and restricting the water supply to the vines are the key quality factors, McDonald believes. Shoot-thinning, leaf plucking and fruit removal give "ripe flavours, deep colour and fine tannins". The grapes are harvested by hand and machine. Yields are low – between two and 3.5 tonnes per acre.

In most years, Vidal releases either a Reserve Cabernet Sauvignon or a Reserve Cabernet Sauvignon/Merlot. "Some years give a great stand-alone Cabernet Sauvignon," says McDonald. "In other years, the Cabernet Sauvignon needs Merlot." The sheer availability of fruit is also a factor. For example, Cabernet Sauvignon came on stream from Ngakirikiri in 1995, but there was no Merlot until 1996.

Vinification is "pretty standard". In some batches the skins are hand-plunged; in others the juice is pumped over during fermentation. The post-ferment maceration lasts up to 18 days. The wine is then pressed and drained to barrel, where it undergoes malolactic fermentation. Maturation is in oak barriques, 90 to 95 per cent French, for up to 22 months. New oak is a key part of the Vidal recipe – each year between 85 and 90 per cent of the casks are new.

Sold at just over $30, Vidal's flagship reds are made in small volumes – 1100 cases in 1996; 300 cases in 1997. McDonald believes the wine's longevity is improving fast, almost on a vintage-to-vintage basis. The 1995, the first vintage to be grown in the Ngakirikiri vineyard, looks set for a very long life.

Vidal Reserve Cabernet Sauvignon and Reserve Cabernet Sauvignon/Merlot have over the last decade been consistently impressive, with concentrated, complex, tightly structured flavours. With the new Ngakirikiri fruit coming on stream, even greater wines lie in the future.

tasting notes

These notes are mainly from a vertical tasting of the 1987 to 1996 vintages, held at the winery in December 1998. The 1997 Reserve Cabernet Sauvignon was tasted in Auckland in November 1998.

1997 ☆☆☆☆☆ (Reserve Cabernet Sauvignon) Bold, bright colour. Rich blackcurrant and mint flavours, very concentrated and supple. Should age superbly, but already approachable. **Drink 2001-05.**

1996 ☆☆☆☆☆ (Reserve Cabernet Sauvignon/Merlot) Bold, youthful, purplish colour. Soft and rich, with intense cassis, plum and mint flavours. Excellent weight. Sustained, supple, finely balanced finish. Great quality for a 1996. **Drink 2000-04.**

1995 ☆☆☆☆☆ (Reserve Cabernet Sauvignon) Bold, inky, purple-flushed colour. Very youthful, vibrantly fruity and densely packed, with great depth of cassis, plum and spice flavour. A monumental red. Still a baby. **Drink 2002-07.**

1994 ☆☆☆☆⯪ (Reserve Cabernet Sauvignon) Full, slightly purplish hue. Closed bouquet. Generous and concentrated, with loads of blackcurrant, plum and spice flavour. Much less herbaceous than most 1994s. Firmly structured, complex and persistent. **Drink 1999-2003.**

1993 Not made.

1992 ☆☆☆☆⯪ (Reserve Cabernet Sauvignon/Merlot) Full colour. Slightly minty. Sturdy, with loads of flavour and impressive complexity, but also highish acidity, reflecting the cool season. **Drink 1999-2000.**

1991 ☆☆☆☆⯪ (Reserve Cabernet Sauvignon/Merlot) Full colour, still reasonably youthful. On a slightly lower plane than the 1990, but still generous, with rich blackcurrant and spice flavours, now softening. **Drink 1999-2001.**

1991 ☆☆☆☆⯪ (Reserve Cabernet Sauvignon) Deep colour. Concentrated and chewy, with a taut finish. Deep cassis and spice flavours, brambly, complex and powerful. Highish acidity. **Drink 1999-2001.**

1990 ☆☆☆☆☆ (Reserve Cabernet Sauvignon/Merlot) Deep, moderately mature colour. Wonderful palate – silky and intense, with enormous complexity. Supple, nutty and very concentrated. Still gorgeous. Hard to spit! **Drink 1999-2000.**

1990 ☆☆☆☆☆ (Reserve Cabernet Sauvignon) Full, maturing colour. Generous, with loads of character. Very deep flavours – brambly, plummy, nutty, softening and ready. **Drink 1999-2000.**

1989 ☆☆☆☆⯪ (Reserve Cabernet Sauvignon/ Merlot) Full, mature colour. Slightly herbaceous on nose and palate. Soft and very full-flavoured. Nutty. Complex. Ready. **Drink 1999.**

1989 ☆☆☆☆⯪ (Reserve Cabernet Sauvignon) Mature colour, good depth. More herbaceous than the 1990. Brambly and concentrated. Cassis/plum flavours, holding up very well. Developing old leathery characters. **Drink 1999-2000.**

1987 ☆☆☆☆☆ (Reserve Cabernet Sauvignon/Merlot) Full colour, still bright. Brambly, spicy bouquet. Big, generous wine with masses of fruit and flavour. Very nutty and complex. Still in superb condition. **Drink 1999-2002.**

Villa Maria Reserve Cabernet Sauvignon/Merlot

CLASSIC

Villa Maria – like the New Zealand wine industry – has been slower to achieve consistent excellence with red wines than with whites. "In quality terms, we're half way to where we can get," admitted Steve Smith, then the company's chief viticulturist, in 1995. "Cabernet Sauvignon has a more exciting future than any other grape variety, except perhaps Riesling."

Villa Maria's flagship red, the Reserve Cabernet Sauvignon/Merlot (a Merlot-based blend in 1992 and 1995) has an outstanding track record in competitions. The 1995 Reserve Merlot/Cabernet Sauvignon won a gold medal and the trophy for champion Cabernet Sauvignon and/or Merlot predominant blend at the 1997 Air New Zealand Wine Awards; the 1996 and 1997 Reserve Cabernet Sauvignon/Merlots both won gold medals at the 1998 Air New Zealand Wine Awards. These are dark, robust, flavour-packed, firmly structured reds with complexity and character.

Not until 1987 did Villa Maria start "getting into the vineyards in a serious way, with very extensive leaf plucking having a significant effect on grape composition". In the same year, the company began to reduce its reliance on seasoned oak puncheons and "got serious" about using new and smaller barrels – barriques.

Chief winemaker, Michelle Richardson, believes the flagship Cabernet Sauvignon/Merlot has continued to improve in recent years. "Its acid levels have dropped considerably, making the wine softer and more pleasureable to drink. Paul Pontallier [of Château Margaux] gave us the confidence to go for low acids

and rely on the wine's tannins to give it aging ability."

The grapes are grown at the company's shingly Ngakirikiri site, near Gimblett Road, and in other Hawke's Bay vineyards. At Ngakirikiri, where the vines are close-planted, heavily crop-thinned and extensively leaf-plucked, "they do a lot of hands-on work," reports Richardson. Devigorating rootstocks, superior clones and carefully timed irrigation also play key roles in obtaining top quality fruit.

The Reserve Cabernet Sauvignon/Merlot is typically based on several varieties; the 1997 vintage is a blend of Cabernet Sauvignon (49 per cent), Merlot (31 per cent), Malbec (13 per cent) and Cabernet Franc (7 per cent). The vineyard lots are vinified separately, "to allow the effects of *terroir* [the total natural environment] to be expressed."

About five per cent of the final blend is barrel-fermented, which Michelle Richardson finds gives "a lift to the palate and chocolatey, raspberryish characters." After the fermentation, in a cool year the wine is quickly removed from its skins, to minimise the extraction of herbaceous characters, but in a warm year, it is held on the skins for up to 10 days, to get "more focused, firmer tannins".

Only French oak is used ("American oak is too 'in

your face', " believes Richardson), although up to and including the 1995 vintage, the wine was handled in French and American oak. Each year, about 40 per cent of the casks are new. After 18 months of barrel-aging, the final blend is selected, the wine is gently fined, very lightly filtered and bottled.

Villa Maria Reserve Cabernet Sauvignon/Merlot is fairly readily available, with an average annual production of 1500 cases. Richardson recommends drinking it between two and eight years old. The

vertical tasting showed that top vintages break into full stride at around five years old.

The distinctive dark labels of Villa Maria's reserve range are a key force among New Zealand's top reds. Rich and complex, with mouth-encircling, spicy, plummy flavour and the firmness of structure to flourish in the bottle, the Reserve Cabernet Sauvignon/Merlot is a consistently distinguished wine. Compared to its rivals at the top of the Cabernet Sauvignon tree, it's modestly priced at $30.

Villa Maria's Ngakirikiri vineyard is increasingly the source of its flagship reds.

tasting notes

These notes are from a vertical tasting of the 1989 to 1997 vintages, held at the winery in April 1999.

1997 ☆☆☆☆☆ Dark, purple-flushed hue. Spicy, slightly minty nose. Vibrantly fruity, with blackcurrant, red berry and nutty oak flavours. Complex style with very good depth and firm tannins, but also a slight lack of warmth, compared to 1995. Needs time. **Drink 2001-04.**

1996 ☆☆☆☆ Deep, purplish colour. Very well made, with plenty of stuffing, but again a fractional lack of warmth. Complex and firm, with deep cassis, plum and spice flavours and a slightly green finish. **Drink 2000-02.**

1995 ☆☆☆☆☆ (Merlot/Cabernet Sauvignon) Deep, youthful colour. Warm, concentrated and rounded. Notably intense, with cassis, plum and oak flavours, supple and chewy. Starting to develop complex, savoury characters. **Drink 1999-2003.**

1994 ☆☆☆☆ Deep, still youthful hue. Slightly herbaceous nose and palate. Tight, with plenty of blackcurrant/plum flavour and chewy tannins. Complex, structured wine. **Drink 1999-2001.**

1993 Not made.

1992 ☆☆☆☆☆ (Merlot/Cabernet Franc) Full, maturing colour. Soft and complex, with deep, brambly, spicy flavours. Delicious wine, currently at the height of its powers. **Drink 1999-2000.**

1991 ☆☆☆☆ Deep colour, starting to brown. Slightly rustic nose. Quite developed wine with plenty of brambly, herbaceous flavour and some leathery complexity. **Drink 1999.**

1990 ☆☆☆☆☆ Full, maturing colour. Very complex and nutty, with excellent concentration. Brambly, leathery and spicy. Warm and ripe. At peak now. A soft, distinguished wine. **Drink 1999-2000.**

1989 ☆☆☆☆ Full, mature colour. Leafy nose. Soft initial impression, but has underlying acidity. Lacks real ripeness, but offers good depth of blackcurrant-like, green-edged, slightly pruney flavours. **Drink 1999.**

Merlot

New Zealand has few classic Merlots, but you can expect a lot more in future. The vine is spreading like wildfire. New Zealand had 10 times more Cabernet Sauvignon than Merlot in 1983, but between 1986 and 1992, the area devoted to Merlot tripled, and during the next three years it doubled again. Within a few years, Merlot will be a more common variety in New Zealand than Cabernet Sauvignon.

Everywhere in Bordeaux, except in the Médoc and Graves, Merlot is more extensively planted than Cabernet Sauvignon. In New Zealand, Merlot's key attraction is that it ripens 10 days to two weeks earlier than Cabernet Sauvignon, and is thus capable of achieving higher sugar levels, lower acidity and riper fruit flavours.

Merlot's stronghold in New Zealand is Hawke's Bay, where over half of the vines are clustered. Much of the fruit is used in blends of Cabernet Sauvignon and Merlot, but the number of straight varietal Merlots is growing fast. Apart from the two classic labels discussed here, two other wines in the Branded Reds section (Esk Valley The Terraces and Te Awa Farm Boundary) have Merlot as a key ingredient.

Syrah

Syrah (usually called Shiraz in Australia) is a noble variety of the northern Rhône Valley, where it yields robust reds with concentrated plum/pepper flavours. As a late-ripener (later even than Cabernet Sauvignon), it has traditionally flourished in hotter countries than New Zealand, but hopes are high that it will perform well in the warm, shingly sites inland from Hastings. Syrah is rare in New Zealand, forming just 0.7 per cent of the national vineyard. Over two-thirds of the vines are planted in Hawke's Bay.

Branded reds

Branded reds, like Cross Roads The Talisman, are not named after their principal grape variety or grape varieties. The winemaker may want to keep all of his or her blending options open, or simply like the idea of using a highly distinctive name.

merlot

syrah

branded reds

Clearview Estate Reserve Merlot

POTENTIAL CLASSIC

Reserve
Merlot

1997
Produced by Clearview Estate
Te Awanga Hawke's Bay
New Zealand

13.0% Alc   750ml

Hawke's Bay winemaker Tim Turvey admits he's "a bit of a gold-digger". With his bold, lush Reserve Merlot, he regularly strikes pay-dirt. The 1994, 1995 and 1996 vintages all won gold medals, and the 1994 and 1996 both collected the trophy for champion Merlot at the Air New Zealand Wine Awards.

Dark, mouthfilling and crammed with ripe fruit characters, Clearview Reserve Merlot is a serious yet sensuous red, with a seductive intensity of spicy, vibrant, almost sweet-tasting flavour. It's a powerful, complex wine with long-term cellaring potential.

Turvey's goal is to make "fruit-driven wines in a Hawke's Bay style. I want my wines to leap unashamedly from the glass and say: 'I'm Hawke's Bay Chardonnay, Sauvignon, Cabernet, Merlot... The reserve reds should show super-ripe fruit, the complexities achieved by extended maceration [skin contact] and French oak influence."

With his Reserve Merlot, Turvey is after "French complexity, rather than just a straight hit of fruit". The shingly, extremely free-draining estate vineyard on the coast at Te Awanga consistently produces robust, very ripe-tasting and flavour-rich reds.

The vines are grown directly behind the winery, in a mix of clay and stone. Merlot ripens about 10 days ahead of Cabernet Sauvignon, but the bunches are highly susceptible to *Botrytis*. "With the sea breezes, we can hold Merlot and hold it, clean as a whistle, until the end of April," says Turvey. "We get it really ripe without getting into the rainy season." The vines, harvested by hand, are extremely low-yielding, with an average crop of two to 2.5 tonnes per acre.

The Reserve Merlot includes a splash (about five per cent) of Cabernet Sauvignon and Cabernet Franc, "to add complexity". During the ferment, extraction is by pumping the juice back over the skins and hand-plunging. Pumping over "gives greater finesse", Turvey believes, while hand-plunging secures greater extraction of colour, tannin and flavour.

The Reserve Merlot spends a total of about 28 days on its skins, including a long period of post-fermentation maceration, and to boost its backbone, the pressings are added back to the final blend. Maturation is for 18 months in French (80 per cent) and American oak, which Turvey says gives "a bit of an Australian influence. The French oak gives finesse and lovely, long, grainy tannins". About 70 per cent of the barrels are new each year.

Clearview's total annual production is a few thousand cases, and with its 400-case supply, the Reserve Merlot ($30) is scarce. Turvey enjoys drinking it at four to five years old, but the vertical tasting suggests top vintages will flourish for much longer.

The Reserve Merlot is not the only red-wine string to Clearview Estate's bow. The lower-tier Cape Kidnappers Cabernet Sauvignon is a chunky red with plenty of warm, ripe flavour. Richly coloured and weighty, the Reserve Cabernet Franc is an

196

Tim Turvey makes one of the country's boldest, richest Merlots.

exuberantly fruity wine with oak complexity and long-term cellaring potential. The Reserve Old Olive Block is a powerful, sensuous blend of Cabernet Sauvignon, Cabernet Franc and Merlot with a seductive fragrance, lush blackcurrant, plum and spice flavours and silky tannins.

Weighty and concentrated, with deep, vivid colour and a powerful surge of ripe, spicy fruit in a fleshy, flavour-packed style, Clearview Reserve is one of the country's first classic Merlots. It's a complex yet upfront wine, "which reflects Tim's personality", laughs Helma van den Berg, Turvey's partner.

tasting notes

These notes are from a vertical tasting of the 1993 to 1997 vintages, held at the winery in December 1998.

1997 ☆☆☆☆☆ Deep, purple-flushed colour. Big, youthful wine with mouthfilling body and concentrated, warm, plummy, spicy, minty flavours, wrapped in sweet oak. Already approachable, but worth cellaring. **Drink 2000-03.**

1996 ☆☆☆☆☆ Bold, youthful colour. Big, chewy wine with deep cassis, plum and spice flavours and oak complexity. Slightly less warm than the 1995, but still highly impressive. Serious, elegant wine. **Drink 2000-03.**

1995 ☆☆☆☆☆ Noble colour, deep and rich. Very generous. More complex than the 1994. Deep flavour and warm, ripe tannins. Excellent concentration and structure. A complete wine

that should mature superbly for many years. **Drink 1999-2005.**

1994 ☆☆☆☆☆ Deep, youthful colour. Big, vibrantly fruity red with loads of cassis/plum flavour, ripe and still quite fresh. A celebration of fruit characters, carrying 70 per cent new oak without effort. Starting to develop some savoury complexity. Powerful, structured finish. Maturing well. The best is yet to come. **Drink 1999-2002.**

1993 ☆☆☆☆☆ (Not labelled Reserve) Fullish, brick-red colour. Big, spicy, slightly herbaceous. Reflects the ultra-cool year. Some fruit sweetness. Maturing solidly. **Drink 1999-2000.**

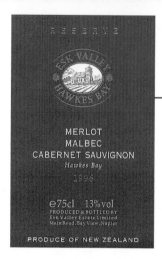

Esk Valley Reserve Merlot-Predominant

Esk Valley's soft, voluptuous reserve red is New Zealand's greatest Merlot, with a host of major awards to its credit. Its exact name (currently Reserve Merlot/Malbec/Cabernet Sauvignon/Cabernet Franc) has evolved over the years, reflecting the varying proportions of minor varieties in the blend, but the wine is always dark, richly perfumed and lush, with intense, plummy, sweet fruit flavours that give it great drink-young appeal, but also the power and structure to mature well for several years.

Why is it a blend of four Bordeaux varieties, rather than a straight varietal Merlot? "We start with a Merlot base (typically 60 per cent of the final blend) and work outwards," says winemaker Gordon Russell. "Merlot provides the heart – a gob full of plums and fruit cake – and we add Cabernet Franc for front-palate sweetness and red-fruit perfume; Malbec for colour and front-palate sweetness; and Cabernet Sauvignon for structure. Each vintage, we build the best wine, given that year's resources. Only in a freakish year like 1998 are all four varieties equally good."

The Esk Valley winery, on the coast at Bay View, is owned by Villa Maria, and Russell attributes the quality of the Reserve Merlot-based red to the group's extensive vineyard resources. "We have a lot of contract growers and, for our company-owned vineyards, we've invested heavily in the shingle country. We have the facilities for small batch winemaking and the company isn't scared to spend on new oak. And our reputation for Merlot keeps us focused, giving us the energy to get even better."

The fruit for the early vintages came from

Malbec grown in The Terraces vineyard adds brilliant colour to Esk Valley's Merlot-based red.

vineyards scattered around the Bay (Fernhill, Bridge Pa, Puketapu, Clive and Gimblett Road), but since 1995 the grapes have come largely "off the stones" – the company-owned Ngakirikiri vineyard, near Gimblett Road, and neighbouring sites. In warm, dry shingle country the fruit ripens earlier, says Russell, "with riper flavours and greater elegance and perfume". At Ngakirikiri, the vines are close-planted and yields are low.

In their pursuit of a "mouth-watering, not mouth-puckering" style of Merlot, Esk Valley's winemakers ferment the wine in open vats and plunge the grapes' skins into the juice by hand every six hours. A proportion of whole (uncrushed) berries in the ferment gives "obvious, lifted fruit characters". After the ferment, the wine is held only briefly on its skins, then matured for 15 months, with regular three-monthly rackings, in thin-staved French oak barriques (70 per cent new).

The Esk Valley Reserve Merlot-based red ($40) is produced in varying volumes – 1500 cases in a favourable year like 1995; 500 cases in a much cooler year like 1997. Gordon Russell recommends drinking the wine "from bottling onwards. People think that because it is so enjoyable young, it may not age, but good wine is all about harmony and texture. It should mature well for up to 10 years."

A star performer on the show circuit, Esk Valley Reserve Merlot-based red has won gold medals for three years in succession at the Air New Zealand Wine Awards, with its 1995, 1996 and 1997 vintages. The 1989 was the runner-up wine of the 1990 Air New Zealand Wine Awards; the 1990 went one better – overall champion wine of the 1991 Air New Zealand Wine Awards. The 1996 recently scooped the trophy for champion wine of the 1999 Liquorland Royal Easter Wine Show.

Dark, vibrantly fruity, and bursting with ripe, sweet-tasting blackcurrant, plum and French oak flavours, Esk Valley Reserve Merlot-based red is one of the country's classiest claret-style reds. Its superb quality, even in cooler years like 1996, makes it an important signpost to the future of Hawke's Bay reds.

tasting notes

These notes are from a vertical tasting of the 1989 to 1997 vintages, held at the winery in December 1998.

1997 ☆☆☆☆ ½ (Reserve Merlot/Malbec/Cabernet Sauvignon/Cabernet Franc) Deep, purple-flushed hue. Plummy and spicy, with slight gamey notes, on the nose. Rich and smooth, with cassis, plum and mint flavours. From a "difficult, cool" vintage, impressively full-flavoured. **Drink 2000-03.**

1996 ☆☆☆☆☆ (Reserve Merlot/Malbec/Cabernet Sauvignon) Full, purple-flushed colour. Beautifully fragrant, soft and rich. Complex, spicy wine with great concentration, warmth and suppleness. A tremendous wine for the vintage. Delicious now. Drink **1999-2003.**

1995 ☆☆☆☆☆ (Reserve Merlot/Malbec/Cabernet Sauvignon) Bold, still very youthful colour. Notably concentrated. Dense, plummy, very spicy, slightly gamey flavour. Splendidly powerful wine. Firmly structured, it should offer outstanding, highly complex drinking in a few years. **Drink 2000-07.**

1994 ☆☆☆☆ ½ Reserve Merlot/Cabernet Sauvignon/Cabernet Franc) Full, rich, still youthful colour. Perfumed wine with strong blackcurrant/plum flavours and a faint herbal edge. Supple and rich, with a spicy finish. Shows a slight lack of warmth, but is developing real complexity with age. **Drink 1999-2004.**

1993 Not made.

1992 ☆☆☆☆ ½ (Reserve Merlot/Malbec/Cabernet Franc) Full, youthful colour, still a bit purplish. Very charming wine with vibrant, plummy fruit characters and balanced tannins. Lacks the backbone Cabernet Sauvignon would have imparted. **Drink 1999-2001.**

1991 ☆☆☆☆ ½ (Reserve Merlot/Cabernet Sauvignon) Full, youthful colour. Strong blackcurrant and plum flavours, fresh, lively and non-herbaceous. Firmer than the 1990, with good concentration and some nutty complexity. Taut tannins. **Drink 1999-2003.**

1990 ☆☆☆☆☆ (Reserve Merlot/Cabernet/Franc) Full colour, showing little development. Very fragrant bouquet of cassis, prunes and cedary oak. Lovely palate – lush and crammed with fresh, vibrant, sweet-tasting, plummy fruit. Mouthfilling and supple. Better backbone than the 1989. Delicious wine, still developing. **Drink 1999-2005.**

1989 ☆☆☆☆ ½ (Reserve Merlot/Cabernet Sauvignon) Full, brick red hue. Leathery, herbaceous bouquet. Soft and smooth, with generous depth of cassis and plum, green-edged flavours. Very easy drinking, with good concentration and a fairly rich finish. Complex and mellow. **Drink 1999-2001.**

HAWKES BAY
Syrah
1997
Grown, produced and bottled at
Stonecroft, R.D.5, Mere Road, Fernhill
Produce of New Zealand
13.5% Vol.   CONTAINS PRESERVATIVE (220)   750ml.
LS701

Stonecroft Syrah

CLASSIC

S yrah (or Shiraz, as the Australians call it) is the foundation of the powerful, peppery reds of the northern Rhône. The noble vine languished in New Zealand until Dr Alan Limmer, of the tiny Stonecroft winery in Hawke's Bay, decided in the mid 1980s that "everything pointed to the fact we'd overlooked a good red-wine variety". With his arresting series of bold, dark, flavour-rich reds, Limmer is the first winemaker in the country to have consistently produced a satisfying Syrah.

With its flashing purple-black hues, rich, peppery perfume, generous body and powerful surge of red-berry, plum and spice flavours, Stonecroft Syrah can be highly reminiscent of a good Crozes-Hermitage. Limmer looks to France rather than Australia for inspiration. "The Australian wines are big, upfront, with jammy fruit and American oak, but they tend to be one-dimensional. Rhône reds have better structure and length. Our reds are heading in that direction; they're New Zealand wines, but more in the mould of the French. For instance, we don't use American oak."

All vintages up to and including the 1997 were grown in Stonecroft's stony, arid vineyard in Mere Road, west of Hastings. The 1998, however, is a blend of Mere Road fruit (which gives "lots of aromatics and a fine palate") with grapes from Limmer's newer Tokarahi vineyard in a warm, sheltered, north-facing bowl at the foot of Roys Hill, which are contributing "denser, more intense flavours".

Syrah is a demanding vine, Limmer finds. "It needs a hard, dry, low-fertility site, because it's a very vigorous grower; it needs a lot of heat to get the fruit

ripe; and being very thin-skinned, it's very susceptible to *Botrytis*. We hang the grapes out as long as we can, until we think they are in danger of collapsing from *Botrytis* or the leaves are falling off. That's when you get the big flavour changes, from herbaceousness through black-pepper characters to violets." The vines are cropped lightly, at between one and three tonnes per acre, and the grapes are harvested by hand.

In the winery, Limmer's views on how to handle Syrah have been changing. "Five years ago, I thought the fruit was the only major quality factor, but now I recognise that the winemaker's input is also very important. The key is knowing what you want to make, knowing what your fruit can give you, and getting that style out of the fruit."

The vinification techniques are aimed at producing an elegant rather than heavily extracted red. In the past, Limmer thought winemaking was "all about extracting as much as possible. My approach was more rustic than anything." Now, to achieve a gentler extraction of the grapes' colour and flavour components, the fermentation is slower and less violent, with less pumping-over. The skins are no longer hand plunged, and after the fermentation the wine is pressed off its skins sooner than before. Maturation is for 18 months in French oak barriques (50 per cent new).

Stonecroft Syrah ($38) is a rare wine, with an annual output of only 400 to 500 cases. Limmer recommends drinking it at four to five years old, "when you get really good aromatics and the palate opens up". Top vintages, like the 1991, can unfold well for a decade.

Alan Limmer doesn't participate in New Zealand wine competitions. The approval that matters to him is when "serious wine people come from Europe and ask me to open the wine. They are struck by the fact that here, on the other side of the world, there's this Syrah reminiscent of what they've had from the Rhône."

There are now about a dozen local Syrahs on the market, but Limmer's not losing any sleep over the emerging competition. "The demand for our wine, especially from the UK and Australia, is so strong. Other serious producers will reinforce the international position of New Zealand Syrah. And if others didn't follow us, it would be a bit strange..."

Alan Limmer produced New Zealand's first distinguished Syrah.

tasting notes

These notes are from a vertical tasting of the 1990 to 1997 vintages, held at the winery in December 1998.

1997 ☆☆☆☆ (Tasted one month after bottling) Rich colour. Youthful, with very good depth of cassis and black-pepper flavours. More muscle than the 1996. Firm tannins. Looks excellent. **Drink 2001-06.**

1996 ☆☆☆☆ Full, purplish hue. More restrained on the nose and less intensely varietal than most years (reflecting the fairly large crop and wet end to the season). Solid wine with a peppery finish. "Needs time" – Alan Limmer. **Drink 2000-04.**

1995 ☆☆☆☆☆ Deep, youthful colour. Very perfumed bouquet – violets and pepper. Searching flavours of cassis, plum and spice. Very concentrated and chewy, with warm tannins. Lovely scale. Good body, flavour and structure. **Drink 1999-2005.**

1994 ☆☆☆☆☆ Big, robust wine, warm and supple. Cassis, plum and pepper flavours, richly spicy. Bold tannins. Opening out splendidly, with great backbone. Beautiful now, but will keep getting better. **Drink 1999-2004.**

1993 ☆☆☆☆ Deep colour. Pungently peppery on the nose, which is also green-edged. Slightly herbaceous palate. Softening. Clearly reflects the abnormally cool year. Ready. **Drink 1999-2000.**

1992 ☆☆☆☆☆ Deep, purplish colour. Very strong peppery characters. Deep cassis and plum flavours, but slightly lighter than the 1991. Fresh and supple, with accentuated spiciness. **Drink 1999-2001.**

1991 ☆☆☆☆☆ Deep, youthful, purple-flushed colour. A standout vintage. Majestic wine – powerful and still youthful, with very concentrated blackcurrant, plum and pepper flavours. Maturing very gracefully. Firm, balanced tannins. **Drink 1999-2005.**

1990 ☆☆☆☆ Deep, purplish colour, amazingly youthful. Strongly peppery on nose and palate. Still fresh and still developing. Vibrantly fruity, with crisp acidity. Less ripe than the 1991. **Drink 1999-2005.**

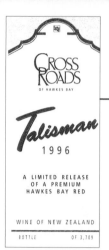

Cross Roads
The Talisman

POTENTIAL CLASSIC

"The Talisman is different to any other New Zealand wine," says Hawke's Bay winemaker Malcolm Reeves. It's a blend of six red grapes whose identities Reeves delights in concealing, but says were chosen after studying the varietal components of Chianti, the super-Tuscan reds, Châteauneuf-du-Pape and Bordeaux. Whatever its varietal make-up, The Talisman is a boldly coloured, highly fragrant, voluptuous red, bursting with sweet, ripe fruit flavours.

From the start, Reeves and his partner, Lester O'Brien, set out to make something unique. "In terms of style, we didn't intend to mimic anything, but felt the grapes had the potential to make an elegant New Zealand red. We're not trying to kill the Aussies with a big red, or rival the sophistication of Pinot Noir. We wanted something that would sit alongside the claret-style reds of Hawke's Bay and be different."

Malcolm Reeves and Lester O'Brien first met in the early 1970s when both were lecturing at Massey University in Palmerston North. When their paths crossed again in Paris in 1981, Reeves suggested to O'Brien that they establish a winery. Hence the company name: Cross Roads.

Lester O'Brien is the general manager. Malcolm Reeves, wine columnist for *The Evening Standard* in Palmerston North, and formerly a senior lecturer in food technology, specialising in sensory evaluation and fermentation technology, is the winemaker. With his research background, Reeves is naturally eager to pursue red wines. "The potential for reds in Hawke's Bay hasn't been fully explored yet," he believes.

Crucial to the wine's quality to date, says Reeves,

is the fact that it's a blend of so many grapes. "That gives us the opportunity to mix and match. The strengths of one variety counter the weaknesses of others."

The grapes are all grown in the estate vineyard on State Highway 50, on the Taradale side of Fernhill, although that may change in future. Much attention is paid to shoot-thinning, leaf-plucking and bunch-thinning, and the vines' yields are limited to around three tonnes of grapes per acre, harvested by hand.

And what are the grape varieties? "A to F," chuckles Reeves, who currently has no plans to divulge their identity. Malbec, a traditional Bordeaux variety which has rich, plummy flavour, brilliant colour and sweet fruit flavours, could be a key contributor to the wine's make-up – but that's just my guess.

The individual grape varieties are fermented separately in small, open vats, and the cap of skins is regularly plunged into the juice by hand. In some years the wine is held on its skins for a lengthy period; in others it is pressed soon after the fermentation has finished. Maturation is in French

Malcolm Reeves keeps pundits guessing about the varietal composition of The Talisman.

and (since 1995) American oak barriques, with a high percentage of new wood.

During its two-year sojourn in casks, the wine is racked frequently to soften its tannins. An initial blend of the various varieties is made after a year, followed by a final blend adjustment at 21 months, prior to bottling.

Production of The Talisman ($36) is rising, but the wine is still in limited volumes. Only 100 cases were made of the debut 1994 vintage, but since then the output has averaged 300 cases and the 1998 vintage yielded 600 cases. Reeves recommends cellaring The Talisman until it is four years old, "for good enjoyment", and suggests a further four years' cellaring will bring a "gentle rise" in form. The early vintages are all maturing strongly.

To blend a red wine from six grape varieties is highly unusual in New Zealand, and to keep their identities a fiercely guarded secret adds to the wine's fascination. Whatever its varietal make-up, The Talisman is a lush, deliciously full-flavoured wine with strong personality.

tasting notes

These notes are mainly from a vertical tasting of the 1994 to 1996 vintages, held in Auckland in January 1999. The 1997 vintage was tasted in Auckland in April 1999.

1997 ☆☆☆☆ Full, bright, youthful colour. Rich, berryish, perfumed nose. Full and supple. A forward vintage, smooth and rich, with sweet oak and upfront appeal. Not highly complex. Soft and spicy, in a rather Australian style. Lacks the power and complexity of a top year. **Drink 2000-02.**

1996 ☆☆☆☆☆ Fullish, purplish colour. Welcoming fragrance, with ripe berry and sweet oak aromas. Plump, velvety, very mouthfilling and rich. Intensely fruity and supple. More forward than the 1995, but still developing. Youthful, complex wine, with excellent weight and real depth of character. The most charming of the quartet. **Drink 2000-03.**

1995 ☆☆☆☆☆ Full, moderately youthful colour. Sturdy, tannic red, developing considerable complexity. Nutty, slightly minty bouquet. Less perfumed than the 1996, and slightly more austere. Sweet, ripe fruit characters. Brambly, nutty flavours, with a long, chewy finish. **Drink 2000-02.**

1994 ☆☆☆☆☆ Dense, still purple-flushed hue. Strapping, highly concentrated wine, built for the long haul. Rich, very deep flavours of blackcurrants and nutty oak in a complex style with chewy but balanced tannins. A top 1994, chock full of cellaring potential. **Drink 1999-2005.**

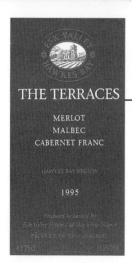

Esk Valley
The Terraces

At $59, The Terraces is one of Hawke's Bay's most expensive reds, but it's also one of the greatest, with enormous scale and bottomless depth. An excitingly bold, dark wine with intense, plummy, spicy, complex flavours, braced by firm tannins, in top vintages it cries out for cellaring for at least five years, ideally a decade.

Soon after Villa Maria purchased the Esk Valley winery (then called Glenvale) in 1987, a steep, north-facing terraced hillside bordering the winery at Bay View, originally planted with vines in the 1940s but later established in pines, was replanted in Merlot, Malbec, Cabernet Sauvignon and Cabernet Franc. Today this densely planted, drought-prone, irrigated vineyard each year yields an exceptional red wine – The Terraces. "I'm the custodian of what is potentially one of New Zealand's greatest vineyards," says winemaker Gordon Russell.

Russell sees The Terraces as continuing "the whole French thing – you take the grapes from the terraced vineyard, put the wine into the barrel and then the bottle. It's very simple". The style of The Terraces, he says, is "what nature gives us". The Cabernet Sauvignon vines were uprooted in late 1995, because it always ripened later than the other varieties. "The rest of the vineyard is so successful, we thought: Why persevere with Cabernet Sauvignon? We don't need it."

The vines, although 10 years old, are still small: "They've had to struggle to survive," says Russell. It's an unusually hot, early-ripening site: "If we planted Chardonnay up there, we could harvest it in February." The vines' yields are very low, averaging only two tonnes per acre.

The hand-harvested grapes are de-stemmed and pumped to open fermentation vats, where the cap of skins is hand-plunged every six hours. "This traditional method is very labour intensive, but it allows a gentle extraction from the skins, resulting in soft-finishing wine without harsh tannins," says Russell.

Near the end of the ferment, the wine is pressed off the skins to complete the ferment in all-new French oak barriques. After the completion of the primary (alcoholic) and malolactic fermentations, The Terraces is barrel-matured for 15 to 18 months, with several rackings during the first year, then egg-white fined and bottled without filtration.

Merlot and Malbec are typically the major ingredients in The Terraces, supplemented by Cabernet Franc. Muscular, with a warmth and concentration rare in New Zealand reds, The Terraces is a dark, spicy, meaty, tannic red, with a distinctive extra dimension that reflects its high Malbec content (30 per cent in 1991; 40 per cent in 1995). Malbec, says Russell, gives the wine "perfume, spice, tannin and brilliant colour".

Production of The Terraces is limited to between 200 and 400 cases per year, and in such unfavourable seasons as 1993, 1996 and 1997, the label does not appear. The wine is not entered in competitions, despite Villa Maria's strong commitment to the show circuit. "It's not a show wine," says Russell. "It's the most expensive wine made by the Villa Maria group –

a symbol of what we can do."

A statuesque red with noble colour, The Terraces offers exceptional depth of splendidly ripe blackcurrant, plum and spice flavours. In 1991, Esk Valley predicted that The Terraces vineyard would "set the standard for New Zealand red wines in the 21st century". A bold prediction, but progress so far has been exciting. 🍇

From The Terraces vineyard flows one of New Zealand's most powerful, concentrated reds.

tasting notes

These notes are from a tasting of the 1991 to 1998 vintages, held at the winery in December 1998.

1998 (Not rated. Tasted as a barrel sample.) Inky, impenetrable colour. Spicy aromas. Hugely concentrated and strapping wine, on the scale of the 1991 and 1995. Should be a classic vintage.

1997 Not made.

1996 Not made.

1995 ☆☆☆☆☆ (Merlot/Malbec/Cabernet Franc) Super-dense colour. Extraordinarily intense, with a tidal wave of flavour – cassis, spice, plum. Buried tannins. Formidable concentration. Still very unevolved. **Drink 2002-10.**

1994 ☆☆☆☆☆ (Merlot/Malbec/Cabernet Franc /Cabernet Sauvignon) Deep, youthful hue. Generous, concentrated wine with blackcurrant and plum flavours. Still very fresh, with a

powerful finish. Needs more time. **Drink 2001-03.**

1993 Not made.

1992 ☆☆☆☆⚡ (Merlot/Malbec/Cabernet Franc) Full, youthful colour. Fragrant and chewy. Slightly less warm than the 1991. Sturdy and very spicy, with good concentration. Will reach a slightly lower peak than the 1991. **Drink 2000-04.**

1991 ☆☆☆☆☆ (Merlot/Cabernet Franc/Malbec/Cabernet Sauvignon) Dense, purple-flushed colour. Very complex fragrance. Serious, highly spiced red with great power. Cassis, pepper and plum flavours of enormous concentration. Becoming very approachable, but still taut. Greatness stamped all over it. **Drink 1999-2006.**

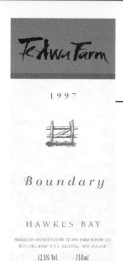

Te Awa Farm Boundary

POTENTIAL CLASSIC

From the start, Gus Lawson's ambition at Te Awa Farm was to produce great red wines. His family's warm, free-draining vineyard site on State Highway 50, near Gimblett Road in Hawke's Bay, is well suited to the task. Another crucial asset is Jenny Dobson, a passionate, widely experienced winemaker who was once the *maitre d'chais* at a well-respected Haut-Médoc *cru bourgeois*, Château Senejac.

Te Awa Farm Boundary is a Merlot-predominant red of rare breed. Subtle, multi-faceted and beautifully harmonious, it is more complex, delicate, savoury and finely balanced than most New Zealand reds. If you're a Bordeaux fan, you'll love it.

"We're making wine to drink with food," stresses Jenny Dobson. "It must be complex and complete, with mouthfeel and texture. To keep the wine lively, you need good structure on the end of the palate, but the tannins should be aromatic, not drying."

It's still early days for Te Awa Farm Boundary (the first vintage, called Boundary Merlot, was 1995), but this is clearly a major new label on the rise. "Our site is important – the soil, climate, *terroir*," says Dobson. "We believe that we have the potential to make great red wine, and are committed to fulfilling that potential by listening to nature and the grapes, rather than trying to change what nature gives us."

The vineyard, says Dobson, is an early-ripening site in which the gravelly soils warm up early in spring and keep the heat at night. "We don't have to do too much work with the vines; we don't get excessive canopy growth or yields." A balanced vine is the goal. "At pruning, you need to leave the right number of buds for the vigour of each vine. We shoot-

thin for an open, balanced canopy, and if you do that well, you don't need to do much leaf-plucking." Irrigation is kept to a minimum: "Just enough to keep the vines going."

The vines crop at between 2.5 and three tonnes per acre, and the grapes are hand-harvested from the most gravelly parts of the vineyard. "Due to the braided soil pattern, we rarely pick a whole row in one go," says Dobson. "Instead, the pickers follow the gravel ridges."

The 1998 Boundary is a blend of Merlot (76 per cent), Cabernet Sauvignon (13 per cent), Cabernet Franc (nine per cent) and Malbec (two per cent). The Merlot was picked from four zones within the vineyard, with each batch reflecting the different soils: "some was plummy, some was spicy; some was structured, some was luscious." The Cabernet Sauvignon from one block was "classic Bordeaux – lean and earthy"; from another part of the vineyard, it was "Australian – big and fat". The Cabernet Franc added "intense perfume", and Malbec "fragrance and spice".

Boundary is fermented in open-top vats at high temperatures – up to 34°C. Extraction is partly by hand-plunging, but Dobson also pumps the fermenting juice back over the skins "to get a gentle extraction of tannin and good immersion of the cap in the wine". The post-ferment maceration (holding the young wine on its skins) is critical. "It's very important for structure and complexity. We taste the tanks every day, looking for a balance of richness and tannins."

Maturation is for 12 to 15 months in French oak barriques, typically 40 per cent new. Dobson is not a fan of American oak. "I prefer the flavour of French oak and the tannins it imparts. American oak gives coarser tannins and its coconut/vanilla characters are not the flavours we're looking for."

At first, only about 500 cases of Boundary ($28) were produced annually, but with the increasing age of the vines, production is heading to 1000 cases.

Dobson sees a good vintage of Boundary as being a 10-year wine, "but its lushness and balance also make it enjoyable soon after bottling." The 1995 vintage is still ascending.

Jenny Dobson doesn't expect Boundary to win a lot of gold medals. "It's not a show wine – it's not flashy. But a group of French winemakers who came here in February [1999] and tasted the 1998 were astounded New Zealand could produce wine like that."

Boundary is a wine that impresses with finesse, subtlety and harmony, rather than brute power. Warm and savoury, with earthy, gamey nuances, it's one of the most deeply satisfying claret-style reds in Hawke's Bay. 🍷

Jenny Dobson's lengthy Bordeaux experience is clearly reflected in her Hawke's Bay reds.

tasting notes

These notes are mainly from a vertical tasting of the 1995 to 1997 vintages, held in Auckland in November 1998. The 1998 barrel sample was tasted in Auckland in April 1999.

1998 (Tasted as a representative barrel sample.) Red/black colour of great density. Hugely mouthfilling and supple, with masses of cassis, plum and spice flavour, very deep and rounded. Warm and soft, with ripe, noble tannins. Astonishing body and flavour – freakish, really.

1997 ☆☆☆☆½ (Tasted soon after bottling.) Deep, youthful colour. Powerful, with very good flavour concentration, oak complexity and fine-grained tannins. Classy wine that should open out well. Not entirely free of herbaceousness, reflecting the cool year, but very generous and harmonious, with lovely

texture. **Drink 2000-05.**

1996 ☆☆☆☆☆ Medium-full colour. Plummy, leathery bouquet. Very subtle and complex red, savoury and mouthfilling. Warm and harmonious. Great effort for a cool year. Developing real interest with age. Distinctly Bordeaux-like. **Drink 2000-03.**

1995 ☆☆☆☆☆ Full, dense colour. Fragrant nose of blackcurrants and spice. Powerful, robust and very concentrated. Warm and non-herbaceous. Crammed with ripe, sweet fruit, wrapped in nutty oak. Chewy, balanced tannins. Highly complex wine, developing well. **Drink 2000-03.**

Making great **Pinot Noir** is not easy. The variety demands a cool climate to conjure up its most magical scents and flavours, and is highly vulnerable to spring frosts and bunch rot. "It's an on-going challenge," admits winemaker Larry McKenna. Yet Pinot Noir may prove to be New Zealand's greatest red-wine gift to the world.

Pinot Noir is the princely grape variety of red Burgundy. Basic Pinot Noir is simple and raspberryish, but at its best Pinot Noir is a gorgeous wine – substantial and rich, complex and supple. Only in cool-climate regions does it reveal its full class, and in New Zealand it has performed best in the Wairarapa and parts of the South Island.

Pinot Noir is the country's most widely planted black-skinned grape (ahead of Cabernet Sauvignon), and between 1998 and 2001 the area of bearing vines will skyrocket by 71 per cent. Much of the crop in Marlborough is reserved for bottle-fermented sparkling wine, but the number of serious Pinot Noirs on the market is expanding swiftly.

From Hawke's Bay to the deep south, Pinot Noir is well established, and in the Wairarapa and Central Otago it is the most extensively planted variety of all. Five of the six classic Pinot Noirs featured in this book are grown in the Martinborough district, which has won an international reputation for the quality of its mouthfilling, richly flavoured, intensely varietal reds.

Would Larry McKenna of Martinborough Vineyard, Clive Paton of Ata Rangi, Neil McCallum of Dry River and Allan Johnson of Palliser Estate have enjoyed equal success, had they gone to Marlborough rather than Martinborough to make great Pinot Noir? Their passion for Pinot Noir and willingness to sacrifice quantity in the pursuit of quality have clearly been critical factors in the Martinborough success story.

In the warmth of Hawke's Bay, the variety has typically yielded sturdy wines that lack the perfume and silkiness of fine Pinot Noir. Many South Island examples lack ripeness and concentration, but a few distinguished wines have flowed from Marlborough, Nelson and Canterbury, and in Central Otago the noble Burgundian grape has discovered another antipodean home.

pinot noir

Ata Rangi Pinot Noir

Powerfully built and concentrated, yet seductively fragrant and supple, Ata Rangi is one of the greatest – arguably the greatest – of all New Zealand Pinot Noirs. Past vintages won a pile of gold medals and trophies, but this consistently top-flight wine is no longer entered in local competitions. "With the styles we want to achieve, our focus is recognition in the international arena, rather than just in New Zealand," says Clive Paton, founder of the small Martinborough winery.

"Intense, opulent fruit with power beneath" is the style Paton is after. "I want firmness and intense fruit. Complexity comes with time. We put enough things in there to make sure it happens. The clonal mix ensures it ages well to 'forest floor' characters" (or what an Ata Rangi blurb called "that funky, wildly sensuous, snuffly, truffly, in-the-barnyard carry-on that is the quintessence of great Pinot Noir!")

In Paton's view, the Martinborough district's crucial advantage is that winemakers can get their grapes very ripe without any loss of varietal character. "In Hawke's Bay, you don't get that fruit intensity. Here, you can hang the grapes out, get them super-ripe, yet still get essential Pinot Noir characters."

Both in the Old World and the New World, methods of handling Pinot Noir vary widely, and the choices made are critical. "You need a really open mind," says Paton, who has made wine in Burgundy three times, and twice in Oregon. "We've always known about the Burgundian techniques, but going over there and actually doing it their way gives you the confidence."

The grapes for Ata Rangi Pinot Noir are drawn from numerous sites in Martinborough, including the estate vineyard, planted in 1980; "Champ Ali", an adjacent vineyard owned by Paton's sister, Alison, and her husband, Oliver Masters; the Fraser block, owned by Murdoch James Estate; the Craighall vineyard, owned by Ata Rangi and Dry River; and the Di Mattina block, leased by Ata Rangi. The range of sites contributes to the wine's complexity, Paton believes: "They're all incredibly different. For example, the Fraser block has six different clones of Pinot Noir, picked at different times over two to three weeks."

In the 1980s, Ata Rangi was quick to adopt viticulturist Dr Richard Smart's ideas about turning "sunlight into wine", including Scott Henry trellising. More recent work with viticulturist Dr David Jordan has focused on balancing the vines in search of improved grape quality.

Paton got his original vines from Malcolm Abel, founder of the now-defunct Abel & Co winery at Kumeu. "When Malcolm was still a customs officer, a vine was confiscated from a guy who'd hopped over the fence at Romanée-Conti [the fabled *grand cru* of Vosne-Romanée], taken a cutting and hidden it in his gumboot. Malcolm got the first vines out of quarantine." That the main clone at Ata Rangi remains unidentified, doesn't worry Paton: "We know what it can do. It gives staying power and elegance." As the vines planted in 1980 mature and develop more extensive root systems, their fruit is showing greater flavour intensity.

Pinot Noir is particularly sensitive to over-cropping, and at Ata Rangi the maximum crop permitted is three tonnes per acre. "We have to be very careful with the year," says Paton. "It's OK to go to three tonnes per acre in a warm season like 1996, but in a cool year we need lower yields."

In the winery, the skins are cold-soaked in the juice for several days prior to the ferment, which Paton finds gives "good colour and tannins which are not harsh at all". The wine is fermented in small batches, with regular hand-plunging of the cap, and up to 15 per cent whole-bunch fermentation gives "stalk-derived spiciness and tautness". The wood maturation is for a year in French oak barriques, typically 25 per cent new.

Ata Rangi Pinot Noir ($40) is available in reasonable volumes, with an annual production of 1500 to 2000 cases. "We could easily sell twice that much," says Paton. "The challenge is for us to make 4000 to 5000 cases of that standard – or better." He recommends drinking the wine at four to eight years old, when, as the vertical tasting discovered, its full personality is revealed.

Although Ata Rangi has now withdrawn from local shows, the 1989 to 1996 vintages won 10 gold medals and seven trophies in New Zealand and the UK. The 1995 vintage was praised by Robert Parker, the American wine guru, as "an amazingly complete wine with a complex Burgundian personality... [that] made me rethink my position concerning the potential for classy red wines from New Zealand."

A stylish, superbly concentrated red with plummy, spicy, smoky flavours and power right through the palate, Ata Rangi Pinot Noir enjoys a cult following in New Zealand – and that's one cult I'm happy to belong to. 🍇

tasting notes

These notes are from a vertical tasting of the 1988 to 1998 vintages, held at the winery in November 1998.

1998 (Not rated. Tasted as a barrel sample.) Densely coloured. Very concentrated, chewy and tight-knit. Should be very powerful and long-lived.

1997 ☆☆☆☆☆ Deep, youthful colour. Chewy tannins. Less seductively fruity than the 1996 at this stage, but perhaps more complex. Very powerful wine, spicy and firm. Serious stuff for the long haul. **Drink 2000-05.**

1996 ☆☆☆☆☆ Full, youthful hue. Robust wine (14 per cent alcohol), crammed with ripe, cherry and plum fruit characters. Very substantial. Still fresh. Lovely mouthfeel. Beautiful wine, potentially very complex. **Drink 2000-04.**

1995 ☆☆☆☆☆ Fullish, still purplish colour. Less opulent than the 1996 or 1994. Mouthfilling, with cherry/plum characters and good flavour density. Slightly restrained at this stage, but still youthful and tightly structured, with good potential. **Drink 2000-02.**

1994 ☆☆☆☆☆ Deep colour, still bright and youthful. Robust, with loads of ripe plum and cherry flavour. Still developing. Very harmonious, with firm but balanced tannins. Maturing well, with lovely richness, structure and complexity. Very classy. **Drink 1999-2002.**

1993 ☆☆☆☆☆ Full, maturing colour. Some barnyard characters on the nose. Big and flavoursome, with concentrated, plummy, spicy fruit. Very generous, with firm tannins and a rich finish. Unexpectedly good for the ultra-cool year. **Drink 1999-2001.**

1992 ☆☆☆☆ Full colour, showing some maturity. Lighter and less ripe than the 1991, with a faint herbal edge but also some attractive savoury characters. Still has some fruit sweetness. A higher-acid style than usual. **Drink 1999-2000.**

1991 ☆☆☆☆☆ Fullish colour of mid-maturity. Very perfumed. Lovely, mouthfilling, generous wine with sweet-fruit charm. Delicious now – warm, complex, supple and very harmonious. A star vintage. **Drink 1999-2000.**

1990 ☆☆☆☆☆ (Reserve) Full, developed colour. Full-bodied, savoury, spicy and mature. Still offering a lot, but very ready. Slightly less seductive than the 1989s. Complex, mushroomy bouquet and good tannins. **Drink 1999.**

1989 ☆☆☆☆☆ (Reserve) Fullish, slightly hazy colour. Bigger, sweeter, more powerful and perfumed than the non-reserve 1989. Remarkably attractive, with lovely richness, complexity and suppleness of texture. **Drink 1999-2000.**

1989 ☆☆☆☆☆ (Not labelled Reserve.) Fullish, red-brown colour. Slightly past its peak, but holding well. Very attractive, fully mature wine, ripe, spicy, savoury and rich. Impressive longevity. **Drink 1999.**

1988 ☆☆☆☆ Browning, slightly hazy. Still hanging in. Very savoury, leathery, mellow and smooth. Still some pleasure to be had here, but be quick. **Drink ASAP.**

Dry River
Pinot Noir

CLASSIC

Drenched with colour and awash with flavour, Neil McCallum's muscular Martinborough red is a startlingly bold Pinot Noir. No other Pinot Noir in the country can match it for flavour density and grandness of scale.

McCallum is well aware that his wine is markedly different from other New Zealand Pinot Noirs. "We don't want a slavish following of 'pretty' wines in New Zealand. I see mine as closer to Vosne-Romanée [the village with Burgundy's grandest *crus*]."

Most of the Dry River vines are of the "Pommard" (no. 5) clone, which yields dark, firmly structured wine. The striking depth of his Pinot Noir, says McCallum, comes from getting the grapes really ripe. "There are strong correlations between ripe fruit and concentration, and between concentration and keeping the vines' crops below 2.5 tonnes per acre." In 1996, the vines yielded just 1.7 tonnes per acre – and the most statuesque Pinot Noir ever made in Martinborough.

In the winery, the juice is soaked on its skins prior to the fermentation, which McCallum finds "extracts more attractive tannins than post-fermentation skin contact". About 50 per cent whole-bunch fermentation, and a lot of whole-berry fermentation of the destemmed fruit, contribute "intense fruit characters".

The Pinot Noir is matured for a year in French oak barriques (25 to 30 per cent new) and not filtered prior to bottling. Throughout the vinification process, the wine is protected from air: "Pinot Noir is very fragile, but if you keep the air away, it can still look good at six or seven years old."

Dry River is a more tannin-laden and slowly evolving wine than other New Zealand Pinot Noirs. This style difference needs understanding and patience from wine drinkers more accustomed to the soft, forward wines McCallum describes as "pretty". In its youth, Dry River is an impressively rich wine, but it takes several years to develop the "forest floor", mushroomy characters prized by Pinot Noir lovers. "Our backbone of tannins gives a slower evolution of the wine – hence its slower development of savoury characters."

McCallum is going for structure and longevity, rather than drink-young appeal. "We want fruit tannin in there, to give the wine the longevity needed to develop savoury characters. Three years [common in New Zealand] is rapid maturation; the 1990 Burgundies are accessible now, and everyone agrees the 1993s are babies."

In McCallum's view, Burgundy's greater heat in summer, compared to Martinborough, gives the French grapes "richer, nicer tannins. New Zealand's cooler maritime climate gives lush fruit but doesn't favour the development of ripe, strong tannins." The Dry River solution is to use whole-bunch fermentation to extract tannins from the grapes' ripe stalks.

With an annual production varying between 600 and 1000 cases, the Pinot Noir ($40) is Dry River's largest volume wine. McCallum doesn't enter his red in competitions, but he relishes its overseas acclaim. "It's been very talked-about in the UK, where they know their Burgundies. The top British wine writers buy my wine – it's in their cellars."

Dry River Pinot Noir is a magnificently full-bodied, dark and spicy, densely flavoured and firm-structured wine. For vintage-to-vintage quality through the mid to late 1990s, the country's two finest Pinot Noirs have been Ata Rangi and Dry River. Their friendly rivalry should produce some great bottles in the new millennium. ♣

From low-cropped vines, Neil McCallum fashions a splendidly robust and concentrated Pinot Noir.

tasting notes

These notes are mainly from a vertical tasting of the 1989 to 1996 vintages, held at the winery in November 1998. The 1997 vintage was tasted in Auckland in August 1998.

1997 ☆☆☆☆☆ Deeply coloured. Highly fragrant raspberry/spice aromas and flavours. Firm, ripe tannins. A lovely, rich, fresh, concentrated, commanding wine, needing time to soften and unfold its full potential. From a cooler season than 1996, it's more intensely varietal in its youth. **Drink 2000-04.**

1996 ☆☆☆☆☆ Dark, purple-flushed, very dense colour. Bouquet redolent of plums, raspberries and prunes. Astonishingly bold wine, awash with flavour. Concentrated and tannic. A powerful beast, built for a decade or longer. **Drink 2001-05.**

1995 ☆☆☆☆☆ Full, youthful colour. Big, fruit-packed wine with bold tannins. Powerful style, chewy, with rich plum/cherry flavours. Slightly lighter than the 1994, but built to last. **Drink 2000-03.**

1994 ☆☆☆☆☆ Deep, still slightly purplish colour. Developing a rich, complex fragrance. Fleshy and firm, with concentrated cherryish, plummy flavour and mouthfilling body. Very

powerful. Superb now, but still developing. **Drink 2000-03.**

1993 ☆☆☆☆☆ Deep colour with a hint of maturity. Superbly fragrant and mouthfilling. Very intense fruit. Powerful and supple, with loads of cherry, plum and spice flavour. Great now, but worth holding. **Drink 1999-2001.**

1992 Not tasted.

1991 Not tasted.

1990 ☆☆☆☆½ Medium-full colour, more developed than the 1989. Savoury and mellow. Very ready, but still highly enjoyable. Full-bodied, flavoursome and supple, with some complexity. **Drink 1999.**

1989 ☆☆☆☆ Medium-full colour, showing moderate age. Very fragrant bouquet of red berries. Full, not hugely complex but highly attractive, with sweet-fruit appeal, some savoury characters and a light tannin grip. Has lasted the distance well. **Drink 1999.**

Gibbston Valley
Reserve Pinot Noir

POTENTIAL CLASSIC

C entral Otago is starting to rival Martinborough for the title of New Zealand's top Pinot Noir region. Gibbston Valley Reserve Pinot Noir 1995 won the champion Pinot Noir trophy at the Liquorland Royal Easter Wine Show in 1997. The 1996 enjoyed even greater success, scooping the trophy for top Pinot Noir at the 1997 Air New Zealand Wine Awards, followed by the prestigious trophy for the overall champion wine of the 1998 Liquorland show – the first time either a Central Otago wine or a Pinot Noir had topped the judging.

The powerful Reserve Pinot Noir is mouthfilling and savoury, with a superb concentration of sweet-tasting, plummy fruit and lovely harmony. Winemaker Grant Taylor is passionate about Pinot Noir. "Every winemaker wants to make a good red," he says. "There's so much more work goes into it, shovelling out tanks of skins and so on; whites are just a warm-up. And Pinot Noir gets winemakers excited. Every year I like it more and more; it's a love affair that lasts."

Most of the grapes are drawn from the relatively warm Cromwell district, where the fruit is "punchy and upfront, with concentrated dark plum flavours". A smaller proportion comes from the cooler Gibbston area, near the winery, where the fruit is "lighter and perfumed and spicy, with good length".

The style of the wine, launched from the 1995 vintage, is already changing, reports Taylor. "The 1995 reflected ripe fruit qualities, but now we're after more structure and tannin. That sort of wine may not show so well in its youth, so we'll hold it back before releasing it. We want a tannic, powerful wine."

Ripe fruit has been the key factor in the wine's

quality, says Taylor. "In the past, the Pinot Noirs from Central Otago were thinner and less ripe. Since 1995, we've been able to get away from herbal, tomato-stalk characters, and get real concentration of flavour in the wine."

In the vineyards, Gibbston Valley encourages its growers to keep their crops to below three tonnes per acre, and penalises them financially if they fail. Leaf-plucking is "very important", to ripen the stalks, reduce acid levels and get better colour in the berries.

Taylor has worked several vintages in Burgundy and Oregon to expand his knowledge of Pinot Noir vinification. At Gibbston Valley, the grapes are hand-harvested and the juice is cold-soaked on the skins for up to eight days prior to the ferment, to get maximum colour extraction. About 20 per cent whole-bunch fermentation adds spiciness and tannins, and extended skin contact after the ferment adds "tannins and weight".

Gibbston Valley Reserve Pinot Noir is matured in French oak barriques, 100 per cent new, for between 12 and 18 months. "I like new wood," says Taylor.

SUELLEN BOAG

Winemaker Grant Taylor in Gibbston Valley's cool, romantic, 76-metre-long underground cellars.

"Toasty oak makes the nose much more attractive."

Taylor reports there are times when the winery at Gibbston Valley "feels a bit like a transit lounge". Each year he and his assistant winemaker, Claire Mulholland, chase ripe grapes in the Northern Hemisphere for a couple of months. In 1998, the traffic was two-way. Anthony van Nice arrived from Oregon to assist with the Gibbston Valley harvest, and Frenchman Cyprien Arlaud flew in from Domaine Arlaud in Burgundy.

With the first wines in the bottle, in August the south-north migration began. Taylor took off for Oregon's Archery Summit winery and Claire Mulholland headed for Domaine d'Arlot on the Côte d'Or. Both winemakers describe the spin-off in knowledge and experience as "huge".

Gibbston Valley Reserve Pinot Noir is a rare and expensive ($48) wine, with only 300 to 400 cases made each year. In the future, Taylor is keen to make single district (rather than regional) wines, and perhaps single vineyard wines. Meanwhile, this powerful, fleshy, splendidly rich-flavoured red offers telling proof of the Central Otago region's ability to produce Pinot Noir of exceptional quality. 🍇

tasting notes
These notes are from a vertical tasting of the 1995 to 1997 vintages, held in Auckland in February 1999.

1997 ☆☆☆☆☆ Bold, bright colour. Rich, robust palate with strong blackcurrant/cherry flavours and lots of new French oak showing. Excellent wine, still very youthful. More firmly structured than the 1995 or 1996. Yet to unfold its full personality, it should richly repay cellaring. **Drink 2000-03.**

1996 ☆☆☆☆☆ Full colour, still slightly purplish. Fragrant. Soft, very generous and richly varietal. Deep, sweet-tasting cherryish fruit and balanced spicy oak. Warm, complex and supple wine, much more developed than the 1997, and just starting to break into full stride. Long finish, slightly firmer than the 1995. **Drink 1999-2001.**

1995 ☆☆☆☆☆ Deep colour, still moderately youthful. Lovely, silky palate, soft and rich. Fleshy and crammed with sweet, ripe, plummy, cherryish fruit. Highly seductive now. **Drink 1999-2000.**

Martinborough Vineyard Pinot Noir

SUPER CLASSIC

This was the first consistently distinguished Pinot Noir made in New Zealand. An intensely varietal wine, it is typically fragrant and delicate, with sweet-tasting fruit and cherryish, slightly smoky, persistent, velvety flavours.

The superb 1986 vintage (still drinking well) was one of the first to transcend the simple, shallow style of Pinot Noir that was previously common in New Zealand. Early vintages won the trophy for champion Pinot Noir at the Air New Zealand Wine Awards in 1988, 1989 and 1990, giving the wine an illustrious reputation that lingers today. However, in recent years the Pinot Noirs from Ata Rangi and Dry River have been more consistently outstanding.

Larry McKenna, who made the 1986 to 1999

Martinborough Vineyard produced the region's first outstanding Pinot Noir.

vintages, describes the Martinborough Vineyard style as "not overblown or with super-tannins, but elegant, richly fruity and very complex. Remington Norman [the English wine writer and Burgundy expert] said we have to get away from the Cabernet-isation of Pinot Noir. It's a unique grape variety, relatively light, but complex. To get that complexity, you need mature vines and low yields to get ripe, concentrated fruit; complex fermentation techniques; and quality barrel-aging."

Site, McKenna believes, is the most crucial factor in producing top quality Pinot Noir. "In most of Australia, Pinot Noir ripens too fast. In a cooler climate, its flavours are not burnt out and it develops methoxypyrazines, or a similar compound, which gives it fungal complexity, as in Burgundy. Burgundy can be slightly herbal, but that turns to 'forest floor' complexity."

The grapes for Martinborough Vineyard Pinot Noir are grown mainly on the delineated, shingly Martinborough Terrace, but fruit is also purchased from a block 10 kilometres to the north of the town. "The Martinborough sites are very similar," says McKenna, "but with their variations in rootstock, clones and trellising, we had 22 different lots to ferment in 1998." The crops are restricted to a maximum of three tonnes per acre.

Clonal diversity is a key factor in the search for

complexity. Half of Martinborough Vineyard's Pinot Noir vines (and most of the older vines) are the 10/5 clone, which McKenna says has "small berries and relatively thick skins, giving depth, concentration and good tannin". Clone 5, which accounts for 20 per cent of the plantings, gives "fruitier, softer wine". Clones 6 and 13 are also well established, with new Bernard (Dijon) clones coming on stream.

In the winery, McKenna has found that extraction is a critical issue in handling Pinot Noir. "It typically has big berries and thin skins, so it's hard to make a big, rich wine." Since the early 1990s, extensive use has been made of pre and post-ferment maceration of the skins in the juice and wine, to secure greater extraction of the skins' colour, flavour and tannins.

Most of the grapes are crushed and destemmed, but a small proportion is whole-bunch fermented to extract stalk tannins. After a pre-ferment soak of several days, the wine is fermented with indigenous yeasts in open vats, during which the skins are hand-plunged on an eight-hourly basis. After the ferment, the young wine is held on its skins for a further five to seven days, then matured for a year in French oak barriques (30 per cent new) and bottled without filtering.

With an annual output of around 3500 cases, Martinborough Vineyard Pinot Noir ($35) is readily available. McKenna suggests drinking it at between three and five years old. The vertical tasting showed that lesser vintages peak within three or four years, but for top vintages like 1994, five years is a conservative guide.

The 1992 to 1994 vintages of Martinborough Vineyard Pinot Noir all won gold medals at the Australia National Wine Show in Canberra. However, Martinborough Vineyard's production of a Reserve Pinot Noir in the 1991, 1994, 1996, 1997 and 1998 vintages must clearly have come at some cost to the standard of the non-reserve wine in those years. The label's position as a Super Classic reflects its long, illustrious history, but its status may well be transferred in future to its Reserve big brother. 🍷

tasting notes

These notes are from a vertical tasting of the 1985 to 1997 vintages, held at the winery in November 1998.

1997 ☆☆☆☆☆ Full, youthful colour. Generous wine, with excellent depth of plum/raspberry flavours. Big body (13.5 per cent alcohol.) Stylish wine with sweet fruit, good mouthfeel and texture. Should develop real complexity. **Drink 2000-03.**

1996 ☆☆☆☆☆ Fresh, mouthfilling, spicy and chewy. Still developing. Very good wine, but shows a slight lack of concentration. **Drink 2000-01.**

1995 ☆☆☆☆ Full, bright, youthful colour. Fresh raspberry/plum flavours, crisp and youthful. Slight lack of complexity. Tight, elegant wine that should age well, but clearly a less-ripe year. **Drink 1999-2000.**

1994 ☆☆☆☆☆ Fullish colour, still with a hint of purple. Excellent now, with strong plum/cherry flavours. Sweet fruit. Savoury characters. Subtle array of flavours and balanced tannins. Clearly a top vintage. **Drink 1999-2000.**

1993 ☆☆☆☆ Fullish, mature colour. Big wine with loads of plummy, spicy flavour, but the fruit slightly lacks ripeness. Tastes a bit past its best. **Drink 1999.**

1992 ☆☆☆ Fullish, mature colour. Hint of greenness on the nose and palate. Herbaceous, with highish acidity. A distinctly lesser year, now past its best. **Drink ASAP.**

1991 ☆☆☆☆ Full, mature colour. Mouthfilling, spicy and mellow, with old leathery characters on nose and palate. Drink ASAP.

1990 ☆☆☆ Slightly dull, browning colour. Very herbaceous nose. Light (11.5 per cent alcohol). Lacks ripeness. High acid. Fading. **Drink ASAP.**

1989 ☆☆☆☆☆ Deep, still fractionally purple hue. Surprisingly undeveloped. Very fresh, plummy and mouthfilling, with a silky texture and good concentration. Complex wine with firm tannins. No rush at all. **Drink 1999-2002.**

1988 ☆☆☆☆ Fullish, very mature colour. Mellow bouquet with hints of prunes, liquorice and leather. Robust and mature, with loads of flavour. Now becoming a bit tired and porty, but a powerful wine. **Drink ASAP.**

1987 ☆☆☆☆ Medium-full, mature colour. Very mature nose and palate, but still pleasureable. Very savoury. Slightly high acid, and leaner than the 1986. Starting to tire. **Drink ASAP.**

1986 ☆☆☆☆☆ Full, mature colour with brown edges. Excellent wine – very savoury, mellow and soft. Lots of pleasure here. Big wine that has lasted superbly. Rich fruit. Still shows fruit sweetness. **Drink 1999.**

1985 ☆☆☆ Deep, exceptionally youthful colour for its age. Big and fruity, but not Pinot Noir-ish. Plummy, spicy, high acid wine. A real oddity. Fairly simple, but should live forever. **Drink 1999-2005.**

Martinborough Vineyard Reserve Pinot Noir

POTENTIAL CLASSIC

Such is the reputation of Martinborough Vineyard Pinot Noir, huge interest surrounded the release of the winery's first Reserve Pinot Noir from the 1991 vintage. That bold, smoky, cherryish wine developed quite swiftly – but not before it won the trophy for champion Pinot Noir at the 1993 Australia National Wine Show.

Larry McKenna, who made the 1991, 1994 and 1996 to 1998 vintages, sees the Reserve Pinot Noir as "a cut above the regular label – trophy-winning wine". The goal has been to create "a deeper, richer, better-structured wine, for drinking at five to 10 years, not three to five years".

The grapes are drawn from the winery's vineyards around Martinborough: "We know which blocks are most likely to give us the Reserve grapes," says McKenna, "but they must still reach the required quality level." The Reserve has typically been based on a higher percentage of fruit from the 10/5 clone than the standard wine, principally because the vines are older.

The Reserve Pinot Noir is essentially a selection of the top barrels. When the standard 1991 Pinot Noir was being blended prior to bottling, nine casks from the two top vineyard sites were identified as having particularly high quality. Those barrels were kept apart from the standard wine, blended and then matured in new French oak barriques for a further six months.

Whereas the standard wine typically spends a year in wood (30 per cent new), the Reserve Pinot Noir spends 18 months in the cask, with a stronger (about 50 per cent) new oak influence. McKenna

sees the Reserve label as Martinborough Vineyard's "research and development wine, where we have experimented with innovative techniques, such as extended macerations and long barrel-aging." It is only made in favourable vintages – there is no 1992, 1993 or 1995.

Larry McKenna believes that New Zealand Pinot Noir has a brilliant future. "Just as Sauvignon Blanc took the UK market by storm in the mid eighties, Pinot Noir is now paving the way for New Zealand to be perceived as a quality red wine producer." A decade ago, viticulturist Dr Richard Smart's ideas on trellis design and vine canopy management gave the country's Pinot Noir makers their most important breakthrough. "He taught that in cool-climate viticulture, you need every bunch and leaf exposed to sunlight to gain maximum ripeness, colour and flavour. This gave all varieties, but especially the large-berried, tight-bunched, thin-skinned Pinot Noir, the required level of colour and fruit ripeness expected by an international audience."

New clones also paved the way for better wines. "The search for new clonal material has been partly fired by the desire for increased complexity, texture and structure. John Comerford, chairman of judges at the Air New Zealand Wine Awards from 1986 to 1993, helped steer the move to more complete, fully layered, complex wines."

Does the existence of the Reserve wine lower the quality of the standard Martinborough Vineyard Pinot Noir? "The standard wine should still be gold medal standard," replies McKenna. "If it's not, what would have become the reserve gets blended back in." However, the 1996 Reserve Pinot Noir is a noticeably more substantial, rich and concentrated wine than the standard version.

Only about 500 cases of the Reserve Pinot Noir are made, compared to 3500 cases of the standard wine. At a retail price of $55, it is clearly New Zealand's most expensive Pinot Noir.

The 1994 vintage, currently in devastating form, has been Martinborough Vineyard's most successful wine on the show circuit. After winning the trophy for Best Soft Finish Red Wine at the 1996 Australia National Wine Show in Canberra and the trophy for Best Lighter Bodied Dry Red Table Wine at the 1996 Sydney International Wine Competition, in 1997 it won the Bouchard Finlayson Trophy for champion Pinot Noir at the International Wine and Spirit Competition in London.

At its best, Martinborough Vineyard Reserve Pinot Noir is a majesterial wine, with notable stuffing and richness. Fragrant, mouthfilling and crammed with spicy, dark cherry flavours, it's an exciting mouthful and one of the country's most distinguished Pinot Noirs. 🍇

The majesterial Reserve Pinot Noir seems destined to take over the prestige of the non-reserve wine.

tasting notes
These notes are from a vertical tasting of the 1991 to 1997 vintages, held at the winery in November 1998.

1997 (Not rated, as tasted very soon after bottling.) Very deep colour. Densely packed and very powerful, but still a bit shell-shocked from bottling. Intense plum/cherry flavours. Looks full of potential. **Drink 2001-05.**

1996 ☆☆☆☆☆ Deep, youthful colour. Very big wine, with rich plum/spice flavours and crammed with sweet fruit characters. Great mouthfeel. Very harmonious, with supple tannins. Still youthful. **Drink 2000-03.**

1995 Not made.

1994 ☆☆☆☆☆ Full colour with a hint of maturity. Very big, rich, rounded and long. Highly concentrated plummy, oaky flavour. Velvet-smooth, with tremendous depth and complexity. Notably complete wine, now at its peak of perfection. **Drink 1999-2001.**

1993 Not made.

1992 Not made.

1991 ☆☆☆☆ Mature, slightly brown colour. Very advanced, savoury and leathery. Rich, but now fully mature. Won't have the hoped-for longevity. **Drink 1999.**

Palliser Estate Pinot Noir

POTENTIAL CLASSIC

Until recently, Palliser Estate seemed content to make attractive but not memorable Pinot Noirs that lived in the shadow of its classy white wines. Then came the 1996 and 1997 vintages – both outstanding and both gold medal and trophy winners. The 1997 won the new trophy for champion commercial red wine at the 1998 Air New Zealand Wine Awards.

Winemaker Allan Johnson aims for a "ripe, full and rich" Pinot Noir. Martinborough's climate suits Pinot Noir, he believes. "It's not too hot and not too cold. Compared to Burgundy, we have a longer ripening season but lower temperature peaks, so we get a different fruit expression. The vines have a good balance of foliage and fruit. The rest is Martinborough magic."

Why the sudden leap in the quality of the Pinot Noir, after a string of good but not great wines? "The biggest thing is moving to a lower cropping level," says Johnson. "We've reduced the vines' average yields from four to three tonnes per acre. It was a matter of convincing the company that you have to do that." Due to the reduced yields, the grapes (currently almost entirely of the 10/5 clone, although clone 5 and Bernard (Dijon) clones are being planted) are achieving higher levels of ripeness.

Palliser Estate is also doing much more leaf-plucking than previously. "In Burgundy, with their higher temperatures, they generally don't leaf pluck," says Johnson. "Here, leaf removal warms the berries, so you get riper tannins and better flavour ripeness."

At the winery, most of the crop is destemmed and crushed, but 10 to 15 per cent is fermented as whole clusters. The skins are soaked in the juice for four or five days prior to the ferment, "to enhance fruit characters and colour", and the young wine is held on its skins for a similar period after the fermentation, "to stabilise its colour and increase the tannins".

Over the years, Johnson's handling of Pinot Noir has become more gentle. "You need to be careful, especially following the fermentation, to treat it in a gentle fashion, otherwise you end up extracting harsh phenolic characters." Wood maturation is for a year in French oak barriques (25 per cent new).

Palliser Estate Pinot Noir ($30) is produced in significant commercial volumes (about 4000 cases per year) and enjoys a steady demand in what Johnson calls "the surprise market" – Australia. He recommends drinking the wine at four years old. The vertical tasting indicates that the superior recent vintages will offer rewarding drinking for at least that long.

The outstanding 1996 and 1997 vintages of Palliser Estate Pinot Noir have moved the winery towards the front rank of the district's red-wine producers. This is a highly significant label, as the judges at the Air New Zealand Wine Awards recognised – a top-flight red wine in decent volumes that you can actually go out and buy. 🍷

Winemaker Allan Johnson's most recent Pinot Noirs are easily the greatest yet.

tasting notes

These notes are from a vertical tasting of the 1990 to 1997 vintages, held at the winery in November 1998.

1997 ☆☆☆☆☆ Rich, very youthful colour. Warm, vibrant wine with deep cherry, plum and spice flavours. Crammed with fruit. Much more concentrated than the pre-1996 vintages. Powerful and firm. More complex than the 1996. **Drink 2000-03.**

1996 ☆☆☆☆☆ Fullish, youthful colour. Lovely surge of sweet, supple plummy flavours. Mouthfilling. A big lift in concentration, compared to the older wines. Vibrantly fruity. Subtle smoky oak. Sturdy, warm and likely to be long-lived. **Drink 2000-02.**

1995 ☆☆☆☆ Medium-full colour, still slightly purplish. Full-bodied, with attractive berryish flavours, spicy too. Crisp and moderately complex. Slightly lacks warmth, but maturing well – still bright and youthful. **Drink 1999-2001.**

1994 ☆☆☆☆ Medium-full colour, much less developed than the older wines. No delights on the nose. Full, with quite good concentration. Still fairly fresh. Raspberry and spice flavours. Slightly crisp, with some sweet-fruit charm and complexity. Maturing well, but will never be a great bottle. **Drink 1999-2000.**

1993 Not tasted. "Lighter, herbal style" – Allan Johnson.

1992 ☆☆☆ Mature colour of moderate depth. Very mature, with some savoury, complex characters, but lacks real richness. **Drink 1999.**

1991 ☆☆☆☆ Mature colour of medium depth. Fairly quiet nose. Still alive. Savoury. Ripe berryish flavours, but not highly complex. Plenty of flavour. Good now but doesn't have great depth. **Drink 1999.**

1990 ☆☆☆ Mature colour, reasonable depth. Scented and savoury, with overtones of strawberries. Sliding into advanced maturity. Slightly lacks concentration, with crisp acidity. Still enjoyable. **Drink ASAP.**

 Index

Glossary

Acidity: A crisp, refreshing taste factor usually derived from natural grape acids (although winemakers sometimes add acid). Excessive acidity makes a wine tart; too little leaves it flabby.

American Oak: Cheaper than French oak and less subtle, American oak barrels add a perfumed, sweetish character to wine, which experienced tasters can easily pick. More winemakers use American oak than admit it.

Barrel-Fermented: Premium Chardonnays and some other white wines are partly or fully fermented in barrels, rather than stainless steel tanks, to enhance their complexity.

Barrique: Bordeaux name for small oak barrels of 225-litre capacity which are widely used in the top chateaux.

Botrytis: The fungus *Botrytis cinerea* causes botrytis bunch rot, which can have an adverse effect on yield and quality. Botrytised sweet wines are effected by the desirable form of Botrytis, known as 'noble rot'.

Brix: A measure of the approximate concentration of sugars in grapes.

Clone: Different clones of the same grape variety are descended from different mother vines. There is a special interest in Pinot Noir clones, whose performances vary widely.

Cool Climate: The term applied to the world's cooler grape-growing regions, including northern France, Germany and most of New Zealand.

French Oak: From forests all over northern France, French oak is highly regarded, imparting more subtle characters to wine than American oak.

Herbaceous: New Zealand's cool climate accentuates the grassy, herbaceous nature of Sauvignon Blanc. Red wines made from unripe grapes can also be herbaceous.

Leaf-plucking: Removing leaves around the grape bunches helps to reduce disease and improve ripening.

Lees-aged: Maturation of premium Chardonnays, bottle-fermented sparklings and other wines on their yeast lees (dead yeast sediment) adds flavour, richness and complexity.

Lees-stirred: Regular stirring of the yeast lees (see Lees-Aged) encourages the pick-up of yeast-related flavour complexity.

Malolactic Fermentation: A secondary bacterial fermentation which softens and stabilises red wines. It is less common in white winemaking, but can be used to add complexity and lower acidity.

Maceration: The process of dissolving tannins, colours and flavours from grape skins into juice or wine.

Méthode Traditionnelle: A term that has recently replaced méthode champenoise to describe the complicated method of making Champagne that is now widely used to make other bottle-fermented sparkling wines.

PH: A measure of the effective acidity in wine which effects wine taste and longevity.

Scott Henry: A vine-training system that can improve grape quality by dividing the canopy vertically, thus reducing fruit shading problems.

Tannin: Derived from grape skins, pips and oak casks, tannin acts as a preservative and adds firmness to the palate.

Tirage: The period during which a bottle-fermented sparkling wine matures on its lees.

Whole-Berry Fermentation: Traditional Beaujolais technique for producing fruity, soft reds.

Whole-Bunch Fermentation: Traditional red wine fermentation method in Burgundy in which the grapes are not de-stemmed.

Whole-Bunch Pressing: A gentle juice separation technique by which winemakers reduce skin contact and boost flavour delicacy by loading bunches of hand-harvested grapes straight into the press, bypassing the crusher.